Lexical Processing in Second Language Learners

SECOND LANGUAGE ACQUISITION
Series Editor: Professor David Singleton, *Trinity College, Dublin, Ireland*

This series brings together titles dealing with a variety of aspects of language acquisition and processing in situations where a language or languages other than the native language is involved. Second language is thus interpreted in its broadest possible sense. The volumes included in the series all offer in their different ways, on the one hand, exposition and discussion of empirical findings and, on the other, some degree of theoretical reflection. In this latter connection, no particular theoretical stance is privileged in the series; nor is any relevant perspective – sociolinguistic, psycholinguistic, neurolinguistic, etc. – deemed out of place. The intended readership of the series includes final-year undergraduates working on second language acquisition projects, postgraduate students involved in second language acquisition research, and researchers and teachers in general whose interests include a second language acquisition component.

Full details of all the books in this series and of all our other publications can be found on http://www.multilingual-matters.com, or by writing to Multilingual Matters, St Nicholas House, 31-34 High Street, Bristol BS1 2AW, UK.

SECOND LANGUAGE ACQUISITION
Series Editor: David Singleton, *Trinity College, Dublin, Ireland*

Lexical Processing in Second Language Learners
Papers and Perspectives in Honour of Paul Meara

Edited by
Tess Fitzpatrick and Andy Barfield

MULTILINGUAL MATTERS
Bristol • Buffalo • Toronto

Library of Congress Cataloging in Publication Data
A catalog record for this book is available from the Library of Congress.
Lexical Processing in Second Language Learners: Papers and Perspectives in Honour of Paul Meara
Edited by Tess Fitzpatrick and Andy Barfield.
Second language acquisition: 39
Includes bibliographical references and index.
1. Second language acquisition.
I. Meara, P. M. (Paul M.) II. Fitzpatrick, Tess III. Barfield, Andrew
P118.2.L485 2009
401'.93–dc22 2009009447

British Library Cataloguing in Publication Data
A catalogue entry for this book is available from the British Library.

ISBN-13: 978-1-84769-152-1 (hbk)
ISBN-13: 978-1-84769-151-4 (pbk)

Multilingual Matters
UK: St Nicholas House, 31-34 High Street, Bristol BS1 2AW, UK.
USA: UTP, 2250 Military Road, Tonawanda, NY 14150, USA.
Canada: UTP, 5201 Dufferin Street, North York, Ontario M3H 5T8, Canada.

Copyright © 2009 Tess Fitzpatrick and Andy Barfield and the authors of individual chapters.

All rights reserved. No part of this work may be reproduced in any form or by any means without permission in writing from the publisher.

The policy of Multilingual Matters/Channel View Publications is to use papers that are natural, renewable and recyclable products, made from wood grown in sustainable forests. In the manufacturing process of our books, and to further support our policy, preference is given to printers that have FSC and PEFC Chain of Custody certification. The FSC and/or PEFC logos will appear on those books where full certification has been granted to the printer concerned.

Typeset by Datapage International Ltd.
Printed and bound in Great Britain by MPG Books Ltd.

Contents

Contributors vii
Preface
Alison Wray xi

1 Introduction: Meara's Contribution to Research in
   L2 Lexical Processing
   John Read and Paul Nation 1
2 Putting Yes/No Tests in Context
   John Shillaw 13
3 Tangled Webs...: Complications in the Exploration of
   L2 Lexical Networks
   Clarissa Wilks 25
4 Word Association Profiles in a First and Second Language:
   Puzzles and Problems
   Tess Fitzpatrick 38
5 Revisiting Classrooms as Lexical Environments
   Marlise Horst 53
6 A Close Look at the Use of Pocket Electronic Dictionaries for
   Receptive and Productive Purposes
   Hilary Nesi and Atipat Boonmoh 67
7 Repeated L2 Reading With and Without a Dictionary
   Jim Ronald 82
8 Exploring Productive L2 Collocation Knowledge
   Andy Barfield 95
9 The Messy Little Details: A Longitudinal Case Study
   of the Emerging Lexicon
   Huw Bell 111
10 Meaning-Last Vocabulary Acquisition and
   Collocational Productivity
   Brent Wolter 128
11 Acting on a Hunch: Can L1 Reading Instruction
   Affect L2 Listening Ability?
   Richard Pemberton 141
12 Taking Stock
   Andy Barfield and Tess Fitzpatrick 154

References 159
Index 172

Contributors

Andy Barfield teaches in the Faculty of Law at Chuo University, Tokyo, Japan. His doctoral work focused on exploring second language collocation knowledge and development, and his research interests also cover learner autonomy in second language education. Andy's book publications include *Reconstructing Autonomy in Language Education: Inquiry and Innovation* (coedited with S. Brown; Palgrave Macmillan, 2007) and *Researching Collocations in Another Language: Multiple Interpretations* (coedited with H. Gyllstad; Palgrave Macmillan, 2009).

Huw Bell 'learnt everything he knows about language' while working with Paul Meara at Swansea, where his PhD dealt with the assessment of lexical richness in L2 text. Huw is now a Senior Lecturer at Manchester Metropolitan University, UK, where he is programme leader for the MA TEFL. His research interests include how teacher and learner attitudes affect learning outcomes, particularly in minority/heritage languages.

Atipat Boonmoh is a lecturer in the Department of Language Studies, King Mongkut's University of Technology Thonburi (KMUTT), Bangkok. He has presented conference papers on the use of electronic dictionaries, and wrote his MA thesis on this topic. He is currently studying for a PhD in English Language Teaching at the Centre for Applied Linguistics, University of Warwick. His PhD research focuses on Thai university students' use of pocket electronic dictionaries for academic purposes.

Tess Fitzpatrick is a Senior Lecturer in Applied Linguistics at Swansea University. Her doctoral thesis investigated ways of using word association tasks and word frequency bands to elicit and measure L2 vocabulary, and described the design and implementation of an innovative test of productive vocabulary knowledge. Tess' research interests remain in the areas of vocabulary acquisition, storage and retrieval, with a specific focus on word association studies and vocabulary measurement tools, and she supervises research students working in these areas. A qualified and experienced EFL teacher and teacher trainer, she has also worked on projects exploring extreme language-learning methodologies and the role of formulaic sequences in second language use.

Marlise Horst is an Associate Professor at Concordia University in Montreal, where she teaches courses in applied linguistics, TESL methodology, language testing and the history of English. Her research addresses vocabulary development through reading, computer-assisted vocabulary learning and contrastive language awareness in francophone learners of English. A study of extensive ESL reading, done with Paul Meara as part of her doctoral research (Horst *et al.*, 1998), is cited regularly in investigations of incidental vocabulary acquisition. She also enjoys needlework and is an active member of the Village Quilters of Hudson, Quebec.

Paul Nation is Professor of Applied Linguistics in the School of Linguistics and Applied Language Studies at Victoria University of Wellington, New Zealand. He has taught in Indonesia, Thailand, the USA, Finland and Japan. His specialist interests are language-teaching methodology and vocabulary learning. His latest books include *Learning Vocabulary in Another Language* (Cambridge University Press, 2001), *Focus on Vocabulary* (with Peter Gu; NCELTR/Macquarie, 2007), *Teaching Vocabulary: Strategies and Techniques* (Heinle Cengage Learning, 2008), *Teaching ESL/EFL Listening and Speaking* (with Jonathan Newton; Routledge, 2009) and *Teaching ESL/EFL Reading and Writing* (Routledge, 2009).

Hilary Nesi publishes in the fields of corpus linguistics and dictionary design and use, and is a Professor in English Language at Coventry University. Paul Meara supervised Hilary's PhD studies and coauthored two papers with her (1991: 'How using dictionaries affects performance in multiple choice EFL tests' *Reading in a Foreign Language* 8:1, and 1994: 'Patterns of misinterpretation in the productive use of EFL dictionary definitions' *System* 22:1). Hilary is now a supervisor herself, and is coauthoring a chapter in this book with Atipat Boonmoh, a PhD student from Thailand.

Richard Pemberton is Associate Professor in TESOL in the School of Education at the University of Nottingham. Previously he taught for nearly 15 years at Hong Kong University of Science and Technology, and before that in Papua New Guinea, Zimbabwe and the UK. His PhD thesis investigated the ability of Hong Kong learners to recognise very frequent words in connected English speech. His research interests include spoken word recognition, and technology-assisted vocabulary learning in formal and informal settings. He has coedited *Taking Control: Autonomy in Language Learning* (Hong Kong University Press, 1996) and *Maintaining Control: Autonomy and Language Learning* (Hong Kong University Press, 2009).

John Read is an Associate Professor and Head of the Department of Applied Language Studies and Linguistics at the University of Auckland, New Zealand. He has taught applied linguistics, TESOL and English for academic purposes at tertiary institutions in New Zealand, Singapore and the USA. His primary research interests are in second language vocabulary assessment and the testing of English for academic and professional purposes. He is the author of *Assessing Vocabulary* (Cambridge University Press, 2000), as well as numerous articles and book chapters on aspects of vocabulary learning and assessment. He was coeditor of *Language Testing* from 2002 to 2006.

Jim Ronald's interest in vocabulary began with work as assistant editor on the second edition of Collins COBUILD English Dictionary. His main concerns since then have been with two aspects of the use of dictionaries by language learners. The first is the use that language learners make of dictionaries: choices they make regarding dictionary use and factors that affect these choices. The second aspect is the effect of dictionary use on the vocabularies of language learners. This has also been the focus of his doctoral research and the topic of his PhD thesis, completed in 2006.

John Shillaw is Professor of English Language Education at Nanzan University, Nagoya, Japan. John's interest in lexical research stemmed from his work on the use of corpora for selecting words for vocabulary tests. John's PhD studies examined Yes/No vocabulary tests as a measure of learners' vocabulary size. The results of his early research threw up a number of issues that seriously questioned the validity of the test format. Using the Rasch model to analyse large sets of test data, John's later studies demonstrated that a simpler form of checklist test was valid and more reliable than the Yes/No format.

Clarissa Wilks is Associate Dean of the Faculty of Arts and Social Sciences at Kingston University. She studied with Paul Meara first on the MA in Second Language Learning and Teaching at Birkbeck College, London and then on the doctoral programme at Swansea, completing her PhD in 1999. Her research interests are in second language lexical networks and in attitudes to discriminatory language in France.

Brent Wolter is Assistant Professor and Director of the TESOL program at Idaho State University. He was awarded his PhD in 2005, which focused on developing a computer test for assessing depth of word knowledge. His research interests include using psycholinguistic and cognitive approaches to understanding lexical acquisition. His work has been published in journals such as *Applied Linguistics*, *ELT Journal*, *Second Language Research*, *Studies in Second Language Acquisition* and *System*.

Alison Wray was part of Paul Meara's PhD supervisory team at Swansea from 1996 to 1999, but Paul's considerable positive influence on her research began almost a decade earlier, when he acted as a valued informal mentor during the last stages of her doctoral work, in which she developed and described a new model of language processing (University of York, 1988). The main focus of Alison's current research is the status of multiword items (formulaic language) as part of the lexicon, and how, in the L2 context, different approaches may be taken to their learning and processing. She is now a Research Professor at Cardiff University in the Centre for Language and Communication Research.

Preface
A Research Network Model

ALISON WRAY

Between 1996 and 1999 I had the privilege of working as Paul Meara's colleague in the Centre for Applied Language Studies, University of Wales Swansea, where I assisted with the running of the PhD programme of the Vocabulary Acquisition Research Group (VARG). It was a tremendous training for me, a young academic with much to learn about how research can and should be conducted, and how best to nurture postgraduate students. Without question, it has made me a better supervisor than I would otherwise have been. In this short account, I shall try to pinpoint what makes the VARG programme so special, and show how Paul has distilled into its design – and the practice of its day-to-day management – the essence of excellent research training.

PhD Programmes: The Challenge

We must begin with a consideration of the wider context in which the VARG programme operates. The PhD is a different creature in different countries but in the UK financial constraints and established traditions tend to funnel full-time students into three years of narrow and solitary investigation. In many other countries, less speed and more breadth would be the norm, with a mixture, over a longer time frame, of PhD research and taught components focused on both academic content and research training. In the UK, the training component is normally undertaken first, as a Masters course in research methods, and one obvious disadvantage is that it precedes the development of the student's own empirical work.

In truth, the most effective learning will occur during the process of carrying out research for oneself. The combination of front-loading the training and imposing a tight completion deadline sometimes means that UK PhD students gain rather little breadth of practical research experience. Some projects entail only one, large, data collection, and therefore the design of only one investigative instrument and only a small number of analytic techniques. Even the extent to which a student learns to engage critically with the research literature is not uniform. Critical skills take time and experience to develop, and are best nurtured through tightly focused vignettes that receive detailed feedback from the supervisor. Many students, unfortunately, launch directly into an extensive, under-focused literature review that favours quantity over critical quality, and they can miss out on the opportunity to draft and redraft their account until it fully and appropriately integrates with their own investigatory aims.

Given the intractable constraints of time and resources, how can supervisors provide the best possible training experience for their PhD students? There are certain design features that a programme needs, if it is to support the development of critical insight, facilitate the acquisition of breadth and depth in research experience, and create a solid knowledge-base for original ideas. These features include a good balance between freedom to explore one's interests and hunches and a structured operational space; regular feedback on work from specialists in the field; opportunities to air one's ideas in a safe environment; a strong sense of community; and *time*. I think it is no accident that the VARG PhD programme at Swansea, expressly designed to provide this combination of experiences, is dedicated entirely to part-time students.

The Marks of Success

The success of the VARG PhD programme can be measured in many ways:

- a spectacularly high pass-rate at first submission (PhDs in the UK often do not pass first go);
- excellent onward career trajectories for its graduates;
- the respect and recognition of international experts in the field;
- recognition from the Economic and Social Research Council as a research training programme eligible for its studentship funding;
- an international reputation amongst would-be students, resulting in a highly competitive application process and a waiting list for places.

VARG students think for themselves, question everything, and view not only other people's but also their own work with critical circumspection. VARG graduates tend to display a striking combination of confidence founded on real knowledge and insight, and modesty derived from their understanding of where their own work fits into the bigger picture.

So, what is it about the programme that reliably produces these markers of success? Many things: its design, the expertise and commitment of its staff, the calibre of the students it recruits, and, importantly, the maintenance of just the right number of students to balance experience with renewal. The numbers on the VARG programme have settled, through trial and error, at around 25. Typically, in any given year, four new entrants begin the programme and three to four people complete it.

Commitment from a team of experts

VARG is unquestionably Paul Meara's programme, and his strong leadership is integral to its international stature. But he has drawn in colleagues over many years to share ownership and responsibility, thereby providing them with an opportunity to develop their own skills in supervision and teamwork, while broadening the base of expertise offered to students. In-house staff supporting VARG have included (in chronological order) Jim Milton, Ann Ryan, myself, Nuria Lorenzo-Dus, Geoff Hall, Chris Butler, Chris Shei, Tess Fitzpatrick (a VARG graduate herself) and Cornelia Tschichold. In addition, many academic visitors from home and overseas have made valuable contributions, most notably by being 'stars' at the annual conference (see later).

Valuing the part-time student

The entire VARG enterprise is geared to the constraints and opportunities associated with part-time, distance study. Other than on the UK's excellent Open University programmes, part-time distance students in the UK often get something of a raw deal. Unable to attend seminars, reading groups and so on, they may often feel like unwelcome interlopers on the full-time programme. VARG, however, recognises and exploits the many advantages of being part-time. For example, students usually take part-time registration because they have a full-time job. Often construed as a problem, in fact it means they are financially solvent and can factor in the work-study balance from the start, in contrast to the many full-time postgraduates without scholarships, who find their need to earn money in direct conflict with their study. Furthermore, as most VARG students don't have just any old job, but a career – usually in language teaching – they have a clear rationale for their study, can see tangible benefits in completing it, and have a professional future planned out. They have, in short, both security and motivation. A third benefit is that, working in an environment directly relevant to their research, VARG students normally have no difficulty gathering linguistic data – often finding research subjects in their own classroom – whereas a full-time student may have to make considerable efforts to access a cohort of subjects.

Most importantly, part-time registration takes the pressure off that tight three-year window, and creates many opportunities for reading, investigations and reflection that the frantic full-timer can easily miss. Data collected from a cohort of language learners might reveal patterns that invite a follow-up of the same cohort a year later, or a comparison with the next cohort. A part-timer's scope to do that is much greater than a full-timer's. Part-timers also get more bites at the cherry when it comes to annual conferences.

Structure, routine, progression, feedback

Of course, part-time registration has potential disadvantages too. One inherent difficulty for many students is that, with other calls on their time and such an apparently distant thesis submission deadline, weeks or months easily go past with very little work being done. The VARG programme's solution is to impose across the entire five-year registration period a highly structured schedule of small, manageable pieces of work with set deadlines. These mini-projects are in response to two strands of activity: a personal annual programme of work, based on a template but adapted to the individual's stage and research trajectory; and the monthly mailing, sent out to all students. For a busy part-timer, it is a lot easier to start and complete a series of small, well-defined tasks than to motivate oneself regularly to put time into a single, open-ended activity of unknown duration. Small tasks have other benefits too: the chance to try out new skills and new ideas, get feedback, and try again. Rather than investing all one's hopes in one huge analysis of a single dataset, it becomes possible to try out different approaches, and develop insights and confidence along the way.

The monthly mailing is the means by which the set tasks for the entire cohort are administered. All students are required to complete at least six of the eight tasks set during the year (there are eight 'monthly' mailings per year, to allow for vacations). The tasks are strongly focused, following a particular theme within the area of vocabulary acquisition (e.g. lexical richness, word association). They usually entail the critical evaluation of a research paper or part of a book, written up as a short report. The responses are read and commented on by the staff member that set the task. In the next mailing, some of the responses are circulated, along with the staff member's own commentary – both on the paper itself and on how the students engaged with the task. In this way, a kind of virtual seminar takes place. Students receive not only feedback on their own work, but also the opportunity to see how others approached the same activity. Over a period of time, the effect is to induct students into an approach to critical evaluation that emulates best practice. In short, VARG students learn not only to regard with healthy scepticism and a discerning eye aspects of published papers that others might accept on trust, but also to justify their criticisms in a structured and explicit way. One particularly valuable aspect of these exercises is the fine-tuned examination of statistical analyses. Most Applied Linguistics students lack experience in, and confidence with, statistics, but VARG students soon learn what to look for, and thereby develop the ability both to understand reports of quantitative analyses, and to run their own statistical tests.

The annual schedule for each student focuses on targeted reading and the building of a portfolio of empirical studies, each written up at the time, to become part of the final thesis. In Year 1, the student undertakes a modified replication of a published study. Replications are a highly valuable, and typically much underused, tool for learning: by developing an existing design and analysing the data in a comparable way, one is guided safely through the investigatory process and comes out the other end with results that can be compared to the original. One learns much about what can arise in the course of investigations, and one also learns how important it is to write up one's own work in a way that will allow others to replicate it. From Year 2, students undertake their own original experiments or other investigations. Usually they will conduct one investigation in each of Years 2 and 3, and increase the number to two per year after that.

For some students there is a natural progression from the first experiment to the second and onwards, as different variables are manipulated, or as the same cohort is tested on successive occasions. For others, each experiment comes at the central question in a different way, so that the final write-up provides several windows on a phenomenon, reflecting the student's developing understanding of complex issues. There is a good chance that, in the course of creating the investigatory portfolio, a range of different designs and analytic tools will be needed, and several statistical tests will be used. Through this structured apprenticeship, VARG students are initiated into many of the different practices of the Applied Linguistics community, and provided with the means to become experts in their field of enquiry.

There are other components, too, of the annual schedule. Everyone writes a book review, subsequently circulated to the group and often submitted to a journal for publication. Students are encouraged to review books that others on the programme might otherwise not access, including ones written in languages other than English. Students are also required to prepare presentations for conferences: typically a poster in Year 2, and papers thereafter.

The portfolio approach to research means that there is never a point at which the student has to face a blank page – or empty computer screen – with the challenge of 'starting to write up'. Rather, the 'writing up' phase is essentially a matter of joining into a coherent narrative the work that has been done. Thus the danger of not completing the thesis is minimised.

The annual conference

The annual VARG conference is a major and highly significant part of the programme. Students and staff meet over three days to present and discuss their work both formally and informally. Typically, part of the time is given over to a workshop led by a member of the VARG staff, but the central activity is the students' chance to present on some aspect of their research and get feedback on it from the staff and other students. There are special guests at each conference: key international researchers in the field of vocabulary acquisition, who, besides presenting their own work, comment on student presentations and provide a useful 'outside' view. Paul insists that everyone at the conference adheres to a key principle: it is acceptable to challenge someone's ideas, but only while giving due credibility and respect to the person. Care in making this distinction assists in creating an atmosphere in which students dare to express ideas without fear of being made to feel stupid. Thereby, they gain confidence in defending their position before they attend outside conferences. The etiquette of mutual respect also helps everyone appreciate the impact of their own style of expressing their interest and scepticism – an insight that potentially contributes to constructive engagement with others in every aspect of their lives.

The conference provides a community experience in more than just a social way. Students bring to the event their own specialist knowledge to share with others. Skills and information about statistical tests, useful software, research literature and complementary approaches are freely traded in the common pursuit of excellence.

Community

But the VARG community exists all the time, not just at the conference. VARG students can be located anywhere (past members have been in the UK, Hong Kong, Japan, Israel, Spain, Canada and many other countries), and so may rarely meet each other face-to-face other than at the conferences. Through the mailings, and the opportunities afforded by new electronic technologies, the VARG community, although virtual, replicates to some extent the physically located 'lab' environment that students in other disciplines enjoy. In truth, few linguistics departments in the UK are big enough to support the range of activity on-site that VARG can provide through electronic means. VARG has the additional, equally rare advantage that all the students and staff are focused on the same research area, L2 vocabulary acquisition, making more or less everything that anyone is doing interesting and relevant to the others.

The VARG community is not restricted only to registered students and supervisory staff. It also has 'lurkers'. Lurkers do not submit work, but they do receive the mailings, so it is a status that suits both those who, having completed the programme, want to keep up to date with the field, and those who are waiting to start their VARG PhD. Indeed, most of those who have won a place on the programme will lurk for a few months first, giving them a chance to see how things work, and acculturate to the community. In addition, the network usually has a few lurkers who are engaged in similar research at other universities.

There is, of course, a real physical base to VARG too, and many students are able, at some point, to come to Swansea for a few weeks or months to work intensively on their thesis and have face-to-face supervision with the staff. One particular attraction of spending time in Swansea (in addition to the proximity of the beach) is using the print archive of well over 1500 published and unpublished research papers on vocabulary acquisition, including many that would be difficult to access by other means.

Conclusion

Is the VARG PhD programme special? Yes, it is. Few PhD programmes are so well thought out, or have enjoyed such a consistent, caring investment of time and imagination. What one sees in VARG is the translation of Paul's dream into a reality that has proved itself sustainable and unquestionably worthwhile. The programme turns out balanced researchers, with a broad and mature understanding of their field of enquiry and of the processes by which interesting research questions can be robustly investigated – one proof of that fact is this volume. Is the VARG model replicable? In principle certainly, though perhaps few people could match Paul's vision and commitment.

In sum, a great many Applied Linguists owe Paul Meara a big thank you, and many, many more look in awe at VARG and wish they had a PhD programme like it. I'm one of them.

Chapter 1

Introduction: Meara's Contribution to Research in L2 Lexical Processing

JOHN READ and PAUL NATION

Introduction

We are delighted to have been invited to contribute to this volume in honour of Paul Meara because we have long admired his work, as a researcher, a teacher and presenter, a writer, a bibliographer and a supervisor of doctoral theses in the field of second language vocabulary studies. Our perspective is that of outsiders, in the sense that we are the only authors in the book who have not worked closely with Paul as colleagues or research students at Swansea. This puts us in a good position to reflect on the wider impact of his scholarship in relation to our own work and the field generally. We will begin with some personal observations and then go on to review some major strands of his research in a more formal way.

Both of us met Paul for the first time at the AILA World Congress of Applied Linguistics in Greece in 1990, but we had been aware of his work for some time before that. Paul Nation remembers how pleased he was to read Paul's review article 'Vocabulary acquisition: A neglected aspect of language learning', which was published in *Language Teaching and Linguistics* in 1980. At that time, there truly were only a small number of scholars with an interest in L2 vocabulary learning and it was heartening to realise that here was another researcher who was so obviously committed to work in this area. This led to correspondence and a regular exchange of papers, articles and ideas, which has continued to this day. However, for reasons that we will discuss further in a moment, his research and ours have proceeded mostly along separate tracks; Meara and Nation have collaborated only once, on a co-authored article (Nation & Meara, 2002) for Norbert Schmitt's introductory survey of applied linguistics.

After the initial meeting in Greece in 1990, John proceeded straight to London to spend three months on sabbatical, working with Paul at Birkbeck College. This turned out to be a key transition point in Paul's career because he was in his last few months at Birkbeck, having already accepted an intriguing new opportunity to establish a specialised research unit on vocabulary acquisition in what was then the Centre for Applied Language Studies at University College, Swansea. Subsequently, we have both visited him in Swansea and have met him regularly at international conferences. However, we have never been able to entice him to New Zealand. He travels widely in Europe and has an impressive range of collaborations with scholars in his own continent. We know that he also makes trips to Canada, the USA and Japan, but it seems that our part of the world is a hemisphere too far for him. Still, we hope that some day he may visit us and give our students the chance to meet him and hear firsthand one of his stimulating presentations on his research.

It is interesting to note in this regard that the two universities, Swansea and Victoria, which are perhaps the foremost centres in the world for doctoral research in second language vocabulary, are located at opposite ends of the earth. It is stretching the metaphor too far to say that they are poles apart in other respects, but there are certainly differences. The Swansea PhD programme (as described by Alison Wray in the Preface to this volume) is distinctive, if not unique, in its emphasis on distance study and the structured way in which it builds up the candidates' expertise in research methodology, while still giving them the freedom to follow their own interests. The doctoral candidates at Victoria follow a more conventional programme of study, tailored to their individual needs and interests, alongside students working on a variety of other topic areas.

More importantly, there are differences in research orientation. Our work at Victoria grew out of very practical concerns to promote more effective vocabulary learning by students of English as a second or foreign language. In this, we built on the achievements of our mentors at the English Language Institute in Wellington, H.V. George and Helen Barnard, who in turn linked us to the British tradition of vocabulary study represented by giants in the field like Harold Palmer and Michael West. As a result, a great deal of the research effort at Victoria has gone into the development of word lists, vocabulary tests and computer programs to analyse the lexical content of texts – all intended ultimately to be of practical value to teachers and learners. By contrast, the work of Paul and his doctoral students at Swansea is motivated by more theoretical questions about the nature of vocabulary acquisition and the state of the learner's mental lexicon at various stages of development. There is a stronger influence from psychology, seen not only in the research questions, but also in the types of measures and analytical procedures they have used in their experiments. Paul's ongoing interest in theoretical models and computer simulations (of which we will say more later) is further evidence of the impact of psychology on his thinking.

The contrast in approaches has been brought home to Paul Nation on more than one occasion when he has been giving talks in various parts of the world. Members of the audience sometimes ask questions that he struggles to find an answer to, like 'What model of vocabulary storage and learning is this based on?' It usually turns out that the questioner has been in the PhD programme at Swansea. This indicates the distinctive orientation of Paul Meara's work. It also highlights the fact that, after more than 15 years of operation, the Swansea programme has an impressive roll of graduates who are not only challenging inquisitors of other people's research, but also, in many cases, productive researchers in their own right, as can be seen in the contents of this volume.

Paul Meara has noted in the past the lack of continuity in L2 vocabulary research, with many one-off studies where someone had researched an idea and written an article on it, but never followed that up with further research so that the individual studies could be set in the framework of a larger continuing investigation. Paul even produces bar graphs to show the piecemeal nature of the research, as a way of encouraging researchers to pursue vocabulary studies more persistently.

To some degree, it seemed in the 1980s and early 1990s that Paul was something of a dilettante himself within vocabulary research, in that he published a number of short papers in which he explored an interesting concept without apparently taking it further (see Meara, 1990a, 1992d). However, in reviewing his work for this chapter, we have been struck by the fact that there are definite lines of enquiry that he has pursued systematically over many years on his own account and through the work of his doctoral students. We will now move to a more formal analysis of some of the major strands of his work, to identify those continuities and point out connections with the work of others, including our own.

The Yes/No Format

We begin with the aspect of Meara's work that is perhaps closest to our own interests. He brought a significant innovation into the field of second language testing by introducing the Yes/No format, in which learners are presented with a large set of words and simply asked to indicate whether they know each one or not. This type of test had previously been used by L1 reading researchers, going back at least to Sims (1929), under the name *checklist*. A modern version of the format was introduced to L1 research initially by Zimmerman *et al.* (1977) and then by Anderson and Freebody (1983), with one crucial addition to the basic concept: a certain proportion of the words were not real words in the target language, in order to allow the scores to be adjusted for guessing, confusion, overoptimism or whatever else might lead learners to claim knowledge of words that did not exist. Meara was one of the first to propose that this checklist test would be a useful vocabulary measure for second language learners.

Meara and Buxton (1987) introduced the format to readers of *Language Testing* as an alternative to multiple-choice items as measures of word knowledge. They raised various questions about the reliability of these items to assess individual target words, but also argued that a multiple-choice test could not adequately sample the number of words required to make a good estimate of vocabulary size, which the authors saw as the primary purpose of a vocabulary test. Elsewhere, Meara (1996) has expressed the view that up to a level of about 5000 words, vocabulary size is the single best indicator of the state of the learner's lexical development.

It is easy to see how the Yes/No format would appeal to Meara from a variety of perspectives, apart from its effectiveness as a measure of vocabulary size.

- As the format lends itself well to electronic delivery, the design of computer-based Yes/No tests was for Meara an early venture into programming, which has subsequently led to a range of other computerised measures, some of which are now available as freeware under the Lognostics brand (www.lognostics.co.uk).
- Although the test-takers' task is a very simple one, the scoring of a Yes/No test poses a number of challenges and, as discussed further below, has engaged Meara's attention for many years.
- Similarly, the issue of what form the nonwords should take and how they influence the nature of the task continues to intrigue him. Early on, Meara and Buxton (1987) recognised that plausible nonwords in English could in fact turn out to be actual words in the learners' L1, especially if they were speakers of cognate languages like French. This was the focus of a later study in Canada (Meara *et al.*, 1994).
- Apart from its value as a research tool, the format has practical applications in language teaching for placement testing and as a means of monitoring the expansion of learners' vocabulary development over time. Thus, Meara has sought ways to make Yes/No tests widely available to language schools and programmes in various forms, as a product on disk distributed under the auspices of Eurocentres (Meara & Jones, 1990), as a bound set of pen-and-paper tests (Meara, 1992a), and more recently both as a published CD-ROM (Meara & Milton, 2005) and as downloadable files from the Lognostics website (e.g. Meara & Miralpeix, 2006).

The scoring of Yes/No tests has been the major concern. The original basis for scoring was the Signal Detection Theory, as developed to account for the performance of sonar operators in locating enemy submarines, hence the names of the four possible responses: hit, miss, false alarm and correct rejection. Meara has written about Yes/No scoring in several papers (Huibregtse *et al.*, 2002; Meara, 1992e, 1994), identifying the main issue as being the need to find a method of scoring that satisfactorily models the test-takers' response behaviour without, for instance, overpenalising those who respond Yes to a small number of the nonwords. Other researchers have also taken up the question (e.g. Beeckmans *et al.*, 2001; Eyckmans, 2004; Eyckmans *et al.*, 2007; Mochida & Harrington, 2006). An emerging conclusion appears to be that, for most practical purposes, it is sufficient to use a relatively simple scoring formula, such as the proportion of the hits minus the proportion of false alarms (Mochida & Harrington, 2006).

One important application of the Yes/No format has been in DIALANG, the web-based diagnostic assessment system for adult learners of 14 European languages (www.dialang.org). Meara was commissioned to develop for the system a vocabulary size test consisting of 50 actual words (all verbs, to facilitate comparability across the languages involved) plus 25 nonwords. The basic function of the test within DIALANG is to determine the learners' general level of language competence so that, in subsequent tests of various skills, they can respond to texts and items that are broadly at their level of ability. Alderson's (2005) validation research on the English version of the DIALANG measures shows that the vocabulary test is remarkably good as a general measure of competence, as reflected in very substantial correlations (0.61 to 0.72) with the skills tests.

People associated with the Swansea research programme have extended Meara's contributions in various ways. For his doctoral research, Shillaw (1999) investigated the possibility of dispensing with nonwords in Yes/No tests for English learners in Japan and relying instead on the misfit statistics provided by Rasch analysis to identify errant responses. And Milton and Hopkins (2006) have developed a version of the test called Aural_Lex, which presents the test items orally, rather than in written form on the screen. They have used Aural_Lex to investigate whether native speakers of Arabic produce underestimates of their English vocabulary knowledge in written tests because of their well-attested tendency to transfer L1 reading strategies to the decoding of English words (Milton & Hopkins, 2006; Milton & O'Riordan, 2007).

In addition to his research on the validity of DIALANG, Alderson (2005) also re-examined the general concept of diagnosis in language assessment and advocated a greater role for diagnostic tests in the field. If this call is taken up, it will give fresh impetus to the development of vocabulary measures such as Yes/No tests, and Meara's pioneering efforts will be even more widely recognised. There is evidence that this is already happening, as reported in yet unpublished research into computer-based diagnostic testing.

Word Associations

Some of Meara's earliest work on vocabulary acquisition investigated the potential of word association data to give insights into the state of the second language learner's mental lexicon. In fact, his very first published article on vocabulary had the title 'Learners' word associations in French' (Meara, 1978). The basic word association task – presenting subjects with a list of preselected words one by one and asking them to give the first word that came to mind in response – was a well-established research tool with native speakers, which had yielded two findings in particular that were of interest. One was that native speakers produced a remarkably stable set of responses to many common stimulus words, with relatively few 'deviant' items. The other finding was a developmental sequence whereby younger children gave a preponderance of responses that were syntagmatically related to the stimulus word (as in *black–bird*), but there was a clear shift as they grew older to more paradigmatic responses (*black–white*), which predominate in the output of adult subjects (Entwisle, 1966; Postman & Keppel, 1970).

These findings suggested that word association responses would provide interesting data for L2 vocabulary studies. Meara and his students at Birkbeck undertook a number of studies in the 1980s (Meara, 1982b, 1984), which showed that learner responses were much more diverse and less stable than those of native speakers. In addition, learners had a strong tendency to produce 'clang' associations: responses that sounded similar to the stimulus words but were not semantically related at all. Thus, the word association task did not seem such a productive avenue for investigating how learners organised their knowledge of L2 words. Subsequently, Söderman (1993b) found that clang associations were likely to result from a lack of familiarity with the stimulus words, rather than any phonological basis for the organisation of learner lexicons. Singleton and Little (1991) made a similar point, using data from a rather different elicitation task, the C-Test.

In the meantime, Meara moved on to a variety of other ways of exploring the basic concept of word association. One line of development began during the three-month period Read spent at Birkbeck in 1990. He was looking for a practical means of assessing depth of word knowledge and, working with Meara, devised the word associates format (Read, 1993, 1998), which essentially required learners to select appropriate associations rather than supplying them. The items consisted of a target word plus eight other words, four of which were associates (with varied semantic relationships to the target) and four distractors. Although Read has been cautious in his claims for the validity of the format as a measure of deep word knowledge, others have taken it up for their own research purposes and modified it in various ways (e.g. Greidanus & Nienhuis, 2001; Qian, 2002; Schoonen & Verhallen, 2008). Meara himself stripped the format down to its essence by creating a set of French tests (Meara, 1992b) with items comprising pairs of words, some related to each other (*vache* 'cow' and *lait* 'milk') and others not (*avion* 'plane' and *écrire* 'to write'). Bogaards (2000) conducted trials of several of these tests to compare the performance of native speakers of French with that of Dutch native speakers who had advanced levels of proficiency in French, with somewhat mixed results. In both versions of the format (Read's original one and the paired version), native speakers do not always identify the intended associations and there are issues related to the role of the nonassociated elements, so that the format remains an interesting research tool rather than a test in widespread practical use. Meara has largely moved away from seeing depth of knowledge as a useful concept. He believes that it does not help us understand how the lexicon works, although it may be useful in assessing how well individuals know particular words (Meara, 1992d: 69).

A second line of enquiry adopted by Meara has been to use chains of associations to investigate the overall structure of a person's vocabulary, building on the widely used metaphor of the lexical network or web. The original elicitation task involved presenting participants with pairs of words such as *cold...desire* and instructing them to produce a series of words to link the two stimulus ones, as in *cold → hot → passion → desire*. The resulting response chains were analysed using the mathematical principles of Graph Theory, which provides both measures and a visual representation of the density of associations among the words in a person's lexicon. The initial exploratory work at Birkbeck (Meara, 1992c; Welsh, 1988, cited in Wilks & Meara, 2002) led to further research by Wilks (1999, cited in Wilks & Meara, 2002). Despite Wilks' efforts to refine the basic model, these studies were unsuccessful in supporting the hypothesis that the associative chains of L1 speakers would be shorter and denser than those of L2 speakers, partly because participants tended to produce idiosyncratic and unpredictable responses.

Wilks and Meara (2002) took the work a stage further by developing a new elicitation procedure. As with the word associates format, it entailed a switch from supplying to selecting associations – except that in this case, associations were accepted at face value rather than being judged correct or incorrect. The participants received a questionnaire with 40 sets of five randomly selected high-frequency words in French and were asked to circle two of the words in each set that they considered to be associated. The results showed that native speakers identified significantly more associations than L2 learners did. Another interesting finding was that for both groups the number of associations was much greater than had been predicted by computer simulations of the task. An evaluation of their results led Wilks and Meara to conclude that lexical density involved more than simply their basic calculation, the average number of connections. Words varied in the strength of their associations and their centrality to the network.

Another recent study (Wilks & Meara, 2007) raised additional questions about individual variation in performance of the new elicitation task. Moving beyond classical quantitative analyses of the data on a group basis, they explored the strategies used by individual participants in finding associations among the sets of words in the questionnaire, which provided a carefully detailed set of instructions about what the participants were to do where they saw no associations, and where they saw the strongest associations. Wilks and Meara were responding in part to Nation's (2007) call in the same volume for vocabulary researchers to pay more attention to the attitudes and orientations of learners as they undertake vocabulary tests of various kinds.

Productive Vocabulary

A different area of investigation that draws on word association data also represents a crossover to another of Meara's concerns: how to find an efficient measure of productive vocabulary. For this purpose, Meara and Fitzpatrick (2000) devised Lex30, which simply requires the test-takers to write at least three responses to a sample of 30 high-frequency stimulus words, ones that typically elicit a variety of responses from native speakers. A simple computer program scores the test by awarding a point for any word that is not a high-frequency content or structure word in English. The measure correlated well with a Yes/No test of receptive vocabulary and yielded a good estimate of test-retest reliability. However, other efforts to validate Lex30 have produced mixed results (Fitzpatrick, 2007a; Fitzpatrick & Meara, 2004). The test did not distinguish native from non-native speakers as clearly as expected, and it produced rather moderate correlations with two other measures of productive vocabulary. The authors concluded that 'productive vocabulary' was a complex construct, which a simple measure like Lex30 could assess partially at best. Citing Read's (2000: 154–157) distinction between 'recall' and 'use', Fitzpatrick and Meara (2004: 72) acknowledge that Lex30 involves recall of words rather than the ability to use them in actual writing or speaking tasks.

One measure that *is* applied to learner production is Laufer and Nation's (1995) lexical frequency profile (LFP), a calculation of the percentages of words in, say, a student's essay from the first and second 1000 most frequent words, the Academic Word List, and from outside those three lists. Meara has been somewhat critical of the LFP, but has also sought ways to create a more satisfactory measure (Meara, 2006). One result was P-Lex (Meara & Bell, 2001), a program that divides a learner text into 10-word segments and determines how many non-high-frequency words occur in each 10-word segment, resulting in a summary statistic, lambda. A low lambda shows that the text contains predominantly high-frequency words, whereas a higher value is an indication of more sophisticated vocabulary use. Read and Nation (2006) used P-Lex as one measure in their recent project to investigate the lexical features of candidate performance in the International English Language Testing System (IELTS) Speaking Module. The results showed that mean P-Lex scores gave a useful summary index of the lexical sophistication of candidates at various band levels in the test, although – like the other statistics used in the study – it was not sensitive enough to be a reliable measure of vocabulary richness for individual candidates.

Modelling Vocabulary Networks

In discussing the development of the work on word associations, and the Wilks and Meara research in particular, we have already touched on Meara's growing interest in modelling vocabulary knowledge as a network. Recognising that a lexical network must inevitably be highly complex, he has sought to use simplified models that might show how elements of the network interact with one another. Through computer simulation, the models provide the basis for insights that can give quite a different perspective on vocabulary knowledge from more conventional explanations. Modelling also generates predictions that can then be tested on real data from learners in experimental studies. As Wilks *et al.* (2005: 359) put it, 'simulation modelling forces us to make critical analyses of assumptions in a way that is not always necessary in less exacting experimental environments'.

A paper that foreshadowed Meara's subsequent work with computer-based models was 'A note on passive vocabulary' (Meara, 1990a). At the time the distinction between receptive and productive vocabulary tended to be seen as a matter of strength of knowledge: learners need to know a lot more about a word in order to be able to use it productively. In his 1990 article, Meara provided a very different explanation. He saw the receptive-productive distinction as a network issue, in the sense that words that were known only receptively had few if any connections with other words in the mental lexicon. It was only when such connections were well established that a word would become available for productive use. This view was ahead of its time and had not been incorporated into discussions of vocabulary knowledge by other authors until quite recently (e.g. Nation, 2001). The idea that receptive vocabulary was qualitatively different from productive vocabulary led to a very practical suggestion for bringing words into productive use: 'stress links *from* already known words *to* newly learned [receptive] words' (Meara, 1990a). However, by the time of Meara's (1999a) paper on self-organisation in bilingual lexicons, his thinking had moved on and he suggested a different kind of explanation, focusing mainly on Boolean network models.

In his recent work, Meara has shown that computer modelling can give very interesting insights into not only the receptive/productive distinction, but also language attrition, spurts in vocabulary growth, interaction between first language and second language lexicons, switching between L1 and L2, the effect of the age of acquisition on L2 words and the activation and stabilisation of vocabulary networks (Meara, 2006).

The work with models reflects Meara's fascination with the 'black box' – what is going on inside the heads of language learners and language users. Other researchers with a more pragmatic focus on vocabulary teaching and learning can lose sight of the ultimate objective of teaching and learning, which is to help learners develop an integrated and usable system of lexical knowledge. Meara's work always keeps the psycholinguistic perspective well to the fore, and this has acted as a healthy balance to other research that has been less well-grounded in theory.

In addition, the results of computer modelling can challenge and extend the findings of studies undertaken with real learners. The results of such studies are often limited by the specific research questions that are addressed and the particular subjects and context of the experiment. Computer modelling can bypass these limitations and focus more directly on the processes involved. For example, Meara (2005a) published a critical analysis of the LFP, in which he used multiple computer simulations to test the claims Laufer and Nation (1995) made for this measure, and found good reason to question both the reliability and the validity of the LFP as a measure of the productive vocabulary knowledge of learners at different proficiency levels. In her response, Laufer (2005) not only pointed out various ways in which she considered that Meara had misrepresented the original research, but also implied that a study based purely on simulations had little credibility as an account of how real learners might perform. However, we take the view that there is a place for both approaches in L2 vocabulary research, and each can complement the other in advancing our understanding of how vocabulary knowledge develops. Research findings need to relate to theoretical models and theoretical models need to be tested.

Other Contributions

It is important to note some of Meara's other contributions to the field. In the introduction, we referred to his 1980 review article in *Language Teaching and Linguistics*. He followed that up with three volumes of annotated bibliography published by CILT (now the National Centre for Languages) in London (Meara, 1982a, 1987) and as a special issue of *Reading in a Foreign Language* (Meara, 1992c). These were invaluable resources for other researchers in the 1980s and early 1990s, given the disparate nature of L2 vocabulary research during that period. This bibliographical work has continued during the Swansea years with VARGA (Vocabulary Acquisition Research Group Archive), a web-based series of annual lists of references to publications on vocabulary learning and teaching (now available at www.lognostics.co.uk).

Another noteworthy feature of Meara's output as a scholar has been his work as a book reviewer. He is unusual among senior academics in applied linguistics in the fact that he has published reviews virtually every year throughout his career. The reviews are always stimulating to read, written in his clearly recognisable voice and often revealing as much of his own current concerns as of the content of the book itself. A good example is his review article in *Second Language Research* (Meara, 2002) on four of the main books on L2 vocabulary (two of them written by us). Apart from evaluating the individual merits of the four volumes, he considers what they reveal about the overall state of research in the field and finds it depressingly unchanged from the research agenda articulated by Palmer in the 1930s. He laments the lack of interest in the psychological dimension of vocabulary learning, in theoretical models of the bilingual lexicon and in the potential insights to be gained from computer modelling. Modestly, he omits to mention that all three of these topics are prominent in his own work, so that any neglect of them by other scholars is not for want of effort on his part to draw attention to these fresh perspectives and to work through their implications in his own research.

Summing Up

In 1990, Paul had a unique opportunity when he was appointed to set up the research unit at Swansea. He had a vision of what could be achieved through a purpose-built doctoral programme specialising in research on vocabulary acquisition. It was designed so that experienced professionals in language teaching could fit doctoral study in with their work commitments, receiving a thorough grounding in research methodology before they undertook their own studies on a variety of innovative topics in the field. The results of the programme are obvious in the quality of the publications its graduates have produced, as well as the ways in which they have taken many of Paul's original ideas and explored their implications in such depth. It is important to recognise the distinctiveness of the perspective on vocabulary acquisition represented by the Swansea research and its role in complementing what other scholars in the field have done. And we certainly hope that this research agenda will continue to be vigorously pursued for many years to come by the graduates of the Swansea doctoral programme, by new PhD students at Swansea and elsewhere, and not least by Paul himself.

Chapter 2
Putting Yes/No Tests in Context

JOHN SHILLAW

Introduction

The Yes/No test format is, according to Meara (1994), the simplest measure for estimating the number of words that learners know in a foreign language. The tests combine real words, usually selected from a corpus of some kind, and *nonwords*, which are words that look genuine but do not exist in the language. Learners are simply required to check yes or no to indicate whether or not they know each one. Each real word checked as known is designated as a *hit*, whereas a checked nonword is called a *false alarm*. The method of scoring a Yes/No test is based on Signal Detection Theory (Green & Swets, 1966), a model of decision making which posits that the higher a learner's false alarm rate is, the less likely they are to know the real words they claim to know on the test. Test scores are calculated by using a formula that adjusts the proportion of hits according to the number of false alarms; this revised figure is then used to estimate the total number of words a learner knows on a test. Finally, by extrapolation, the total number of words a learner knows in the language is estimated by multiplying the total number of words in a given target word list by the revised proportion of hits on the Yes/No test.

In the 20 years since the first published research into the Yes/No test in second language acquisition (Meara & Buxton, 1987), it has become recognised as a useful measure of vocabulary size for foreign language learners (Nation, 2001; Read, 2000). The test format has achieved the status of being a standard, so much so that the pan-European DIALANG project elected to use computerised versions of Yes/No tests to estimate the vocabulary size of learners of 14 European languages (Alderson & Huhta, 2005). However, despite its popularity, some view the test as controversial. Chapelle (1998), in particular, has been highly critical of Yes/No tests, challenging their construct validity and consequential effects on learners.

It is my intention in this chapter to do two things. In the first part, I will summarise studies that illustrate the evolution of the Yes/No test. Putting the Yes/No test into a *historical context* is essential if we wish to appreciate some of the critical issues that have dogged the test's development. The cumulative evidence gained from these studies,

I suggest, poses serious questions about the continued use of the Yes/No test in its traditional format. In the second part of the paper, I use *context* in a different sense. Here, I will describe a study that uses two forms of the Yes/No test; one in the traditional format compared with one that presents the same words in the context of a sentence. My goal is to determine whether providing context affects learners' confidence in their knowledge of test words and how this may impact on the test's reliability.

Historical Context

Zimmerman *et al.* (1977) were the first to use Signal Detection Theory to estimate vocabulary size in their study of the word knowledge of native English-speaking students at an American university. They gave a test of 300 real words of widely varying frequency and 100 nonwords to 200 subjects who were asked to indicate on a 6-point scale how confident they were that a word was real. Using a method similar to that described in the Introduction, the students' scores were calculated and then compared with scores on the verbal component of the Scholastic Aptitude Test, which the researchers proposed as being the most suitable measure for concurrent validation. From the results, Zimmerman and his colleagues claimed the test method was valid and scores were reliable, even though the two sets of scores only showed a moderate, albeit significant, correlation of 0.6.

Inspired by the work of Zimmerman *et al.*, Anderson and Freebody (1983) investigated the relationship between vocabulary size and the reading ability of fifth-grade (10 to 11-year-old) American children. They chose to emulate the methods used by Zimmerman *et al.* because their earlier research measuring children's vocabulary size (Anderson & Freebody, 1981) had thrown up significant problems with multiple-choice tests for young learners. However, instead of following the original study by using a scaled response test, Anderson and Freebody adopted a Yes/No model. In some respects, this was a surprising decision because Zimmerman *et al.* had demonstrated that when their scaled data was reanalysed in the Yes/No format, the new test was substantially less reliable than the original.

Anderson and Freebody's Yes/No test was made up of 195 real words and 131 nonwords. The real words were selected from a corpus of vocabulary found in the fourth-, fifth- and sixth-grade versions of the Stanford Achievement Test (1973). The nonwords were created by altering one or two letters in real words (e.g. *flirt* to *flort*), or using unconventional base + affix combinations (e.g. *adjustion*), which they called *pseudoderivatives*. The authors hypothesised that because poor readers have weak phonological decoding skills, they would tend to be attracted to *flort* type nonwords. Good readers, on the other hand, would be more prone to morphological errors and be more attracted to pseudoderivative nonwords.

In order to obtain a detailed profile of the words learners knew, the study combined data from Yes/No tests, multiple-choice vocabulary tests, reading tests and oral interviews about word knowledge. The results of the research enabled Anderson and Freebody to argue that corrected scores from Yes/No tests had a stronger relationship with tests of reading ability and thus provided a more reliable measure of vocabulary size. However, despite their confidence in the Yes/No test format, Anderson and Freebody expressed reservations about the reliability of the method used to score the tests. They concluded, rather unconvincingly, that the correction formula '...does passably well at separating word knowledge from the tendency to over- or understate this knowledge...' (Anderson & Freebody, 1983: 253).

White *et al.* (1989) were skeptical about the validity of the Yes/No test format for students from educational and social environments very different from the white, middle-class children who took part in the Anderson and Freebody study. To establish test validity, the researchers administered a battery of Yes/No tests, multiple-choice vocabulary tests and interviews to elementary school children from a broad cross-section of socioeconomic and ethnic backgrounds. Much to their surprise, their study broadly supported most of Anderson and Freebody's research findings. However, White *et al.* included two caveats in the discussion of their study. Firstly, they expressed the same reservation raised by Anderson and Freebody concerning the correction formula. Secondly, they concluded that the margin of error in Yes/No tests suggested they are only accurate enough to estimate vocabulary size for groups of learners, such as by class or by year: they strongly cautioned against using individual scores to estimate the vocabulary knowledge of a specific learner.

Paul *et al.* (1990) conducted a further study that partially replicated Anderson and Freebody's work. Their study differed from the original because its primary goal was to compare young children's reading skills not only to their vocabulary size, but also their depth of knowledge of the words. Like the two previous studies discussed earlier, the researchers elected to compare scores from a Yes/No test, multiple-choice test and oral interview to assess students' lexical knowledge. The results of the research again appeared to show that Yes/No test scores make a good predictor of reading skills. However, the study uncovered a serious flaw in the formula used to correct scores. They noted that if a subject claimed to know all the real words in a test, their corrected score would always be 100%, irrespective of their false alarm rate. Paul *et al.* argued that this error casts a significant doubt over the results of studies that used the same correction formula.

Like the studies cited above, Paul Meara's studies of Yes/No tests were initially inspired by the work of Anderson and Freebody. The most obvious difference between the four American studies discussed earlier and Meara's work is that he and his colleagues concentrated their research on the relationship between vocabulary recognition and the language proficiency of foreign language learners rather than the vocabulary knowledge and reading skills of native English speakers. In their seminal study of Yes/No tests, Meara and Buxton (1987) compared the results from a 100-item Yes/No test (60 real words, 40 nonwords) with those from a multiple-choice vocabulary test in order to determine which test was the best predictor of grades on the First Certificate in English (FCE) examination. Both tests turned out to be very reliable and scores were quite strongly correlated. However, only the scores from the Yes/No test demonstrated a significant relationship with the grades on the FCE. Despite the success of the Yes/No tests, Meara and Buxton identified two issues that may affect the reliability of the test scores. Their first concern was that item analysis showed very few nonwords attracted the attention of the subjects, meaning that most nonwords were redundant in terms of test measurement. Their second concern was that some nonwords were significantly more attractive to French-speaking students than students of other languages, suggesting some form of item bias. The results of two further studies (Meara *et al.*, 1994; Meara & Jones 1988) reveal the same two problems. In fact, the results from the latter study are so inconsistent with the researchers' expectations that it leads them to question the reliability of the tests not only for Francophone speakers, but also for foreign language learners in general.

In a more recent paper, Huibregtse *et al.* (2002) described a new formula, I_{SDT}, derived from an updated model of Signal Detection Theory. They claimed the new formula would provide an improved measurement of vocabulary size because it not only corrects scores for guessing, but also takes into account each individual learner's response style to the items. However, following a study of several correction formulae, including I_{SDT}, Beeckmans *et al.* (2001) had concluded that none was able to handle the response bias found in French language Yes/No tests taken by their Dutch-speaking learners. In the conclusion to their study, the researchers suggested that it is difficult to imagine how Yes/No tests can ever be accepted as reliable until a correction model is found that accounts for response bias. Since then, Eyckmans and her fellow researchers (Eyckmans, 2004; Eyckmans *et al.*, 2007) have conducted a comprehensive series of studies of the Yes/No test method and the results confirm the earlier findings of Beeckmans *et al.* (2001). In the 2007 study, Eyckmans and her colleagues considered the impact of exerting greater control over learners' responses and whether this might reduce response bias. They found that when the scores from a traditional, paper-based Yes/No test were compared with scores from a more controlled, computerised version, both tests exhibited about the same level of bias. Consequently, Eyckmans and her colleagues concluded that there is no obvious way to avoid measurement problems that are inherent to the Yes/No task. Instead of searching for yet another method of correcting Yes/No test scores, they suggest that research be conducted into developing alternative test formats that are less susceptible to variability.

From 1993 to 1998, I conducted several studies to investigate the reliability of Yes/No tests. I was mainly concerned with two issues: possible problems related to correction formulae, and whether the choice of real words and nonwords might affect test scores. Shillaw (1996) described the performance of a group of Japanese university students on three 'standard' Yes/No tests (Meara 1992a) where formulae from three earlier studies (Anderson & Freebody, 1983; Meara *et al.*, 1994; Stallman *et al.*, 1989) were used to correct scores. The results showed that the three formulae produced substantial variation in the corrected scores and that these scores had weak correlations with two tests that included multiple-choice vocabulary items from the TOEFL and FCE. Further analysis showed that very few nonwords elicited any false alarms and that the reliability of the three tests improved considerably if scores from the nonwords were discounted. In effect, the best estimate of vocabulary size turned out to be the uncorrected test score, i.e. the sum of the real words that testees claimed to know. When testees' uncorrected and corrected scores were correlated with the TOEFL and FCE scores, the uncorrected scores had a significantly higher correlation.

As a result of all these findings, I concluded that no correction formula was well suited for the task and that continued use of nonwords was counterproductive. However, this presented a dilemma. If, as the study suggested, we should drop the use of nonwords in favor of using real words, how could we be sure that learners are being honest? Clearly, if the use of nonwords and a correction formula was not viable, a new method had to be found that would provide an alternative way to verify the consistency of learners' responses. One promising solution was to use Rasch Analysis, an approach to test validation that has become well established in the language-testing fraternity (McNamara, 1996) and that has largely supplanted what is generally referred to as classical test theory (see Barfield, this volume). Rasch Analysis differs in a number of important ways from the traditional approach to test analysis. One of the most significant features of the model is that the difficulty of an item and the ability of any person taking the test can be directly compared on a common scale. The model specifically states that when the difficulty of an item and the ability of a person are exactly matched, there is a 50% chance that the testee will answer the item correctly. More generally, the model predicts that when there is a gap between person ability and item difficulty, the probability of success will vary predictably. So, if person ability is higher than item difficulty, the probability of success will be greater than 50%, but if the reverse is true, the probability of success will decrease. Perhaps the most interesting aspect of the model is that *misfits* – improbable responses – are identifiable through statistical measures. Misfits are often the result of a person guessing correctly (or incorrectly) the answer to a question that is inconsistent with their ability.

In a series of studies (Shillaw, 1999) involving Yes/No format tests using verb and noun lemmas from the 100 million word British National Corpus, I was able to demonstrate that Rasch Analysis worked consistently and reliably to measure the vocabulary size of large samples of Japanese university students. As predicted, learners who were inclined to guess were identifiable through their misfitting responses to the items, but they were few in number, usually less than 5% of the test-takers. At the end of the studies, I concluded that Rasch Analysis provided a viable alternative method to the traditional Yes/No test format. I also made a number of suggestions for further research that might help improve test reliability. One proposal was that learners presented with the target test words in a suitable context might answer with greater confidence and test reliability would increase. In the next section of this paper, I describe a study to test this idea.

Study: Contextualised Yes/No Tests

To see if providing a context for words would lead to better and more reliable tests, I needed two groups of learners and three tests: a conventional Yes/No test, a contextualised Yes/No test and a translation test. The study would compare the scores from a group of learners who would take a conventional type Yes/No test with learners taking a test with the words presented in context. Based upon their responses, I would be able to determine if the groups' total test scores varied significantly, and whether there was any significant variation in their response to each word. In common with my earlier studies (Shillaw, 1999) and the work of other researchers (Eyckmans, 2004; Eyckmans *et al.*, 2007), I considered a translation task to be the best criterion for testing that students know the meaning of the target words.

I began by selecting the 30 nouns shown in Table 2.1. Each word had been used in the research described above (Shillaw, 1999). The results of Rasch Analysis from my earlier work indicated that the students would have a high probability of knowing a small number of the test words (e.g. *shopping, medicine*), while a few words (e.g. *solicitor, facade*) would be known by hardly any students. Their knowledge of the majority of the words would lie somewhere between the two extremes.

Table 2.1 Thirty target words

academic	diagnosis	inheritance	medicine	surface
accumulation	discharge	installation	palace	surgeon
ban	entity	investment	pillow	suspicion
brigade	existence	lake	reasoning	thesis
cluster	facade	layout	shopping	urine
company	feast	mammal	solicitor	wagon

Using these 30 nouns, I created two Yes/No tests: a contextualised form and a noncontextualised version. The noncontextualised version looked the same as a conventional Yes/No test with each word listed by itself on a separate line. The contextualised version was made up of 30 sentences, each containing one of the target words, which was underlined. All the sentences were taken from the electronic version of the *Longman Dictionary of Contemporary English* (2005). Most of the target words had what might be described as a primary exemplar sentence, i.e. a sentence embedded in the definition. Some, however, did not, or were illustrated by a partial sentence. In these cases, I selected a sentence from other examples included in the supplementary database provided for each word. I was careful to select examples that I felt the students would understand and in a context they might have come across through their reading.

The format of the translation test was similar to the format of the noncontextualised Yes/No test, with each word printed on a separate line and a space next to it for students to write in their English to Japanese translation.

Subjects

The students who took part in the study were English majors at Nanzan University, Japan. Most were second-year students, attending classes in the first of a two-semester writing course. Four classes were selected for the study; two ($n = 48$) were chosen to take the traditional, noncontextualised Yes/No format test (NC-group), while two ($n = 47$) took the contextualised test (C-group). The department policy is that students are randomly assigned to writing classes according to their student number. This being the case, I assumed there would be no significant difference in the average ability of each class. Unfortunately, this could not be verified, as the students who took part in this study had not taken a common test of English in over a year. However, the Test of English for International Communication (TOEIC) results that the department has collected in recent years have consistently shown the majority of second-year students in the department to be around low-intermediate proficiency.

Method

The study was conducted in two stages. In stage one, the NC-group and C-group were given the different forms of the Yes/No test to complete in class. The students in the NC-group were instructed that each of the 30 words in the test was a noun and that they had to decide whether or not they knew each word in this form. The criteria for 'knowing' a word were defined as the ability to translate or paraphrase the word in Japanese. The test instructions for the C-group were essentially the same as those given to the NC-group, except C-group students were strongly encouraged to use the context provided to help them decide whether or not they knew a word. In both tests, students registered their choice of Yes or No by shading in a small box next to each word. Yes responses were awarded one point, with zero given for a No response. A time limit was not imposed for completing the task, but no student took more than five minutes to finish either test. The second stage of the study took place two weeks later. Both groups were reminded about the Yes/No test they had taken and were informed they were going to take a second test using the same 30 words. Students were instructed to look at each word carefully and to provide either a direct translation or a paraphrase of the word in Japanese. Students were given 10 minutes to complete the task, but almost all of them completed the test in half the allotted time.

The translation tests were assessed by myself and a native Japanese speaker with near-native English proficiency. When we did a preliminary check of the test papers to identify acceptable translations, we came across two problems that had to be resolved. The first was that some Japanese words could be written in such a way that it was not straightforward to determine whether they represented a noun or a verb. This came up so regularly that we chose to adopt a relaxed policy and accept any response that was recognisable as a translation of the English word, as long as it could be construed as being 'noun-like' in form. The second issue involved two words derived from English that some students had written in katakana, the Japanese script used for loan words. The first word, *layout* [レイアウト] is frequently used in Japanese with the same meaning as the original English word. In this case, I judged the katakana translation as completely acceptable. The second word, *wagon,* was translated by many students as [ワゴン], which is a style of car that is popular in Japan. Strictly speaking, *wagon* does not have this connotation in English and no monolingual English dictionary lists such a meaning. However, we discovered two out of the three Japanese-English dictionaries we used for reference included this definition, so I decided to accept the katakana form as partially correct.

Once the checking was complete, the translation tests were scored. The scores were allocated as follows: zero points for no response, one point for an incorrect response, two points for a partially correct response and three points for a completely acceptable response.

Results

The frequency response tables for the Yes/No tests were calculated for the two groups. I was interested here to identify if there were any differences in the frequency of Yes responses for the two groups. As exemplified in Table 2.2, differences in response ranged from 0% for the word *company* to 28.8% for the word *reasoning*. The average difference in the Yes responses for all 30 words was 8.8%. The NC-group answered Yes more frequently than No to 10 of the words, compared to 19 words for the C-group, with one tie.

The total number of words each student claimed to know was also calculated and the scores showed a mean of 18.9 (63%) and a standard deviation of 3.9. A Shapiro–Wilks test established that total scores were not normally distributed ($p = 0.003$), so a Mann–Whitney U-test was done to compare the mean score for the two groups (C-group = 19.39; NC-group 18.13). The result showed that the C-group had a significantly higher score than the NC-group ($Z = -2.260$, $p = 0.024$). In order to examine the responses of the two groups in more detail, additional Mann–Whitney U-tests were carried out to test if there were significant differences for each word. Only five words were found to vary significantly between the two groups. The NC-group had a significantly higher affirmation rate than the C-group on only the word *thesis* (17.2%), compared to the C-group having a higher rate than the NC-group on *discharge* (26.3%), *feast* (20%), *installation* (21%) and *reasoning* (28.8%).

The results at the end of the first stage of the study show that the C-group appears to be more confident than the NC-group in their overall knowledge of the test words. Yet, out of 30 words, the C-group only

Table 2.2 Example frequency response tables

Item	Group	Frequency	Percent
company	No context	48	100.0
	Context	47	100.0
reasoning	No context	26	54.2
	Context	39	83.0

demonstrates a significant difference on the four words discussed above, while the NC-group has a significant edge on one word. At this stage, it appears that providing a context for the words may have had an effect on the C-group, but nothing very substantial. However, until we have considered the results of the translation task, we still do not know if the confidence shown by either group is justified.

The analysis of the translation test scores began with the total score being calculated from the response to each word. Out of a possible maximum score of 90, the mean was 50.2 and the standard deviation was 8.4. The results from a Shapiro–Wilks test determined that the total score was normally distributed. The mean scores for both groups were close (C-group = 50.9; NC-group = 49.6) and a t-test analysis revealed no significant difference between scores.

Further analysis of the translation task results showed the groups differed significantly on only two words. The first word, *company*, was unexpected and was the result of six of the NC-group providing an incorrect translation. Of the five words that emerged as different in the Yes/No test, only *discharge* remained significantly different, with the C-group again scoring higher than the NC-group.

A final analysis involved correlating scores from the Yes/No test and the translation task to determine which group was more consistent in its responses to the Yes/No test. For a group to be considered reliable, we would expect to find a moderate to strong relationship between the total scores on the two tests. Kendall tau-b correlation was used, as one of the two scales is not normally distributed. The scores for the NC-group correlate at 0.512 ($p < 0.01$), while the C-group scores correlate at 0.256 ($p < 0.05$). The results are interesting because although both sets of correlations are significant, the difference in the coefficients reveals a notable disparity in the strength of the relationship between scores. That the C-group correlation is low compared to the moderately strong NC-group correlation suggests that the responses from the latter were significantly more reliable than those of the former.

Discussion

What we have found from the results of the first part of the study is that C-group students reported knowing four words significantly better compared to the one word reported by the NC-group. However, with the exception of the word *discharge*, the results from the translation test do not support this finding. In fact, as the correlation results show, there is good reason to doubt the reliability of the C-group's responses on both tests. To try to find out how students in the C-group had approached the contextualised Yes/No test, eight weeks after the test had been conducted, I invited students to attend a brief feedback session. Nine students from the two classes agreed to meet with me individually. Each was given a copy of their original Yes/No test paper and asked if they could recall the strategies they had used when responding to the words. All except one reported that they had paid little attention to the context, except where a word was 'difficult', 'rare' or 'strange': *solicitor* and *façade* were the words most frequently mentioned in this respect. The one student who claimed she had carefully checked each word in context was the most proficient student from the two classes, having spent most of her secondary education studying in America. She was also the only student from the C-group who claimed to know every word on the Yes/No test, but her total score on the translation test was only 80%. When asked to recall the strategies they had used to complete the translation test, the students unanimously agreed that they did not consciously think about the words in context; in fact, most confessed that they could not recall the sentences used in the Yes/No test.

My impression after the interviews was that the students were initially confident that they knew the meaning of the words that they had responded to positively in the Yes/No test; they also seemed genuinely surprised to find their translation scores were lower than they had expected. If the interviewees were typical of the other members of C-group, it would seem that students had, to some degree, a misplaced confidence in their knowledge of the test words. Could we perhaps extend this argument to the students in the NC-group? Probably, but to a lesser extent, as the difference in the correlation coefficients between Yes/No test and translation test scores seems to show that the NC-group are more reliable in their responses.

Overall, the results of this small-scale study seem to show that testing words in context does have a slight impact on the scores of students who take them. Yet, it would appear that, instead of helping students decide if they know a word, the provision of a context may actually cause confusion in some students or perhaps induce a false sense of confidence with regard to their knowledge of a word. However, this is very much an exploratory work and further studies are needed of other groups of learners to see if these results are replicated. In addition, in order to better determine how test-taking strategies might impact on measuring word knowledge, future studies should minimise the time between test and feedback.

Conclusion

In this chapter I started out by describing the history and development of Yes/No tests and argued that research evidence suggests conventional Yes/No tests are not necessarily reliable measures of vocabulary size. I then argued that a new form of Yes/No test that dispenses with the use of nonwords was a viable alternative if analysed using Rasch Analysis. In the second part of the chapter, I described an experiment to try to determine whether providing words in context assists learners in making a more reliable decision about their knowledge of a word. The results of the study suggest that the majority of students seem to have taken little notice of the context and that providing an example may have actually caused some form of distraction and reduced test reliability.

From a broader perspective, the results of this study do little to support the continued use of Yes/No tests, whether they are conventional or contextualised. But after 20 years of research, and despite the problems that have been highlighted in this chapter, Meara (2005b) remains optimistic that a new method may yet be found to rectify the flaws in the test format. I doubt that we have read the final word on Yes/No tests.

Chapter 3

Tangled Webs...: Complications in the Exploration of L2 Lexical Networks

CLARISSA WILKS

> *Oh what tangled webs we weave*
> *When first we practise to deceive.*
> Sir Walter Scott

> *...And when we've practised for a while*
> *How we do improve our style!*
> Dorothy Parker

Introduction

This chapter discusses some theoretical and methodological complexities that have recently begun to emerge from a particular strand of L2 vocabulary research. The body of work that it builds on is characterised by the fact that it has taken a formal approach to word association data – based upon the basic principles of graph theory – in order to explore and compare some properties of first and second language vocabularies (Deese, 1962a, 1962b, 1965; Kiss, 1968; Meara, 1992d; Pollio, 1963; Wilks & Meara, 2002, 2007; Wilks *et al.*, 2005). One particular concern of this research has been to investigate the powerful and pervasive metaphor of the 'vocabulary network', and to try to test some of the implicit assumptions that it leads us to make in thinking about the mental lexicon. The findings from this strand of research have raised some important questions about the comparative density and structure of L1 and L2 vocabulary networks, but these findings have not been straightforward. The title of this chapter – Tangled Webs – alludes to the notion that there may be even greater challenges associated with the design and interpretation of research in this area than we have previously supposed. Whilst those of us who are working with word association data in this way are clearly not actively 'practising to deceive', it is nonetheless important to be aware of the need to undertake a sustained interrogation of our research findings so as to avoid simply setting up alternative metaphorical constructs and assumptions that may themselves be misleading.

One of the key issues that arises from recent research into L1 and L2 word association networks is the question of the relationship between group and individual data. In much of the word association literature, the data produced by individual informants is aggregated to give group scores for various categories of informants (native speakers, learners of different proficiency levels, etc.). The conclusions drawn from these group data are then assumed to be representative of individuals within those categories. Recently, however, a number of studies have signalled potential pitfalls in such an approach. Wilks and Meara (2007) and Fitzpatrick (2007b) both draw attention to the fact that close scrutiny of data sets for both native speakers and learners reveals high levels of individual variability within the groups – high enough, indeed, to suggest that automatic assumptions about 'typical' word association behaviour for native speakers or learners may be ill-founded. The study reported in this chapter builds directly on the work of Wilks and Meara (2007) and is part of an ongoing project exploring the potential and challenges of using word association data to help model and explore L2 lexical networks. I will briefly summarise the 2007 study by way of background.

Background

Wilks and Meara (2007) compared the average numbers of word associations identified by informants from three groups: native speakers, advanced learners and intermediate-level learners. They used a receptive word association protocol administered in pencil and paper format, which required informants to pick out associations from word sets consisting of 10 randomly chosen, frequent items in French.[1] Their headline finding was that average hit rates increased with proficiency. In the terms of the simple graph theoretical model that they had proposed, this appeared to confirm the 'commonsense' hypothesis that lexical networks become denser as proficiency advances (Wilks & Meara, 2002). Nevertheless, their findings were not straightforward. As part of their analysis of the data, they drew up best fit Poisson curves to describe the distribution of word association hits for each of their informant groups. They matched the curves derived from the group data against the hit-rate profiles of individual informants. Whilst the group curves suggested that the fundamental finding that word association hit rates would rise as proficiency level increased was plausible, the mismatch of individual performance curves to group norms was great enough to raise doubts about the interpretation of the group data. In the case of native speakers and advanced-level learners, Wilks and Meara found that only 50% of the individual profiles could be described as 'regular' in terms of the group curves. For lower-level learners, irregular profiles were found for 67% of informants.

In seeking to account for this unanticipated level of individual variation, Wilks and Meara (2007) raised the possibility that learner attitudes to word association exercises and the approaches they adopted in taking the tests might be interfering with what researchers had previously assumed to be 'spontaneous' word association behaviour. They focussed their attention on two issues in particular: firstly, the question of differential judgements by informants concerning what counted as a legitimate association; and secondly, the possibility that informants in all groups were adopting conscious strategies when taking the test in this format that might impact on hit rates. Their *post hoc* analysis of the written data, and illustrative qualitative data collected from a single informant as an adjunct to the study, allowed Wilks and Meara to raise some intriguing questions in respect of these two issues. They signalled the need for further investigation of these questions, and in particular for further qualitative insights into the perceptions and behaviour of several informants rather than a single test-taker.

The work reported in this chapter is thus an attempt to move this investigation forward. It has two linked aims. Firstly, it sets out to provide supplementary qualitative information that can further our understanding of how informants perceive and approach word association tests, and of how this may impact on what the data from these tests can tell us. Secondly, it aims to help us construct a principled framework for future research design and the systematic analysis of written data.

The Study

Six informants, five females and one male, participated in this phase of the project. All were native speakers of English, who ranged in age from 21 to 46 years and who were either studying or working in a British university. All of the informants were advanced learners of French, who in addition to studying to at least A-level standard had spent a minimum of one year in a French-speaking country. More detailed information on each of the participants (L3 knowledge, additional proficiency information, etc.) was also recorded for the purposes of individual mapping, as discussed in **Data Analysis and Discussion**.

Data were collected from two word association tests and from a semistructured interview with each informant. First, informants completed the same 20-item word association exercise used in Wilks and Meara (2007). They did this individually in the presence of the researcher. The researcher first ran through the written test instructions and example question with the informants to ensure that they had understood what was required. They were then given 15 minutes to complete the exercise.

Table 3.1 Example questionnaire item and informant responses

Example set of 10 lexical items				
a: sérieux	b: pays	c: sonner	d: gêner	e: empêcher
f: pauvre	g: couler	h: fête	i: adresse	j: peindre
Example informant responses				
Informant	Associations			
02 Barbara	f–b g–j h–c			
03 Chris	h–g f–e c–i			
06 Frank	f–b			

Source: Wilks and Meara (2007)

The test asked informants to pick out as many, or as few, associations as they saw in word sets of 10 lexical items chosen randomly from the *Francais Elémentaire* list (roughly the 1000 most frequent items in French; Gougenheim *et al.*, 1956). The example in Table 3.1 shows the presentation format and gives some exemplar responses from three of the informants.

Immediately after the exercise, the informants took part in a semistructured interview that focussed on three issues: (1) informants' attitude to, and overall experience of, the word association exercise; (2) the criteria they had used to decide on what counted as an association; (3) their approach to the task of looking for associations in the word sets. The interview schedule consisted of six open questions:

- How easy/difficult did you find the exercise?
- Did you know all the words in the exercise? If not, which ones didn't you know? Even if you did know all the words, were some of them less familiar than others/were there some you were less sure about?
- Did you have as much time as you needed to complete it? Would you have done anything different if you had had more time?
- What criteria did you use to decide what to count as an association?
- When deciding if words were associated, which features of the words were most important (e.g. meaning, sound, spelling, etc.)?
- How did you approach the task of looking for associations in the word sets? Did the form in which the test was presented affect how you worked in any way?

The interview format allowed informants to elaborate on their answers as they wished and gave them the opportunity to make further comments not covered by the pre-prepared questions.

Six months later, the participants completed a second word association exercise. On this occasion, the test consisted of only 12 word sets; the reduced format was designed to minimise the risk of 'questionnaire fatigue' or boredom amongst participants on taking the test a second time (see Nation [2007] for a discussion of the impact of 'learner attitude' on individual variability in vocabulary test performance). Ten of the 12 word sets were identical to the first 10 items of the first exercise, although presented in a different order. The two remaining items were new word sets, included in the test as distractors in an attempt to prevent informants simply remembering their responses from the first test. Data from the two distractor items was disregarded in subsequent analyses. The purpose of the second test was to provide insights into the consistency of test approaches and behaviour for individual informants.

Data Analysis and Discussion

The very rich data generated by these various interventions (tests and interviews) can be analysed in a number of ways. First, basic hit-rate performance on the word association tests can be measured for a simple comparison of informants' performance with learner behaviour from earlier studies using this same test. Secondly, interview data for all subjects can be coded to discern common themes emerging from the group in relation to each of the three categories described above: experience of and attitude to the test; criteria applied for deciding on associations; strategies adopted in approaching the exercise. Finally, data from each informant's interview can be mapped on a case-by-case basis against particular features of their actual individual performance on the two tests, such as hit rate or consistency of word association responses. The approach adopted here is motivated by the desire to build on earlier findings and to exploit 'the reflexive relationship between theory and methodology' referred to by Wilks and Meara (2007: 181). They argued for an approach in lexical research '...in which systematic analysis of data leads us to frame emerging theoretical positions in a manner [...] analogous to the principles of Grounded Theory' (Glaser & Strauss, 1967).

It is not possible within the scope of this chapter to present the detail of all of the findings emerging from these analyses. I will concentrate here on the most important issues arising from the thematic analysis of the interview data, but I will also feed into our discussion some headline findings that emerge from the individual mapping exercise.

Basic quantitative data

The basic quantitative results from the word association tests can be very simply presented. Table 3.2 shows the mean number of word association 'hits' for the group of informants taken together across both word association tests.

In terms of mean word association hit rates, our small group of informants is broadly in line with what we would expect from learners at this level. Group data from learners of this proficiency level tested in Wilks and Meara (2007) showed a mean hit rate of 2.86 hits per word set.

The second point to make here, however, is that looking at Table 3.2 and Table 3.3 together provides a salutary reminder of the kind of individual variability that is masked by the presentation of group results. It is true, of course, that the impression of individual variability is exaggerated by the very small size of the group, but it does nevertheless offer further corroboration of the heterogeneity within groups that we have referred to earlier. Here we see there are quite marked differences within our small group in terms of average hit rates. The average hit rate on the first test ranges from just 1.6 hits per word set for Frank, to 6.1 hits for Elaine, and on the second test, from an average hit rate of 1.0 hits (Alex) to 5.9 hits (Elaine).

The data presented in Table 3.3 show that, in terms of consistency of numbers of associations found per test item, individual informants tend to be fairly consistent across the two tests. Five out of the six participants have a slightly lower average hit rate in test two, but the differences are

Table 3.2 Group mean number of hits per word set[a]

	Test 1	Test 2	Test 1 and 2 together
Mean hits for group	3.25	2.73	2.99
n	6	6	6

[a]Data are presented in this format to allow comparison with earlier work. Clearly, with such a small group, standard statistical operations are not meaningful or appropriate

Table 3.3 Comparison of individual association test scores on Test 1 and Test 2

Informant	Mean hits Test 1	Mean hits Test 2	Range Test 1	Range Test 2
01 Alex	2.45	1.0	1–5	0–2
02 Barbara	1.9	1.6	0–4	1–3
03 Chris	2.9	2.4	0–6	1–3
04 Denise	4.6	3.6	2–8	1–8
05 Elaine	6.1	5.9	3–10	3–8
06 Frank	1.6	1.9	0–5	1–4

very small, with the possible exception of Alex where the drop is more marked. Naturally, we cannot hazard any conclusive view of hit-rate performance on the basis of this small sample. Nevertheless, the data do suggest a possible pattern that merits future investigation in a larger data set. The scores indicate that informants may fall into two broad types: they are either 'big hitters' (e.g. Denise and Elaine) who identify large numbers of associations per item or 'small hitters' who are more parsimonious in their identification of associations.

The apparent tendency for individual informants to identify more or fewer associations will merit further investigation in the future. Detailed individual profiling for the informants in this group has, so far, not found any obvious patterns of correlation. For example, there do not appear to be any clear correlations between hit-rate behaviour and any of the more obvious variables: detailed proficiency level, knowledge of L3 or explicit test-taker strategies. Fitzpatrick (2007b) has suggested that as regards individual preferences in word association response types, we may need to look to more complex characterological or cognitive variables (creativity, intelligence, memory type, etc.). These wider considerations may also be useful in attempting to account for individual behaviour in identifying associations.

Interview data: Key themes

Experience of/attitude to the test

As regards the difficulty of the exercise, participants' responses were fairly homogeneous, all respondents reporting that they found the test interesting and rating it as neither easy nor difficult ('moderate'; 'easy but challenging'; 'not too difficult'). The most challenging aspect of the exercise, as reported by all informants, was that it contained vocabulary items that they either did not know at all, or that they were unsure about. They were consistent in reporting that they had consciously avoided all such items in identifying associations. When asked to recall unfamiliar items, informants cited between two and six words that they were sure they did not know. Of these, the words *forgeron* (= blacksmith) and *ficelle* (= thread, type of loaf) were the most commonly reported, being cited by four informants in each case. These particular examples are a reminder that frequency lists are very culturally specific and that they date fairly rapidly. As we have indicated, the items were randomly selected from a list that is now over 50 years old (Gougenheim *et al.*, 1956); some items that were part of a 'core' vocabulary in France in the 1950s may very well not be part of the 'fundamental' vocabulary for London-based learners in 2007, either in terms of their L2 exposure or via the medium of their L1. Having said this, however, scrutiny of the word sets used in the exercise reveals that there was only one other lexical item, *moisson* (= harvest), which could be characterised as 'outdated' in this way.

Another theme emerging from the data was informants' suspicion about the test. Three of the six interviewees reported that they believed that the word sets must have been manipulated in some way to plant associations so that they should have been 'looking for something' (Barbara). They confirmed that they had felt this despite the reassurances given to them in the written and verbal instructions that there were no 'right' or 'wrong' answers and that they should work instinctively. Interestingly, one informant further commented that the inclusion of 'social' words in the word sets (e.g. *pauvre*) had made the task seem more 'serious' (Chris).

These findings are intriguing in that they may add a new perspective to the question of 'learner attitude', an issue singled out by Nation as one of the most significant factors affecting the validity of vocabulary measures (Nation, 2007: 35). Nation's concern is that informants do not take tests seriously, that they may simply not care about how they respond and that this will skew test results. For the informants in the current study, this is clearly not the case; indeed, if anything, they are at risk of trying too hard. Nevertheless, their suspicion regarding the design and intentions of the test may have interfered with their ability to respond spontaneously, just as much as the boredom and unwillingness to cooperate identified by Nation. This observation reinforces the notion that we need to be conscious that the most explicit test instructions may be 'subverted' even by well-meaning test-takers who, quite understandably, react with suspicion and a certain self-consciousness when faced with tests of this kind.

The findings in this respect also raise important methodological issues. We might speculate that the suspicion of the informants in this case was unwittingly fostered by the conditions under which the test was administered. Data were purposely collected in supervised conditions in order to ensure that informants completed the task independently and without recourse to dictionaries. However, in mimicking a classroom exercise – a pencil and paper test supervised by the researcher in the role of 'invigilator', the administration of the test may have contributed to informants' sense that particular responses were expected of them. If this is the case, then we may be prompted to speculate that a belief in the existence of 'naïve' subjects, as widely accepted in the psychological and other scientific literature, may be overoptimistic. At the very least, we may conclude that such informants are hard to find. While informants in the current study had no prior knowledge of either the experimental protocol or the vocabulary research it was feeding in to, they were nevertheless 'sophisticated' in terms of their experience of test-taking in general and may therefore have applied nonspontaneous techniques developed over the course of their wider educational experience.

Criteria used in identifying word associations

An initial observation that emerges very clearly from this category of the data is that all respondents reported experiencing doubts about what should count as an association, with three of them volunteering the same comment that their selections were 'a bit tenuous' in places. All informants were also aware that there was a considerable degree of personalisation in their selection of associations; they referred to the importance of personal memories and experiences ('whether I'd seen or experienced them together') in guiding their decisions. This finding triangulates well with the evidence of earlier work that suggested an unexpectedly high degree of idiosyncrasy in larger sets of data generated by both native speakers and learners using a variety of elicitation tools (Wilks, 1999; Wilks & Meara, 2002, 2007).

Another important and complex theme emerging from participants' reports of the criteria used to identify associations concerns the question of the extent to which their associations were semantically driven. The informant feedback here can perhaps offer a further wrinkle to debates in the research literature concerning the questions of what, if any, types of associations are typical of different categories of informants (e.g. adults, learners of different proficiency levels, etc.) and of how we should classify these associations. Recently, Fitzpatrick (2006, 2007b) has argued for a more elaborate taxonomy of associations to expand and refine the conventional categorisation into *syntagmatic, paradigmatic* or *clang* (i.e. phonologically motivated) associations (Politzer, 1978; Söderman, 1993a). She proposes a classification into three broad groupings, 'meaning-based', 'position-based' and 'form-based', each with subcategories, and adds a further category of 'erratic' associations to account for inexplicable associations.

Whilst the arguments that Fitzpatrick advances for moving beyond the oversimplified syntagmatic/paradigmatic/clang split are convincing, it is nevertheless worth noting the mismatch that emerges from the qualitative data reported in this chapter between expert classification and learner perceptions. All participants in the study stated explicitly and unequivocally that they had only considered the meaning of items when deciding on associations. They contrasted this with the fact that they had not focussed at all on sound or spelling.[2] When expanding on these comments, they reported a range of association criteria that they had invoked. Examples include:

- 'similar meanings' [Barbara];
- 'definitions' [Denise];
- 'opposites – vaguely' [Frank];

- 'words that often go together' [Alex];
- 'words that go together in a phrase' [Frank];
- 'nouns that go with a particular verb' [Elaine, Frank].

Despite the informants' clear understanding that all of these criteria were related to the meaning of items, this is not necessarily how they would be classified in Fitzpatrick's terms. The list of examples, in fact, embraces what for her would be both meaning- and position-based associations. The last three examples in the list, for instance, sit more comfortably as position-based associations in Fitzpatrick's taxonomy, despite the fact that the learners themselves clearly perceived the associations that they had identified according to these criteria to be motivated by meaning. It goes without saying, of course, that we should not expect informants to articulate a meta-analysis of the dimensions of word knowledge in the same way as vocabulary researchers. Nevertheless, these data do act as a useful reminder that, having 'unpacked' some of the complexities of lexical knowledge, we need subsequently to reapply a more holistic perspective that emphasises and assesses the relationships between them. Fitzpatrick's more sophisticated and sensitive classification system may unwittingly imply that her three main categories each relate to each other in the same way as distinct and equal classes. The qualitative data reported here seem to suggest, however, that the distinction between 'meaning' and 'form' is in fact by far the most salient for language users. They seem to perceive 'meaning' and 'form' as distinct and contrasting aspects of lexical items, whereas 'position' appears to be understood as a subcategory of 'meaning'.

Having said this, we are of course very alive to the fact that informants' *post hoc* reflections on what drives their identification of associations cannot necessarily be assumed to provide a complete picture of what actually motivates their association behaviour. The following individual insight from the interview data illustrates this point very clearly.

One informant reported a very interesting process in respect of her responses to test item 10, which presented the following word set:

a: passeport   b: quai   c: conduire   d: profond   e: village
f: vache   g: pouvoir   h: progrès   i: mari   j: mouche

Among the six associations that she identified in the word set was the pair *mari-mouche* (= husband-fly). In her follow-up interview, she singled out this association when asked about the criteria she had used for deciding on associations. She reported that she had made the link instinctively and then had no time to change it. However, she had realised after writing down the pair that she had been prompted by the sound correspondence between the French item *mouche* (= fly) and the Russian word муж [IPA] (= husband) that she recalled from a beginner's course she had taken three years earlier.

This individual's retrospective account encourages two observations. Firstly, it foregrounds the fact that, at least in a timed condition, test-takers may not be fully aware of what motivates their apparently 'intuitive' responses. Secondly, it may underline the difficulties inherent in classifying types of word association even with the benefit of *post hoc* informant feedback. The *mari-mouche* association is interesting: the link from *mari* to муж is semantic; the mapping from муж to *mouche* is phonological. It thus appears to be a kind of hybrid response, combining both 'clang' and semantic motivation, mediated by L3 interference and yet 'intuitive' or automatic. Clearly, this is only a single instance, and could be classed as an 'erratic' association. However, to simply stop at this classification might be to miss a potentially interesting insight that can feed in to the long-running debate over formal versus semantic organisation in the L2 lexicon (Meara, 1978, 1980, 1982b, 1984; Singleton, 1993, 1999; Singleton & Little, 1991).

Test-taker strategies

Wilks and Meara's *post hoc* scrutiny of their written data found some evidence that informants appeared to be employing conscious strategies in responding to the test format that undermined the spontaneity of their responses. In particular, they identified a 'systematic checking strategy', whereby informants 'worked their way alphabetically through the word sets looking first for any links with word "a", then for links with word "b" and so on. For example: *ab aj bc bj ce ch*' (Wilks & Meara, 2007: 178). This strategy was used by 22% of their native speaker informants (eight out of 36), but by only two of the learners in their study, both of whom were in the higher proficiency group. Wilks and Meara pointed to the need for further qualitative data to help us to identify possible test-taker strategies that might be less visible in the written data.

The interview data in this study reveal that three of the six advanced learners (Chris, Elaine and Frank) participating in the qualitative study had used the systematic checking strategy – working through the word set from item (a) looking for associations – but all of them had abandoned it early in the test, either because it took too long or because they 'couldn't be bothered' (Denise). Of the three other informants, two reported that they worked entirely randomly. A sixth informant reported that she had concentrated on the most familiar words in the sets and had looked for the associations that she could find with these items.

This last insight is interesting in that it complements the finding reported above that participants consciously avoided words that they were not sure about. It may be, then, that in receptive word association protocols, learners' sense of how *well* they know a word, even within a core vocabulary of very frequent words, is an important inhibiting factor in the way they approach the task. Having said this, however, it is clearly important to be wary of assuming that this test-taker characteristic applies uniformly to all learners. Our earlier discussion alerts us to the possibility that 'caution' in identifying word associations may rather be another characterological variable that will have a different impact for individual L2 test-takers.

As regards test-taker strategies, therefore, the qualitative data we have so far collected do not suggest that informants are employing an array of unsuspected approaches. One reason for this that emerges clearly from the interview data is the effect of time constraints. Five of the informants reported that they had been aware of having to work quickly, and four of these reported that if they had had more time, they would have gone back over their answers to look for additional associations. It seems, then, that the timed test condition is working as intended for L2 informants in curtailing systematic test-taking approaches to some extent. It is not clear, however, what, if any, time pressure would be sufficient to have this effect for native speakers.

Conclusions

The findings from the qualitative study that we have reported in this chapter supplement the quantitative information collected from earlier work. They highlight a number of theoretical and methodological issues in word association research of this kind.

The data gathered further corroborate earlier speculations concerning the substantial degree of variability within what much previous research had assumed to be homogeneous groups (learners of different proficiency levels, native speaker, etc.). In our analysis of the basic quantitative data, we found heterogeneity in the word association behaviour of our group of advanced learners, but observed that individual informants did themselves appear to be consistent in some aspects of their test performance (e.g. hit rate). We further noted that the detailed profiling of informants that is currently being undertaken does not so far suggest that there is any obvious variable that could account for these individual patterns (proficiency, test-taker strategy, L3 knowledge). Therefore, in future work, it will be important to find ways to explore how different, and perhaps less 'convenient', kinds of factors may explain the different degrees of caution or liberalism that individual informants display in identifying word associations. It may be that individual characterological traits (such as creativity or risk taking, for example) may have a role to play in determining association behaviour.

As regards particular test-taking strategies employed by informants, we found only one informant using a strategy other than the 'systematic checking' approach identified by Wilks and Meara (2007). We noted the importance of time pressure in constraining nonspontaneous behaviour. However, our discussion would also lead us to suggest that the advantage of the time-constrained test condition may be offset by the possible disadvantage of shaping informants' expectations of the nature of the test. The 'suspicious' approach of our informants led us to question the existence of the genuinely 'naïve' subject. This is an important matter in that it may impact on our thinking about how far word association tests such as this can provide a window – even a misty one – into the organisation of the mental lexicon.

The data I have presented in this chapter are neither easy nor convenient. Indeed, they are the classically 'messy' data that, as a stand-alone entity, Paul Meara has rightly cautioned generations of research students about. Nevertheless, as one part of a wider, ongoing research project – a 'durative' project in Singleton's terms (Singleton, 1999) – data of this type do have a valuable contribution to make. They allow us to refine our interpretations of the findings of quantitatively orientated empirical studies and large-scale simulations, and assist in the attempt to derive informed frameworks for future research design.

Notes

1. The elicitation tool used was developed from an instrument trialled in an earlier study (Wilks & Meara, 2002) and has parallels with the V-Links on-line instrument devised by Meara and Wolter (2004).
2. The question of the impact on association behaviour of receptive versus productive tasks has been flagged in earlier work (Wilks, 1999: 161). However, the contrast in findings between the data in this study and that reported by Fitzpatrick (2006, 2007b) suggests that this issue merits more sustained and systematic investigation in the future.

Chapter 4
Word Association Profiles in a First and Second Language: Puzzles and Problems

TESS FITZPATRICK

Introduction

Word association tasks, with their apparent capacity to expose lexical connections in a way not muddied by syntactical considerations, are an attractive proposition to those of us interested in L2 lexical processes. However, findings from the application of word association task data to even the most fundamental questions in second language processing have been far from straightforward. We might ask, for example, whether more proficient non-native speakers are likely to produce broadly the same response words, or to make the same kinds of association, as native speakers. Many studies conclude, tentatively, that this is indeed the case, either in terms of the actual lexical items produced (e.g. Sökmen, 1993) or in that L2 and L1 adult users seem to prefer paradigmatic to syntagmatic responses (e.g. Greidanus & Nienhuis, 2001; Rüke-Dravina, 1971). However, a number of other studies have produced findings that question these conclusions, with Kruse *et al.* (1987) finding no correlation between proficiency and native-like-ness of response, and Orita (2002) suggesting that the type of association made is more dependent on the choice of cue word than the proficiency of the learner. This lack of clarity is particularly frustrating in the face of a wealth of literature from first language studies and psychology, where word association tasks seem to have revealed more consistent and insightful findings. Work by Ervin and Entwisle in the 1960s, for example, led to the accepted notion of a syntagmatic-paradigmatic shift in the L1 word association behaviour of children (Entwisle, 1966; Ervin, 1961). For over a century, the psychology literature has used word association behaviour in the identification and exploration of disorders such as schizophrenia and dementia (e.g. Gewirth *et al.*, 1984; Kent & Rosanoff, 1910; Merten, 1993; Schuessler & Cressey, 1950; Sommer, 1901).

Despite its established role in psychology and L1 research, the use of word association to explore second language phenomena was relatively unexplored when, in 1982, Meara published 'Word associations in a foreign language'. There are crucial exceptions to this, of course, which had started to test the potential applications of word association tasks to the L2 context. These early studies include the work of Riegel and Lambert and their colleagues in the 1960s and 1970s (e.g. Lambert, 1972; Lambert & Rawlings, 1969; Riegel, 1968; Riegel *et al.*, 1967; Riegel & Zivian, 1972), and studies such as those by Rüke-Dravina (1971), Politzer (1978) and Randall (1980). Meara himself had already started to explore this area of research with a study investigating learners' word associations in French (1978). However, Meara (1982b: 32) rightly dismissed much of this earlier work (including his own) as 'content merely to describe the sorts of responses learners produce'. The 1982 paper, on the other hand, represents an important leap forward in L2 word association research for two reasons. Firstly, it was bold in its suggestion that word association studies offer a methodology that can be used to answer the pivotal question 'what does a learner's mental lexicon look like, and how is it different from the mental lexicon of a monolingual native speaker?' (Meara, 1982b: 29). Secondly, it was honest in that it admitted to, and addressed, a number of 'methodological puzzles and problems' (Meara, 1982b: 29) inherent in word association research.

In this 1982 paper, Meara, like others before him (e.g. Riegel & Zivian, 1972), found non-native speaker responses to 'differ fairly systematically from those produced by native speakers' (Meara, 1982b: 30), both in terms of homogeneity of response (they produce a much more varied set of responses than native speakers) and in terms of the actual responses given; Meara (1982b: 30) claims that 'in extreme cases, it is possible to find instances of stimulus words for which the list of native speaker and learner responses share practically no words in common'. This apparent difference between L1 and L2 responses, together, perhaps, with Meara's tantalising suggestion that word associations might provide an insight into the mental lexicon, led a number of researchers to pursue L2 word association studies in the 1980s and 1990s. Most of these (e.g. Kruse *et al.*, 1987; Schmitt, 1998a; Söderman, 1993a; Sökmen, 1993) were based on the assumption that the difference between a learner's word association behaviour and that of a native speaker would decrease as proficiency increased. In other words, the more proficient a learner became, the more her/his associations would resemble those of a native speaker. However, Meara had already pointed out, in a volte-face from the position taken in his 1978 paper, that 'teaching a language aims to produce people who are bilingual, not mere replicas of monolingual speakers' (Meara, 1982b: 34). Regardless of this reminder, the assumption that the L2 mental lexicon will become more native-speaker-like with increased proficiency continues to pervade much of the L2 word association literature.

Puzzles and Problems

This brings us to a more detailed consideration of Meara's (1982b: 29) 'methodological puzzles and problems'. In addition to the problematic assumption about the development of L2 associations mentioned above – there being neither a theoretical nor a consistent empirical basis for assuming that L2 associations will become more native-speaker-like as proficiency progresses – he lists two major methodological concerns. The first of these is the traditional categorisation of word association responses into paradigmatic, syntagmatic and clang. As Meara notes, these categories allow for comparison with L1 language development (see Ervin, 1961; Entwisle, 1966), but 'personally, I have always found that this distinction is very difficult to work in practice, especially when you cannot refer back to the testee for elucidation, but this difficulty is not generally commented on in the literature' (Meara, 1982b: 30). The second problem concerns the number and the choice of words generally used as stimuli in these tasks. Some studies use as few as four stimulus words (Rüke-Dravina, 1971), and words are usually chosen from high-frequency lists such as the Kent Rosanoff list (1910). Frequent words tend to produce predictable responses, and produce similar responses in L1 and L2, making it impossible to decide whether non-native-speaker responses are produced 'via translation into the mother tongue and back again' (Meara, 1982b: 33). In addition to this, early on in the learning process a small number of frequent words are acquired that 'form the hard core of the learners' L2 vocabulary' (Meara, 1982b: 33) and which, Meara argues, are probably not representative of the lexicon in acquisition.

In light of these concerns, it is perhaps unsurprising that researchers who have risen to the challenge of applying word association techniques to the second language acquisition context have failed to produce consistent or conclusive findings. There is a general agreement that word association studies can tell us something about the L2 lexicon (e.g. Politzer, 1978; Riegel, 1968; Schmitt, 1998a; Sökmen, 1993), but this is tempered by a growing realization that exactly what they tell us is unclear (Kruse *et al.*, 1987; Söderman, 1993a; Wolter, 2001). There is some indication that clang responses occur more frequently in less proficient non-native speakers (Meara, 1982b) and that paradigmatic responses occur more frequently in more proficient non-native speakers (Politzer, 1978; Söderman, 1993a), but the findings of at least one recent study contradict this (Nissen & Henriksen, 2006). It seems that the word association-driven insights into the mental lexicon that Meara hinted at in 1982 are frustratingly elusive.

Designing Methods to Tackle the Puzzles and Problems

The experimental work that I present in this chapter constitutes the third in a series of studies (see also Fitzpatrick, 2006, 2007b), where I have taken on the challenge of addressing Meara's 'methodological puzzles and problems'. The first of the problems that I considered was the traditional classification of responses as either paradigmatic, syntagmatic or clang. These distinctions are difficult to define and, in any case, are too broad to show precise differences in response patterns (for a fuller discussion of these problems see Fitzpatrick, 2006: 125–127). In these studies, I address the categorization problem by introducing a more detailed and transparent classification system, consisting of subcategories under the three main headings of meaning-, position- and form-based responses (see Table 4.1). The design of this system is informed both by an analysis of response data from previous studies, and by consideration of the literature concerning aspects of word knowledge, such as the taxonomy proposed by Nation (2001: 27). A more detailed discussion of the rationale behind these categories can be found in Fitzpatrick (2006: 129–131). It is clear from the left-hand column of Table 4.1 that there are overlaps here with the traditional paradigmatic, syntagmatic and clang categories. This system, though, allows for two stages of analysis for each association. First, the researcher determines whether the response is based on a meaning-, position- or form-connection. Depending on which of these categories is selected, the researcher then determines which of the four (meaning-based), three (position-based) or two (form-based) subcategories the association belongs to. It is these subcategories that hold the potential for more precise analysis of word association behaviour; 'conceptual associations', for example, represent a considerable proportion of responses, but are often almost impossible to categorise as paradigmatic or syntagmatic, as the example 'immigration > politics' demonstrates. In terms of being user-friendly and transparent, the categorisation system in Table 4.1 may offer an improvement on the paradigmatic, syntagmatic, clang classifications.

Meara's second problem related to the way in which stimulus words are selected for word association tasks. Traditionally, these have been high-frequency content words with predictable responses (again, the issues associated with the selection of cue words are discussed more fully in Fitzpatrick, 2006: 123–124). In this series of studies, I have used items from the Academic Word List (AWL; Coxhead, 2000), which excludes the 2000 highest frequency English words, and which contains relatively few concrete nouns (a class that tends to produce predictable responses). The example cue words in the right-hand column of Table 4.1 are from the AWL. By using cue words from the AWL, we are avoiding the frequent,

Table 4.1 Categories and subcategories for processing response data

Category	Subcategory	Definition	Example cue > response
Meaning-based association	Defining synonym	x means the same as y	*purchase > buy*
	Specific synonym	x can mean y in some specific contexts	*consultation > talking*
	Lexical set/context relationship	x y same lexical set/coordinates/meronyms/superordinates/context relationship	*goals > football*
	Conceptual association	x and y have some other conceptual link	*immigration > politics*
Position-based association	Consecutive xy collocation	y follows x directly (includes compounds)	*negative > reaction*
	Consecutive yx collocation	y precedes x directly (includes compounds)	*assurance > life*
	Other collocational association	y follows x in a phrase but with other content word/words between them	*specific > disability (specific learning disability)*
Form-based association	Change of affix	y is x plus and/or minus a prefix or suffix	*construction > constructive*
	Similar form only	y looks or sounds similar to x but has no clear meaning link	*label > lapel*
Others	Erratic association	y has no decipherable link to x	*involved > brow*
	Blank	no response given	

early-acquired words that Meara warns may not be representative of the learner lexicon. Rather, it is probable that the list contains, for intermediate and advanced learners, words which have been acquired later, or are 'at the periphery of (their) vocabulary' (Meara, 1982b: 33), and therefore are more typical samples from their L2 lexicon.

Questioning the Assumptions Underlying the Puzzles and Problems

As well as tackling these methodological issues, my aim in these three studies has been to carefully examine the assumptions on which earlier word association research has been based. The least sound of these is almost certainly the assumption, mentioned above, that non-native speaker word association patterns differ consistently and systematically from those of native speakers, and that we can use this difference to make judgements about the developing lexicon of an individual L2 learner (Politzer, 1978; Riegel, 1968; Schmitt, 1998a; Söderman, 1993a; Sökmen, 1993). In the first of the three studies (Fitzpatrick, 2006), I investigated differences in native and non-native speaker responses to a word association task, using the new categorization system and a list of 60 stimulus words selected from AWL. The study found significant differences between the word association behaviour of native and non-native speakers, but only in certain categories of response. Native speakers produced more collocational responses and more exact synonymous responses. Non-native speakers produced more responses with looser conceptual or contextual links, and more form-based responses. The most important finding, though, was that there was no significant correlation between non-native speaker proficiency – as measured by a vocabulary size test (Meara & Jones, 1990) – and the number of responses given in those categories that differentiate between native and non-native speakers. In other words, these learners did not appear to be moving towards more native-like response behaviour as their L2 proficiency increased. In order to explain this finding, not only did the learner response behaviour need to be further scrutinised, but the hitherto accepted construct of 'native speaker response behaviour' also needed to be unpacked.

With the aim of determining how useful the notion of 'native speaker response behaviour' might be, in my next study I set out to investigate homogeneity and consistency of response in a native speaker subject group, by comparing word association task data produced by individuals on two separate occasions (Fitzpatrick, 2007b). What clearly emerged from this study was that, contrary to the assumptions of previous research, native speakers cannot be regarded as a homogeneous group in terms of word association behaviour: between subjects, native speakers vary greatly in their association behaviour. Interestingly, though, it seems that native speakers do have preferred response profiles as individuals: the response profile that any single subject produced for the first association task was very similar to their profile for the second. In other words, within subjects, native speakers respond to cue words in a consistent way. Put crudely, this means that whereas one individual may produce a lot of straight collocational responses, another might produce a high proportion of defining synonyms as responses, and so on, and, crucially, those individuals will display the same behaviour in subsequent word association tasks.

Research Questions

Having established that individuals seem to demonstrate preferred response profiles in their L1, I decided that the logical next step was to investigate whether these preferences are also noticeable in second language word association behaviour. This study, then, compares subjects' word association behaviour in their L1 (in this case English) with their word association behaviour in their L2 (in this case Welsh), in order to answer the specific questions:

(1) If we have individual response profile preferences in our L1, do the same preferences apply to our L2 too?
(2) As proficiency increases, does an individual's word association behaviour in the L2 become more like their L1 association behaviour?

The Present Study

In order to investigate these two questions, data were collected from a group of participants ($N = 37$), who completed two word association tasks, one in English and the other in Welsh. Each task presented 100 cue words, and the participant was required to provide a single word in response to each cue, in Welsh for the Welsh cues and in English for the English cues. The responses were categorised according to response type (as listed in Table 4.1) in order to create a profile for each task, and subjects' individual profiles for the two tasks were compared.

The participants in this experiment were speakers of English and Welsh. All were expert users of English and proficiency in Welsh varied from 'modest user' to 'expert user'. Participants self-rated their proficiency level according to an adapted version of the International English Language Testing System (IELTS) band descriptors, which required participants to tick the description that best described their use of Welsh (see Table 4.2). The majority of participants rated themselves at a high level of proficiency, with 18 of the 37 claiming to be 'expert users'.

Table 4.2 Scale used by participants to self-rate their Welsh proficiency

User level	*Descriptor*	*No. of respondents*
1: Limited	My basic competence is limited to familiar situations. I have frequent problems in understanding and expression. I am not able to use complex language.	0
2: Modest	I have partial command of the language, coping with overall meaning in most situations, though am likely to make many mistakes. I should be able to handle basic communication in my own field.	1
3: Competent	I have generally effective command of the language despite some inaccuracies, inappropriacies and misunderstandings. I can use and understand fairly complex language, particularly in familiar situations.	3
4: Good	I have operational command of the language, though with occasional inaccuracies, inappropriacies and misunderstandings in some situations. Generally, I handle complex language well and understand detailed reasoning.	8
5: Very good	I have fully operational command of the language with only occasional unsystematic inaccuracies and inappropriacies. Misunderstandings may occur in unfamiliar situations. I handle complex detailed argumentation well.	7
6: Expert	I have fully operational command of the language; appropriate, accurate and fluent with complete understanding.	18

At this point it is important to acknowledge that the Welsh language has an interesting status in Wales, which sometimes makes it difficult to categorise as a first or second language for an individual speaker. Bilinguals often have distinct (and largely separate) contexts of use for either language, with Welsh, for example, used as their domestic language and English as their professional or academic language. Some Welsh speakers, who would claim Welsh as their mother tongue, in that it was the language of their early childhood and their first acquired language, have not operated regularly in Welsh for most of their lives. As an example of this, one participant in this study identified Welsh as his first language and gave his age as 60, but when asked

'For how many years have you regularly communicated in Welsh?' answered 'Five'. He had operated in English from when he was three years old until, on retiring, he decided to relearn Welsh. This kind of complicated personal linguistic history was not uncommon among participants in the study. For the purposes of our investigations into the productive mental lexicon, though, there are advantages to the sort of bilingualism found in these minority language contexts. It is probable that, on any given day, the participants in this study would operate in both English and Welsh, so we might expect that their lexicons in both languages are relatively active. Another advantage of using Welsh as the second language in this study is the fact that there are relatively few cognates between Welsh and English. Academic words in many European languages tend to be Latinate in origin, which means that in Romance languages, and in other languages whose academic vocabulary is derived from Latin (e.g. German, Swedish), many cognates appear when AWL words are translated. In a word association task, the inclusion of cognates increases the possibility of participants processing their L2 associations via the L1, thus making it more difficult to interpret the data with any confidence.

The materials used in the study consisted of one word association task in English, comprising 100 words from the AWL, and one word association task in Welsh, comprising a different 100 words translated into Welsh from the AWL. The words used in the two tasks were matched for frequency and word class to minimise any potential effects of these factors on response behaviour. Meara (1982b) suggests that frequency of cue word affects response behaviour, and a number of studies (e.g. Deese, 1962b; Nissen & Henriksen, 2006) suggest that cue words of certain grammatical classes produce responses in certain classes. The practical disadvantage here in terms of data collection, of course, was that, because the cues are infrequent words, in Welsh as well as in English, participants had to have an above-intermediate command of Welsh in order to complete the tasks. Potential participants who were unsure whether their Welsh proficiency was fit for the task were sent a sample list of 10 items translated into Welsh from the AWL to self-assess their knowledge. As Table 4.2 shows, almost all those who did eventually participate in the study rated their Welsh proficiency at 'good user' or higher.

The completion of the word association tasks resulted in two sets of data for each participant: 100 stimulus-response pairs in English and 100 stimulus-response pairs in Welsh. The responses were now categorised under the 11 headings listed and described in Table 4.1. The English responses were categorised by an English native speaker (myself) and, after training and a practice session, the Welsh responses were categorised by a Welsh native speaker.

Results

The categorisation process resulted in two profiles for each participant, an example of which can be seen in Table 4.3.

In this sample profile, for example, we can see that this subject made a relatively high number of 'xy collocation' responses in both her English (e.g. *occupational > hazard*) and Welsh (e.g. *atal > pleidlais*) tasks,[1] but whereas she made 21 'yx collocations' in Welsh (*cynaladwy > fferm*), she only gave 13 of this type of response in English (*assessment > continuous*). There seem to be differences too, for this subject at least, in the distribution of conceptual association responses (*migration > birds, dirwasgiad > tlodi*) and specific synonym responses (*precise > right, enillion > elw*), while the number of defining synonym responses (*minimal > least, hanfodol > angenrheidiol*) is similar in both languages. An overview of the data from all participants (Table 4.4) allows us a group perspective on these similarities and differences.

We can make a number of preliminary observations about this group data before moving on to tackle our specific research questions. Most responses for both Welsh and English tasks were categorised as 'specific synonym', 'conceptual association' or 'xy collocation'. This differs slightly from the native speaker responses reported in Fitzpatrick (2007b), where the most popular response type was also xy collocation, but the next most popular response was 'defining synonym', accounting for 22% of responses as opposed to 4% (Welsh data) and 15% (English data) in the current study. This is counterbalanced by the number of

Table 4.3 Sample response data from one participant

Category	Welsh	English
Defining synonym	7	5
Specific synonym	9	13
Lexical set/context relationship	7	6
Conceptual association	12	19
Consecutive xy collocation	44	42
Consecutive yx collocation	21	13
Other collocational association	0	0
Change of affix	0	1
Similar form only	0	1
Erratic association	0	0
Blank	0	0

Table 4.4 Overview of word association data

Category	Mean (SD) Welsh	Mean (SD) English	Significant difference between Welsh and English responses?
Defining synonym	4 (4.08)	15 (9.74)	Yes ($t = 6.304$, $p < 0.001$)
Specific synonym	18 (12.87)	24 (13.31)	No
Lexical set/context relationship	3 (2.66)	4 (2.4)	No
Conceptual association	17 (6.52)	24 (8.51)	Yes ($t = 4.112$, $p < 0.001$)
Consecutive xy collocation	24 (13.14)	19 (12.88)	No
Consecutive yx collocation	13 (7.32)	7 (6.58)	Yes ($t = 3.842$, $p < 0.001$)
Other collocational association	0 (0.16)	0 (0.16)	No
Change of affix	4 (5.3)	2 (3.52)	No
Similar form only	3 (5.09)	1 (0.95)	No
Erratic association	4 (4.59)	1 (1.36)	No
Blank	10 (12.49)	4 (8.71)	No

'specific synonym' responses: only 9% in the 2007 native speaker study, but 18% (Welsh data) and 24% (English data) in the current study. 'Conceptual associations' account for 17% (Welsh data) and 24% (English data) in the present study, but only 12% of the native speakers in the 2007 study. One of the findings from Fitzpatrick (2006) might shed some light on these differences. That study found significant differences in the numbers of defining synonyms and conceptual associations given by native and non-native speakers, with the former providing more defining synonyms and the latter more conceptual associations. Given that, as described above, the labels 'native' or 'non-native' are not as straightforwardly binary in the case of Welsh-English speakers, it is perhaps not surprising that many of our participants are not as clearly native-like in their behaviour as the 2007 group.

One factor that does, unarguably, tally with the findings reported in Fitzpatrick (2006, 2007b) is the high standard deviations in each response category. For example, though the mean number of yx collocation responses was 13 for the Welsh data, the actual number of these responses ranged from 2 to 30, and the mean of 4 masks the fact that the actual number of responses consisting of an affix change ranged from 0 to 21. The findings here, then, support findings from previous studies that indicate a wide variance in individual word association responses.

Discussion

The first of my research questions asked whether individual response profile preferences in the L1 apply in a similar way to the L2. In order to answer this, it is necessary to calculate the degree of 'proximity' between the English and Welsh association data sets. 'Proximity' here refers to the Euclidean distance, which is calculated by squaring the differences between each subcategory pair in the data set, and then taking the square root of the sum of the squared differences (if we make this calculation for the data presented in Table 4.3, we see that the Euclidean distance between that subject's Welsh and English data is 11.83, which is in fact well below the mean of 28 [see Table 4.5] for within-subject proximity – this subject's L1 and L2 profiles were very similar to each other. Two identical profiles would score a proximity distance of 0). I made this calculation firstly for the 37 between-subject data pairs (English and Welsh association profiles for each subject), and secondly for the 1332 between-subject data pairs (each subject's Welsh profile with every other subject's English profile). Each data pair was awarded a proximity score, and these scores are summarised in Table 4.5.

The 'within-subject proximity score' tells us how similar an individual's Welsh association data profile is to their English association profile. The 'between-subject' score tells us how close their Welsh profile is to every other subjects' English profile. The mean scores in Table 4.5 indicate that on average the within-subject profiles are 'closer' than the between-subject profiles. To confirm this finding, a comparison was made between the two sets of proximity scores using an independent t-test analysis, and the resulting t-value was $t = 4.679$ (df 1367, $p < 0.001$). In other words, the distance between an individual's Welsh and English profiles is significantly smaller than the mean distance between their Welsh profile and the other subjects' English profiles.

Figure 4.1 represents these data as a scatter plot, and we can see that for all but four of our subjects, the distance between their own two language profiles (x axis) is smaller than that between their Welsh and all

Table 4.5 Proximity score for data pairs

	n	Mean	SD
Within-subject proximity	37	28	11.08
Between-subject proximity	1332	38	13.46

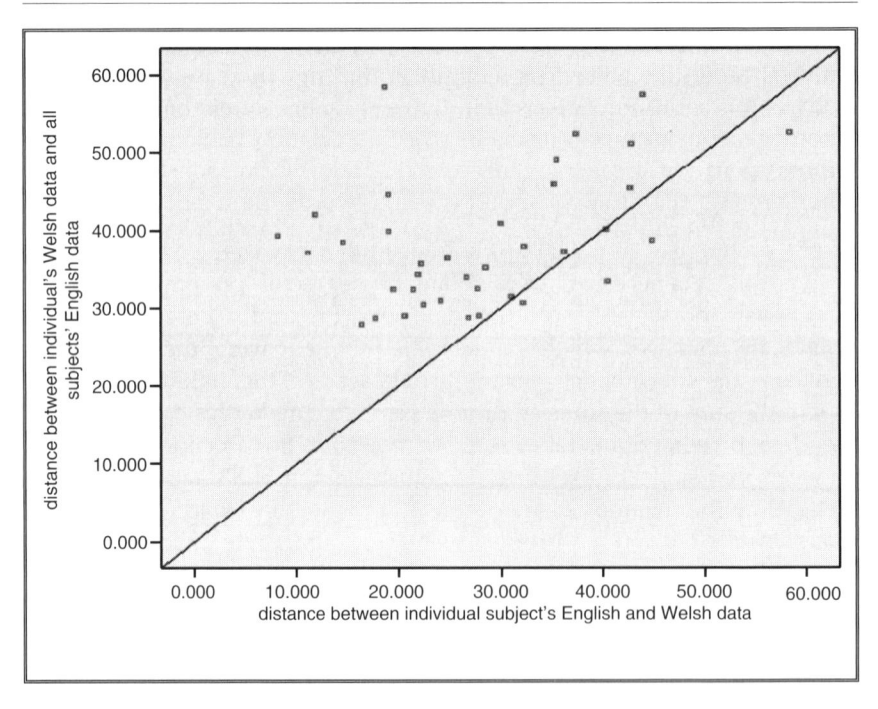

Figure 4.1 Comparison of within- and between-subject proximity scores

the other subjects' English profiles (y axis). Interestingly, when we look back at the proficiency data for those four subjects who fall well outside this pattern (i.e. well underneath the line in the chart), we see that none of these subjects rated themselves as 'expert users' of Welsh. In other words, their self-assessments placed them in the lower proficiency half of our subject group (cf. Table 4.2).

This leads us neatly into a discussion of the second research question, that of the relationship between Welsh proficiency and the closeness of the Welsh and English profiles. The correlation between proficiency and within-subject proximity score is in fact $r_s = -0.370$ ($p < 0.05$). While this is not a strong correlation, it is significant, and it indicates that as L2 proficiency increases, an individual's word association behaviour in the L2 does indeed become more like their L1 association behaviour.

Revisiting the Puzzles and Problems

So, how much closer has this study, and its predecessors, brought us to solving the puzzle of word association behaviour? We know from Fitzpatrick (2006) that there are significant differences between the word association behaviours of native speakers and non-native speakers of English, at least in certain categories of response. That study also found that non-native speakers do not appear to move towards more native speaker-like behaviour as their proficiency increases. The second study in this series informs us that native speakers cannot be regarded as a homogeneous group in terms of word association behaviour, but that individual native speakers seem to have 'preferred' response profiles; in other words, that they respond to cue words in a consistent way (Fitzpatrick, 2007b). The study that I've presented in this chapter enables us to fit two more findings into the word association puzzle. For individuals, L1 association behaviour seems to be reflected in L2 association profiles and, as proficiency increases, an individual's word association behaviour in the L2 becomes more like their own L1 association behaviour. These are, so far as I can tell, new findings that might indeed bring us closer to an understanding of why earlier studies, which focussed on the concept of homogeneous native speaker responses, produced such inconclusive results.

The puzzles and problems are far from resolved, of course, but these findings do indicate that the notion of native speaker norms is a misleading one. Further to this, they suggest that the reason so many studies have failed to find convincing correlations between proficiency and word association behaviour, is that they have looked for evidence of individual learners' word association behaviour moving towards this notional native speaker group norm. The findings I have reported here suggest that we should look, instead, for learners' word association behaviour to move towards their own, individual, L1 behaviour as proficiency increases.

These findings also raise, in their turn, three further questions about word association behaviour and about the relationship between word association data and the mental lexicon. The first of these stems from our having established that responses vary between individuals, but are internally consistent: we have still to explore what, if any, characteristics of an individual might predict what their response preferences will be. Some hints as to the directions we might take here can be found in studies from the field of psychology, such as Merten (1995) (word associations and psychosis, verbal intelligence and personality), Merten and Fischer (1999) (word association and creativity), Hirsch and Tree (2001) (word associations and age) and even Banay (1943) (word associations and emotional maturity).

Secondly, there is an important methodological question, which we have until now conveniently ignored, but which must be addressed if we are to continue with the sort of research methods described in this study. That is the question of whether our results do truly reveal information about the organisation and accessing of the mental lexicon, or whether approach to task has a confounding effect on findings. The word association tasks used in the studies described here have deliberately clear and simple instructions to 'Please write down the first word you think of when you read each of the words listed below', in an attempt to dissuade participants from editing their responses. It is possible, though, that participants interpret the objective of the task in a certain way and assume, for example, that the researcher is asking for synonyms, or definitions. In this case, our results would tell us much more about the subject's approach to a task than about the organisation of their mental lexicon.

Finally, it is certainly the case that word association tasks are often favoured because they appear to give a more spontaneous set of response data than more formal language tasks that might set out to elicit specific target words or lexical connections. However, it is important that we do not assume that all the word association responses in our data have the same degree (or any degree) of spontaneity, but that we explore the possibility that some kinds of association are more automatised than others.

The findings reported in this chapter certainly endorse the view that word association studies should remain central to our investigations into the L2 mental lexicon. Though bold, Meara's claim that such studies might answer the question 'What does a learner's mental lexicon look like, and how is it different from the mental lexicon of a monolingual native speaker?' (Meara, 1982b) seems to have been typically prescient.

Acknowledgements

I would like to express my gratitude to Gwenllian Awbery (Cardiff University, Centre for Lifelong Learning) and Osian Rhys (Swansea University Welsh Language Officer) for their help in processing the Welsh language material and data for this study.

Note

1. Language note: *atal pleidlais*=withhold (one's) vote; *fferm cynaladwy*=sustainable farm; *dirwasgiad*=(economic_depression), *tlodi*=poverty; *enillion*=winnings, *elw*=profit; *hanfodol*=essential, *angenrheidiol*=necessary.

Chapter 5
Revisiting Classrooms as Lexical Environments

MARLISE HORST

Introduction

If you were asked to associate Paul Meara with a place, one choice might be Birkbeck, where Paul did much of his landmark research. Or perhaps Spain comes to mind and the Spanish students who joined the doctoral program that Paul headed in Swansea. There is also Palmyra in Syria for the obvious reason and, of course, Wales. But for me, an important association is Montreal because I first met Paul there. He had come to work with research colleague Patsy Lightbown at Concordia University where I was a student. She introduced me to the visitor in hiking clothes, and soon after, I joined the Swansea program. Today I live and work in Montreal, thanks at least in part to this memorable encounter.

So it is fitting that the research reported in this chapter revisits the Quebec context that Paul Meara, Patsy Lightbown and Randall Halter explored in a 1997 study entitled 'Classrooms as lexical environments'. This study examined the lexical richness of speech samples produced by teachers of English as a second language (ESL) in Montreal-area classrooms with a communicative language teaching orientation. Communicative classrooms, where instruction is typically varied and meaning focused, can be expected to provide a rich lexical environment, and the researchers set out to determine whether this was in fact the case in intensive ESL programs where young French-speaking learners were exposed to many hours of spoken English. The premise was that a large number of medium and lower frequency words in the input would be indicative of speech that was rich in opportunities for new word learning. To arrive at counts of infrequent words, the researchers tallied the numbers of different lemmas that occurred in 500-word stretches of teacher talk and categorized them according to frequency, using the GSL (West's [1953] *General Service List*) and the UWL (Xue & Nation's [1984] *University Word List*, a list of words with medium frequency in the language at large, but that occur frequently in academic texts). A lemma is defined as a base word such as *talk* along with inflected forms *talks, talked* and *talking*; thus various occurrences and forms of *talk* in the data were counted as a single type. There were five frequency categories: basic function words, the first 1000 most frequent English words (GSL), the second 1000 (also from the GSL), words from the UWL and less frequent words that did not appear on any of the four other lists. This last category of 'off-list' words was the main focus of the study; the more types in this category, the richer the input was assumed to be.

The authors were struck by the homogeneity of their findings: total lemma counts did not differ greatly across the 10 teachers they investigated, and the numbers of off-list lemmas the teachers used were consistently low, ranging from 0 to 6 per 500-word sample. The authors' initial conclusion was that the speech environment in all 10 cases was lexically poor. But extrapolation of the findings to a full school day indicated that the young learners were probably exposed to about 50 different off-list lemmas per day or about 250 per week. Seen this way, the input was perhaps not so impoverished after all. There was also the possibility that they were hearing 1000- and 2000-level words that they did not know, making the input even richer from the perspective of these learners. But without concrete information about their prior word knowledge, it was difficult to be sure how rich the teacher talk really was.

Despite this uncertainty, the study has characteristic strengths. First, it is typical of Meara in that it does something original. At the time of writing, frequency lists had been used in developing measurement tools such as Nation's Levels Test (1990) and the Eurocentres Vocabulary Size Test (Meara & Jones, 1990). Laufer and Nation (1995) had based their Lexical Frequency Profile software on the GSL and UWL lists and tested its ability to assess learners' written production. But Meara appears to have been the first to apply the frequency framework to the speech that learners are exposed to. In fact, his first study in this vein was a 1993 exploration of the lexis of English lessons broadcast on the BBC in comparison to the lexis of a Tintin comic (Meara, 1993). The 1997 research discussed here (Meara *et al.*, 1997) is the first I know of that uses frequency lists to examine classroom teacher talk.

The connection to a Really Big Question is also typical of Meara's work. The researchers examined small data sets based on just 15 minutes of teaching, but it seems clear that the goal was to establish basic counts that could be extrapolated to whole days, weeks and even years of exposure to classroom teacher talk. Quantifying the opportunities for acquiring new vocabulary in major amounts of teacher talk would make it possible to test Krashen's claim about the efficacy of exposure to comprehensible input (Krashen, 1982, 1985). The study exemplifies how one might start to transform a rather vague claim into an empirically testable theoretical model. In a discussion of approaches to research that also appeared in 1997, Meara argued that applied linguists would do well to formulate and test formal mathematical models, and that this should be done on a scale large enough to allow for possible deficiencies of the model to be identified and corrected (Meara, 1997: 113–114). Establishing a baseline number of potential learning events in the Quebec classroom study clearly fits this picture. With the input variable in place, a probabilistic model of incidental vocabulary acquisition can then be proposed, tested and found viable (or not).

Why return to this study 10 years after it was published? With the availability of new computer tools and large specialized corpora, it may be possible to answer the lexical richness question more conclusively than was previously possible. But more importantly, questions about acquisition through exposure to speech remain largely unanswered. Perhaps because written input is easier to access, studies of incidental vocabulary acquisition have tended to focus on reading rather than listening. Certainly, one of the obstacles Meara and his co-researchers faced was the difficulty of finding long stretches of transcribed classroom speech and they were obliged to rely on short (500-word) samples. Recently, however, a large corpus of teacher talk was collected in the same Quebec classroom setting by my colleagues Laura Collins and Joanna White (2005), so the analysis used in the 1997 study can now be applied to a much larger data set. As Collins and White also collected a corpus of writing samples produced by learners in some of the classrooms where the teacher talk was recorded, the problem of identifying what the young listeners already know can be overcome. In the study reported below, these writing samples were analyzed to derive a list of words likely to be well known in the learner population.

The rest of this chapter reports an investigation that set out to shed more light on some of the same questions posed in the original research as well as several new ones. The research questions are as follows:

(1) How many different words does a learner typically hear in a day of intensive ESL? How many of these are off-list?
(2) Does the lexical richness of the spoken input vary from one teacher to another? Does it change over time?
(3) Does lexical richness depend on the type of instructional activity?
(4) How many words are typically available for learning in a day of teaching?
(5) Which frequent English words are *not* heard in teacher speech?

Method

Teacher data

The speech data explored in the study come from three instructors who teach in intensive ESL programs in French elementary schools in Quebec, the same context that was investigated in the 1997 study.

The students they teach are in their sixth year of schooling (11 to 12-year-olds). The programs devote close to half of the regular school year to the learning of English and differ from traditional immersion models in that they are not content-based: the regular curriculum (science, math, history, French language arts, etc.) is completed in French in a condensed format that frees up time for an extended block of ESL. Typical themes in the ESL classes are food, hobbies and pets. Each of the three teachers was filmed for an entire day on four occasions; the 12 video recordings represent about 50 hours of teaching in total. The four filming sessions were spaced so that approximately 100 hours of classroom teaching had transpired between each one. The recordings were transcribed in their entirety for a project that examined the occurrence of selected grammar features in the input (Collins *et al.*, 2007). The data were also categorized according to the following activity types: classroom procedures, language-related episodes (explanations of words or structures and corrective feedback), written texts presented aloud, text-related discussion and meaningful interaction (e.g. personal responses to topics). The corpus is about 104,000 running words in length.

Learner data

The written narratives used to determine words that were likely to be known by participants were produced by 210 beginner-level francophone learners of English in intensive ESL programs in Quebec. About one third of the writers were students in the classrooms where the teacher speech was recorded. The texts were written in response to four picture prompts selected to be age-appropriate and easy to respond to. One depicted the discovery of a nest of kittens, another a schoolyard altercation. The lexical characteristics of the 80,000-word learner corpus are described in detail in Horst and Collins (2006).

Analysis

The initial analyses followed methods used in the original research. As in the 1997 study, words in the teacher talk (proper names excluded) were classified according to five categories based on frequency lists. This was achieved by using word family counts produced by the online programs *Familizer* and *Vocabprofile* (Cobb, 2000). A word family includes the base word and its inflected forms (e.g. *talk, talks, talked, talking*) and also basic derived forms (e.g. *talker*). Off-list words that the programs cannot 'familize' automatically were grouped into families manually. The frequency lists used to categorize the data were the same as those used in the original study – except in the case of academic words. The online tools draw on Coxhead's Academic Word List (2000), a list that was not available at the time of the earlier research. To identify words in the learner corpus that could be assumed to be already known, a criterion of 10 occurrences was used. That is, if a word family had been used 10 times or more in the entire corpus, it was assumed to be familiar to all of the learners, even though not all of them had used it in their narratives. The resulting list of 'known' words consisted of 412 families.

Results

Number of words encountered in a day of teacher speech

Table 5.1 shows the number of word families in the teacher speech and their distribution over five frequency categories. One transcript (Teacher A, Time 3) proved to be atypically short due to special events at the school and was therefore excluded. The means shown in the bottom row indicate that in an average full day of ESL teaching (about 4.5 hours), learners in the intensive programs are exposed to 700 different word families, of which half are on the GSL list of the 1000 most frequent families. They also hear well over 100 from the second most frequent 1000 families and around two dozen AWL families. The mean number of off-list families – the main indicator of lexical richness in the 1997 research – amounts to 131. The authors of the earlier study ventured a conservative estimate of 50 off-list lemmas per day based on the smaller 500-word samples. The findings reported here show that in terms of opportunities to hear off-list words, the teacher talk is easily as rich as they estimated.

Table 5.1 Numbers of word families by frequency used by Teachers A, B and C

	Function	1K	2K	AWL	Off-list	Total
A, Time 1	64	275	82	8	67	496
A, Time 2	69	343	122	22	137	693
A, Time 4	61	292	97	24	98	572
B, Time 1	70	376	107	28	98	679
B, Time 2	66	373	161	37	161	798
B, Time 3	65	375	164	34	191	829
B, Time 4	72	398	136	34	135	775
C, Time 1	75	404	168	40	164	851
C, Time 2	67	312	100	21	105	605
C, Time 3	67	324	101	19	141	652
C, Time 4	72	366	144	25	141	748
Mean (SD)	68 (4)	349 (41)	126 (29)	27 (9)	131 (36)	700 (113)

Richness across teachers and over time

The counts of running words (tokens) for the full days of teacher talk varied considerably, ranging from 5300 to 13,900. Although they present an interesting picture of whole days of teaching, the varying amounts of speech make comparisons difficult. So, to address the questions about differences in lexical richness between teachers and over time, transcripts of equal length were analyzed. Figure 5.1 shows the number of families in the various frequency levels in 6000-word stretches of talk produced by each of the three teachers at the four different times. There are only two bars for Teacher A because two of the transcripts did not reach the 6000-word criterion.

As in the original study, there is a great deal of homogeneity in the samples. The teachers all use around 600 different word families, of which around 100 are off-list. There are variations in the data, but no one teacher's speech appears to be consistently richer than that of the other two. Over time, the teachers might be expected to use more families overall and more unusual words as the proficiency of the learners increases. But there is no evidence of this in the data as shown in Figure 5.1. Although

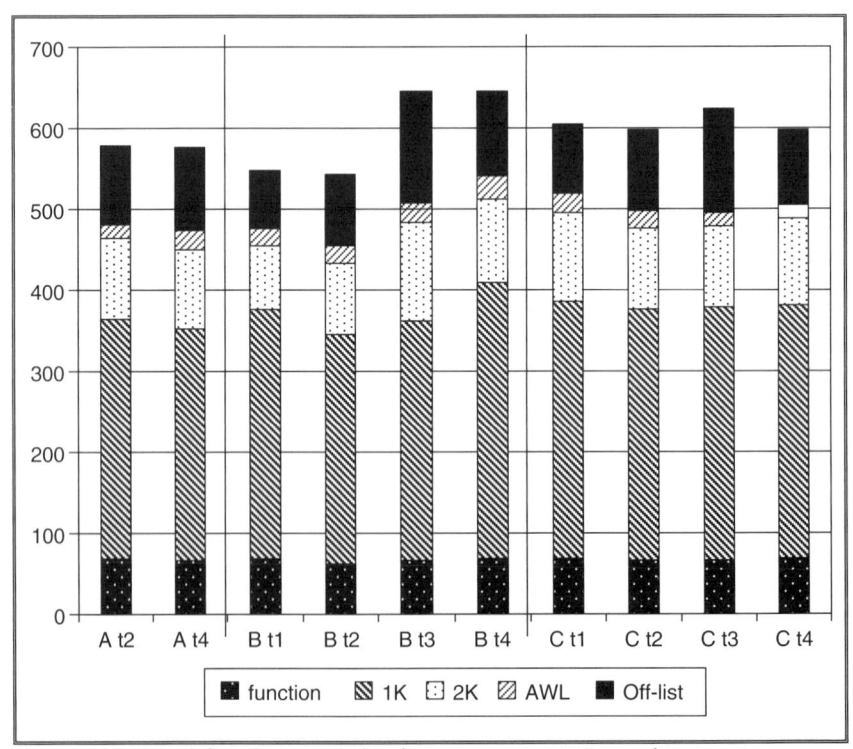

Figure 5.1 Word family counts by frequency in 6000-word excerpts

heights of the whole bars and the off-list sections are taller for Teacher B at Times 3 and 4 than at Times 1 and 2, the pattern is not found for Teachers A and C. Thus, the variations that occur are apparently due to something other than the teachers' personal styles or their learners' proficiency.

Lexical richness and activity type

It is possible that the small variations in lexical richness in Figure 5.1 could be explained by differences in the types of discourse used on a given day. There is certainly reason to expect richness differences in varying kinds of speech. For instance, Meara (1993) found songs and comic book speech to be richer than the talk in BBC radio English lessons. For another example, a follow-up investigation to the 1997 study by Lightbown *et al*. (1998) found teacher talk in communicative classrooms to be substantially richer than that of audio-lingual classes. These findings prompted the third research question about the lexical richness of the speech used in different kinds of instruction. Five types of instructional activity had been identified in the corpus, but two were not present in sufficient amounts to be analyzed. Findings for the three remaining types – classroom management, language-related episodes and texts read aloud – are shown in Figure 5.2. Each bar represents the numbers of off-list families in a 3000-word speech sample that is made up of three 1000-word samples, one from each of the three teachers at Time 3.

As written texts generally feature more medium- and low-frequency words than speech (Nation, 2001), I expected that texts read aloud would offer the most opportunities to meet infrequent word families. However, the richest genre proved to be talk about language with 135 off-list families. Text read aloud and classroom management talk proved to be substantially less rich with 87 and 84 off-list families, respectively. The transcribed segment below illustrates the colorful character of the talk-about-language genre (off-list words are underlined).

Student: How do you say it... *cacao* (French)?
Teacher: We say cocoa. Okay. So the cocoa with no sugar is very bitter and if you have dark chocolate like Carole said made with no sugar, it's bitter. I don't know if you've ever seen the baker's chocolates? You know what I mean? It has absolutely no sugar. Very bitter, just like cocoa. Did you ever taste cocoa?
Students (in chorus): Yeah.
Teacher: Yeah. That's a very good example of bitter. Also, something that's bitter and you can taste this time of year is.... What's the plant you asked me about yesterday?

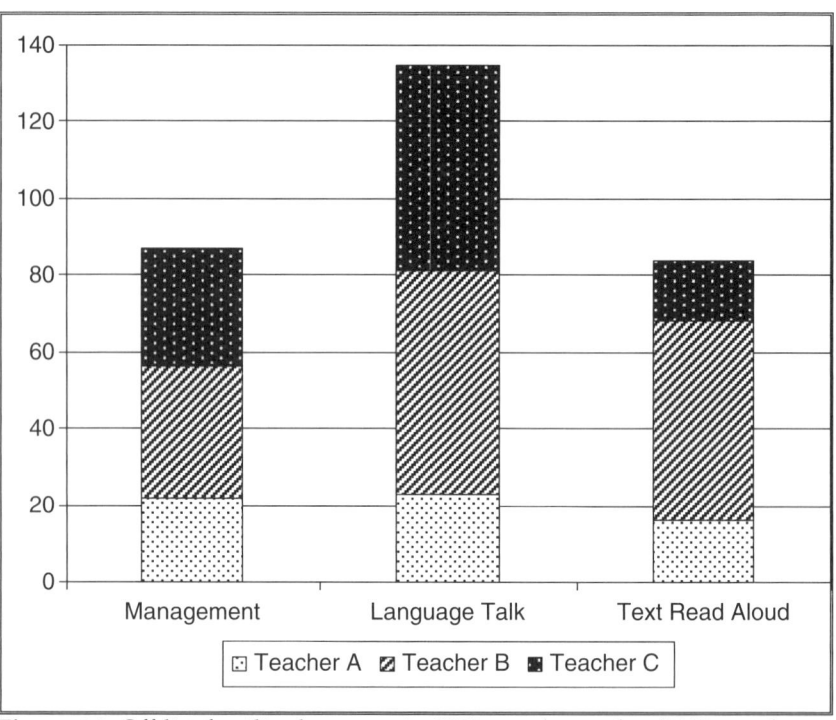

60 Lexical Processing in Second Language Learners

[Bar chart showing values for Teacher A, Teacher B, and Teacher C across three categories: Management, Language Talk, and Text Read Aloud. Y-axis ranges from 0 to 140.]

Figure 5.2 Off-list families by genre in 3000-word samples (1000 words per teacher)

Student: Dandelion.
Teacher: Dandelions! Okay. Do you know what a dandelion is?

But this lexically rich talk that engages learners in attending to new forms is not what the learners hear most. The focus-on-language episodes account for only 17% of the entire corpus, while 74% is taken up by the relatively impoverished talk that centers on classroom procedures. An example of the latter follows below; the only off-list item is *okay*, a word that is hardly likely to be new.

Teacher: So raise your hand if you've filled, if you've completed the sheet. Anybody? Missing just two words? Well that's, that's fine, normal, because there were a lot of words to place, eh? It's a long song. Who writes very well and quickly? To go write the answers on the board. Who wants to do that? Somebody who writes well, clearly and quickly. Philippe? Yes, Philippe does write well. Okay, come bring your sheet, Philippe. So raise your hand to say the answer and Philippe will write it on the board. Okay. Philippe write in columns on the board, starting at the top. Okay.

The findings for text presented aloud raise a basic question about lexically rich environments and how they may facilitate vocabulary acquisition. The bar for this genre in Figure 5.2 shows that a disproportionately large number of the off-list family types occurred in Teacher B's sample (52 of 84). Examination of the transcripts reveals that her text was an extended narrative, while the samples provided by Teachers A and C were songs, chants and tongue twisters. While Teacher B's story text scores high on lexical richness, learners in the other classes were probably better positioned to retain the new vocabulary they were exposed to. Though they heard relatively few unusual words (only 16 in both samples), the words they did hear were repeated many more times in the songs and poems.

Number of words available for learning in a day of teaching

Ideally, the spoken input would provide the best of both scenarios above: exposure to many less frequent word families *and* opportunities to hear them used repeatedly. In answering the fourth question about new word-learning opportunities in the intensive setting, an unknown word family was considered to be potentially learnable if it occurred 10 times or more in a whole day of teacher talk. The choice of 10 or more exposures is based on studies of learning new vocabulary through reading that place the numbers of contextual encounters required for reliable retention between six and 15 (see Zahar *et al.*, 2001, for an overview).

As in the original study, a word was considered unusual and a potential target for learning if *Vocabprofile* analysis identified it as off-list. The off-list families that met the 10+ exposures criterion in full days of teacher talk recorded near the end of the session (Time 4) are shown in the third column of Table 5.2. There were only six in the transcripts of Teachers A and C; Teacher B produced 13. However, these figures are probably unrealistically low. As Meara and his colleagues noted in 1997, there is a problem with designating off-list vocabulary as the main growth area for young learners in the intensive programs. As they are beginners, there are probably many other words they do not know. For this reason, I decided to try defining learnability in a different way. As mentioned earlier, this involved checking whether a word family had been used repeatedly in the learner corpus. If it had not, the family was considered to be available for learning, regardless of whether or not it was off-list. The results of this analysis are shown in Table 5.2 in the fifth column labeled 'Off-learner-list families'. These families all occurred 10 or more times in the teacher talk, but did not appear on the list of families that the learners presumably already knew.

Table 5.2 Learnable word families (10+ occurrences) in a single day of teacher talk

Teacher	Transcript length	Off-list families	Total	Off-learner-list families	Total
A	5300 words	jacket, leap, magazine, okay, recess, scrapbook	6	active, board, complete, dive, eliminate, excellent, few, jacket, leap, letter, magazine, noise, page, paper, pencil, rain, ready, right, scrapbook, sing, sport, team, use	23
B	10,300 words	basement, fairy, fuzzy, locker, okay, portfolio, sketch, tale, twister, veal, vinegar, wuzzy, yeah	13	absolute, ahead, art, basement, chair, church, comment, connect, desk, difficult, easy, English, evaluate, even, example, express, fairy, fine, fuzzy, hole, hot, kind, leave, library, locker, mean, mistake, Monday, noise, part, point, portfolio, practice, preach, raise, ready, right, section, sheet, sign, sketch, sound, suggest, tale, team, title, tongue, twister, use, veal, vinegar, voice, way, which, wine, wuzzy	56
C	8600 words	agenda, chip, homework, insist, locker, shorts	6	active, agenda, already, April, avenue, board, bottom, build, chip, count, country, dive, follow, homework, insist, leave, locker, map, mean, page, paper, paragraph, part, partner, passenger, pencil, per, point, probable, quiet, ready, right, ship, short, shorts, should, still, table, team, thirty, trip, twenty, use, way	44

This way of identifying unusual words results in larger, more plausible lists of learnable families, ranging in size from 23 to 56 items. However, they contain words such as *page, paper* and *pencil* that were almost certainly not new. This is explained by the topics of the stories in the learner corpus. In responding to a picture of newborn kittens for instance, the young writers had no logical reason to use words like *pencil* or *paper*, which meant they did not appear in the list of families that were excluded from the teacher talk lists. If common classroom words like *pencil* are manually removed from the lists of off-learner-list families in Table 5.2, about one or two dozen families remain, depending on the teacher. Thus, a figure of about 20 learnable families per day could be a reasonable baseline number in an experiment involving testable models of the type Meara has proposed.

Frequent words not heard in teacher speech

The results in Table 5.1 indicate that about half of the 700 families that occurred in a typical day of teacher talk were on the GSL list of the 1000 most frequent English words. As these frequent words represented such a large proportion of the language that the intensive learners were regularly exposed to, I thought it would be useful to know whether the teaching exposed learners to a wide range of 1000-level families or whether they were hearing the same few hundred recycled repeatedly. As roughly 75% of the words in English texts are on the GSL list of the 1000 most frequent words, and coverage of conversation is even higher (Nation, 2001), the importance of knowing this basic vocabulary well can hardly be overstated. In the absence of full transcriptions for every day of the courses, it is not possible to provide a truly comprehensive answer to this lexical richness question. However, the 12 transcripts sampled in three different classrooms over four intervals seemed well positioned to show the range of 1000-level vocabulary typically used.

The entire teacher talk corpus was analyzed using *VP Negative,* a feature recently added to *Vocabprofile* that identifies GSL and AWL words that are *not* present in a submitted text. The output showed that all but 199 of the 1000 most frequent families occurred at least once; thus there is some reason to suppose that over five months of intensive ESL, learners would be exposed to the full set. However, a look at the missing items suggests otherwise. Families not heard in the teacher speech fall into several thematic groups. One of these is discourse markers such as *although, moreover, neither* and *thus*. These are characteristic of the written mode and would hardly be expected to occur in speech addressed to 12-year-old ESL learners. It is also not so surprising to see that 30 words related to business and commerce did not occur. Examples are *account, manufacture, profit, receipt, tax* and *wage*. It is perhaps more of a concern to note that about 60 items pertaining to knowledge of the physical world did not occur. Examples include *bridge, coast, desert, distance, fact, flow, gold, length, moon, mountain, river, shore, surface* and *west*. Another group of over 30 pertained to history and social studies, e.g. *ancient, castle, faith, independent, justice* and *poor*. It is possible to argue that these omissions are flukes and that classes on other days might have focused on themes that naturally required these words. However in Quebec, science, history, mathematics and other core subjects must (by law) be studied in French. For this reason, teachers in intensive programs may avoid topics that might be seen as teaching 'content' in English. The 1000-level words not spoken may reflect this concern. Yet another set of missing word families pertained to armed conflict, including *army, battle, command, defeat, enemy, victory* and *wound*. No doubt, such items go unheard because teachers find this topic unsuitable.

Discussion

The results of the study provide new insights into the nature of the lexis of ESL teacher talk and refine those of the previous studies. In answer to the first research question about the numbers of word families encountered in a single day (about 4.5 hours of teaching), the study showed that the mean for the speech addressed to beginner-level child learners was 700 per day or 155 per hour. The mean number of off-list families per day was 130, which amounts to about 29 per hour. If we assume that the off-list words were unfamiliar, then the teacher talk clearly provided learners with hundreds of opportunities to hear new vocabulary in use over the entire session. Using the corpus of learner productions as a measure of known and unknown vocabulary allowed the word-learning opportunities to be specified more closely than was previously possible. This methodology identified items like *dive* (repeated 10 times), *tale* (21 repetitions) and *fuzzy* (24 repetitions) and others shown in Table 5.2 as off-learner-list words that stood a good chance of being acquired through exposure to the teacher talk. Though identifying precisely which words are both new and repeated often enough to be learnable remains a challenge, it was possible to arrive at a plausible baseline figure of around 20 families that could serve as a useful starting point in testing a mathematical model of vocabulary uptake. It would also be interesting to investigate teacher talk in other ESL contexts, e.g. adult learners in intermediate- or advanced-level classes.

Perhaps the most interesting result is the variation found within the teacher speech. The lexis of speech that focused specifically on language proved to be much richer than that of other kinds of teacher talk (though a storybook read aloud also proved to be rich when considered apart from other more repetitive text types). The talk-about-language finding raises the question of how learners benefit from exposure to vocabulary-focused speech like the excerpt above where the teacher builds a rich associative network around the words *cocoa*, *bitter* and *dandelion*. In a preliminary study of the transcripts (Horst *et al.*, 2007), my colleagues and I found that language-focused episodes occurred frequently – even though most of the class time was taken up by other kinds of talk. The number of treatments (of an individual word or structure) totaled 703 in the entire corpus, of which the overwhelming proportion (80%) focused on lexis. The mean number of vocabulary interventions per day was 47 – which amounts to roughly 10 per hour. Clearly, a great deal of lexically rich talk about vocabulary goes on in these classrooms; the extent to which this results in learning is a subject for future study.

The finding that many but not all of the 1000 most frequent GSL families occurred in the teacher talk has interesting pedagogical implications. I observe that in communicative ESL classrooms in Quebec (and elsewhere), teachers encourage learners to share opinions about many topics, but often avoid those that may provoke controversy. They are uncomfortable with discussions of religious beliefs, social values and views of current events; in the Quebec intensive context, primary teachers may also avoid material they perceive as overlapping with the science and social studies curriculum taught in French. But these omissions appear to do learners a lexical disservice; basic vocabulary related to precisely these subjects was found to be missing. Can intensive course teachers be encouraged to take on topics they may perceive to be off limits? I would like to think that they can, and that learners are interested in learning about the world they live in and the controversies that surround them – in English.

Conclusion

In sum, the study by Meara and his colleagues asked important questions, provided a useful methodology for answering them and paved the way for new explorations. I recall that a required element in the doctoral program at Swansea is a replication study, and again, I see that the experience has proved its value. I have new respect for the technique of counting word families and increased awareness of the challenges of modeling uptake from speech. As a teacher of future language teachers, I am eager to continue investigating the characteristics of teacher talk – vocabulary-focused speech, in particular – and its potential benefits for language learning. Fortunately for all of us, there are many more studies like this one to explore. Paul Meara has written a great deal – both on his own and in collaboration with others – and visiting or revisiting any one of these contributions is guaranteed to be worth the journey.

Acknowledgements

I am grateful to *Fonds québecois de recherche sur la société et la culture* for generous support of the research project of which this study is a part. I would also like to recognize the valuable contribution of student research assistants, research associate Randall Halter, and project team members Laura Collins, Pavel Trofimovich, Joanna White and Walcir Cardoso – all colleagues at Concordia University.

Chapter 6
A Close Look at the Use of Pocket Electronic Dictionaries for Receptive and Productive Purposes

HILARY NESI and ATIPAT BOONMOH

Introduction: Paul Meara's Work with Computers and Dictionaries

Paul Meara was one of the first researchers to exploit the potential of the computer as a means of assessing vocabulary knowledge and the comprehension of dictionary information. One early example of his skill in this area was the computer-based Eurocentres Vocabulary Size Test (EVST) (Meara, 1990b; Meara & Buxton, 1987; Meara & Jones, 1988), designed as a quick and effective means of placing learners in language classes at an appropriate level.

The EVST also proved to be a useful tool for assigning experimental subjects to comparably proficient groups, and was used for this purpose by Nesi and Meara (1994) in their experiment with dictionary-defining styles. The same method was employed in subsequent studies examining the effect of language and culture on the comprehension of dictionary entries (Nesi, 1994), and the effect of dictionary examples on the understanding of word use (Nesi, 1996). For all three of these studies, Meara also created the software that underpinned the experimental design: subjects were presented with dictionary definitions on screen, and their responses were recorded on disk. Meara's contribution was essential to this research, although this was probably inadequately acknowledged at the time, especially in the two single-author papers.

Another piece of software designed by Meara helped Ann Ryan investigate Arabic-speaking students' perceptions of word forms (Ryan & Meara, 1991). Subjects were required to judge whether they were viewing the same word or a different one when it appeared on a computer screen for about a second, disappeared and then reappeared in an identical or altered form. The experiment was conveniently administered via a hand-held pocket electronic organizer – very cutting edge at a time when pocket electronic dictionaries (PEDs) were still in their infancy.

Meara's foresight in recognising the potential of the computer as a tool for vocabulary learning and vocabulary research was one of the prompts that led us to look more closely at dictionaries in electronic form. This chapter tells the story of the development of PEDs, considers their influence and describes a recent investigation into their use.

The Evolution of Pocket Electronic Dictionaries

Lexicographical materials have been stored on computer since the 1960s, initially for research purposes, and then as a tool for dictionary compilation. However, only specialists had access to these early, computerised dictionaries. PEDs and CD-Rom-based dictionaries came later, following markedly different development paths. The publishers of dictionaries on disk worked with lexicographers, and generally looked to the new technology to improve lexicographical practice and presentation, for example by making possible new search functions involving wildcards and Boolean operators. On the other hand, the people who designed the first PEDs worked in consumer electronics, and were more interested in creating new kinds of toys and gadgets than in lexicographical innovation.

Primitive PEDs were adaptations of electronic calculators. Two of the first were the *LK-3000* (Lexicon, 1978), a translator with a calculator-style keyboard, and Texas Instruments' *Speak & Spell* (1978), a toy that exploited new developments in speech synthesis so that words could be 'spoken' aloud. In 1979, Texas Instruments used the same technology to move into the market for hand-held translating devices; other speaking translators soon followed, manufactured by companies such as Sharp Electronics, Canon, Casio and Franklin.

'First generation' PEDs were technologically exciting, but lexicographically very limited. They drew on printed dictionary sources, but could only contain a very small number of headwords and definitions. The first of the 'second generation' PEDs, containing the full texts of several published print dictionaries, was reportedly the Seiko *TR-700* in 1982 (Nakamura, 2003: 346). Seiko later manufactured the first monolingual English learners' dictionary to appear as a PED, the *Hand-Held Longman Dictionary of Contemporary English* (1995). Since the 1980s, PEDs have become progressively bigger in capacity and smaller in size. Some of the more expensive PEDs now contain the contents of 30 dictionaries or more, and offer scanning facilities, pronunciation of extended text, and speech recognition to translate between languages. Increasingly, PEDs contain the full text of at least one monolingual dictionary from a major publishing house, such as the *Oxford Advanced Learner's Dictionary*, alongside bilingual material of varying quality.

Pocket Electronic Dictionaries in the Classroom

PEDs are undoubtedly popular with students, particularly in East-Asian countries. In Deng's (2005) survey of 80 Chinese college students, 70% were found to be PED users, and in Midlane's (2005) survey of English as a foreign language (EFL) teachers, all those teaching in China, Indonesia, Japan, Korea, Malaysia, Taiwan and Vietnam reported that their students brought PEDs to class. Boonmoh and Nesi (2008) questioned 1211 undergraduates from King Mongkut's University of Technology Thonburi (KMUTT) in Thailand, and found that although only 40% owned PEDs and 82% owned print monolingual dictionaries (generally the intermediate-level *Longman Active Study Dictionary* bought on the recommendation of their university teachers), most students aspired to own a PED, and very few planned to progress from an intermediate to an advanced monolingual learner's dictionary in book form. Of the 1097 respondents who answered the question: 'If you do not have a dictionary or if you plan to buy a new dictionary, what type of dictionary would you like to buy?' 75% named a PED, as opposed to 16% who wanted a print bilingual dictionary and only 8% who wanted a print monolingual dictionary. There was very little interest in monolingual dictionaries on CD-Rom (only 1% of respondents chose this option).

Research suggests that teachers, on the other hand, typically take a much more negative view of PEDs. The act of PED consultation itself is a cause for concern. Stirling (2005), for example, describes classroom situations where learners concentrate on looking up words in their PEDs instead of listening to the teacher or taking part in discussion. Teachers interviewed by Taylor and Chan (1994) voiced fears that the ease and speed of PED access would hinder the development of reading skills. Sharpe (1995) and Stirling (2005) worry that the vocabulary information in PEDs, so easily extracted, might just as easily be forgotten. Teachers not only object to the PED consultation process, but also to the quality of PED content. Deng (2005) complained that the PEDs used by his students in China did not supply English definitions, inflectional forms or examples. Several of the 11 EFL teachers interviewed by Stirling (2005) also complained about 'inaccurate meanings' and 'insufficient examples'. Israeli teachers objected to PEDs because they lacked 'word meanings, word families, parts of speech, tense, usage and idioms, etc.' (Koren, 1997: 7).

Many of the 30 KMUTT English language lecturers surveyed by Boonmoh and Nesi (2008) were highly critical of PEDs as tools for language learning. Typical comments were:

- A PED does not provide usage, examples. And as a consequence, students are likely to make mistakes.

- It doesn't give the correct meaning and doesn't tell students clearly how to use the word in different contexts.
- It is not as detailed as a dictionary in book form.

However, more than half the KMUTT lecturers admitted that they had no idea whether the PEDs their students used contained monolingual English dictionaries. Only four actually owned a PED themselves, and only one had used a PED out of preference, and then only in combination with other sources:

- I will use it only when I cannot think of English vocabulary. However, I will have to check how that word is used from a monolingual either in book form or on CD-Rom.

Several researchers have commented on teachers' 'widespread lack of knowledge of what PEDs can commonly do' (Midlane, 2005: 87), and in fact, many of the supposed defects of PEDs must also apply to hard-copy dictionaries, given that nowadays they generally contain the same lexicographical content. Without access to empirical data concerning PED use, however, it is impossible to judge the extent to which teachers' complaints are justified, or whether they are jumping to conclusions about PED quality, perhaps recalling the inadequacies of first generation PEDs.

Methods of Researching Pocket Electronic Dictionaries Use

There are many practical difficulties surrounding PED research. Learners are inclined to be secretive about their use of PEDs, especially when they suspect that their teachers might disapprove. There are no PED class sets, and it is often the case that many different models are in use within the same classroom. Moreover, with a display area so much smaller than a computer screen or the printed page, it is rather difficult for teachers to see what is happening during a student's PED consultation, even if the student is inclined to share the experience. 'Spy' software has some potential as a means of observing online dictionary use (through keystroke logging and screenshots), but it cannot be loaded into the standard PED. Thus, with regard to PEDs, few teachers are in a position to follow the recommendation of Atkins and Varantola (1998: 115) and find out 'exactly what their students are doing with their dictionaries, what they expect from them, and how easily they are satisfied during the process of consultation'.

Most prior research into the PED phenomenon has been confined to quantitative ownership surveys and qualitative investigations into teacher and student attitudes and beliefs. The occasional researcher has worked alongside users and discussed their PED consultations (e.g. Tang, 1997) and a few simple experiments have been conducted, such as a look-up 'race' between PED and print dictionary users (Weschler & Pitts, 2000), but there have been no close analyses of exactly what happens when PED users look up words. The 'Light Bulb' experiment, described below, is an attempt to address this research gap.

The Light Bulb Experiment

This experiment aimed to discover how Thai students used their PEDs to read a passage in English and write a summary in Thai. This was judged to be a typical activity in the Thai university context, where non-English majors rarely have to write in English, but are frequently required to read and paraphrase the information in English-medium textbooks.

Subjects

Initially, 20 subjects were chosen from a cohort of 580 students enrolled on a foundation English programme at KMUTT in Thailand. KMUTT is a science and technology university that does not offer English as a degree subject, although it provides supplementary English language courses for all its students. KMUTT students typically read in English, but write their assignments in Thai, and according to questionnaire surveys, they use their dictionaries most frequently when translating.

The 20 subjects were chosen because, in an earlier questionnaire survey (reported in Boonmoh & Nesi, 2008), they had claimed to possess and use PEDs, had stated a preference for word-processing their assignments (rather than writing them on paper) and had indicated a willingness to participate in the experiment. All the subjects had already received dictionary skills training in their English language courses. Potential subjects attended a first meeting prior to the experiment and answered questions about their current dictionary-using habits. At this stage, three subjects were dropped because they were no longer PED users.

Procedure

Of the 17 subjects who underwent training in the think aloud technique, six more were rejected because they required too much prompting and tended to repeat the written instructions rather than voicing their own thoughts. The remaining 11 subjects completed the summary task in individual sessions. Of these, eight were selected for particular study because of the quality and completeness of their performance while thinking aloud, because they were at the same intermediate level of language proficiency (according to their English language course results) and because they owned comparable PED models that were popular among the student body as a whole. The eight subjects came from a range of disciplines (the computer sciences, engineering, maths, microbiology and multimedia). They used *TalkingDict* or *CyberDict* PEDs with a variable combination of bilingual and monolingual English dictionaries (the *Concise American Heritage Dictionary* for *TalkingDict* PEDs, and the *Oxford Advanced Learner's Dictionary* or the *Longman Dictionary of American English* for *CyberDict* PEDs). In all cases, an English-Thai dictionary was the default that they first accessed when they keyed in an English word.

Subjects were asked to summarise a news article taken from a BBC webpage entitled 'Light bulbs: not such a bright idea' (Prescott, 2006), which discusses ways to solve the world's energy problems:

Light bulbs: Not such a bright idea

Governments are wrestling with problems of rising energy demands, rising costs and the spectre of climate change. In this week's Green Room, Dr Matt Prescott argues there is an easy first step to dealing with all three issues – banning the traditional light bulb.

Listening to most politicians, you would think the world's energy problems can be solved only by building ever bigger power stations and burning ever more fuel. Not so; and it certainly cannot solve the coming climate crisis.

After turning off unnecessary pieces of equipment, improved energy efficiency is the cheapest way for developing countries to maximise their use of limited energy supplies, and for developed countries to achieve cuts in their carbon dioxide emissions. One quick and simple option for improving energy efficiency would be to make greater use of compact fluorescent light bulbs. Each one of these bulbs produces the same amount of light as an incandescent light bulb whilst being responsible for the emission of 70% less carbon dioxide.

Nobody would suffer; every energy-saving bulb would save money and help to curb climate change. It is truly a win-win solution.

This text had been piloted with a comparable group of volunteers, and had proved to be appropriate in terms of topic, difficulty level and length (193 words). Subjects were asked to think aloud while they summarised the text. The task was undertaken in individual sessions, in the presence of one of the researchers who also observed every word looked up and completed an observation check sheet. The check sheets were used to help us record the words and meanings the subjects looked up, and were also used as notes to ask some specific questions during the retrospective interviews conducted with each subject at the end of the session:

- Can you explain how you normally use your PED for reading?
- Did you have any problems when you did this task?
- I noticed you looked up this word, why?
- What were your criteria in selecting which words to look up?
- Are there any differences between your electronic dictionary use for this task and the way you use it normally?
- Do you normally use an English-English learner's dictionary in your PED? If yes, how often? If no, why?

Data analysis

Findings were derived from consideration of four data sources:

- subjects' written summaries in Thai;
- observation notes;
- think aloud protocols, recorded and then transcribed;
- retrospective interviews, recorded and then transcribed.

Words or sentences in the think aloud transcriptions were highlighted in bold when they represented the subjects' own thoughts, and were not highlighted when they were extracts repeated from the text. This enabled us to distinguish between 'read aloud' and 'think aloud' data, and facilitated analysis.

The transcribed think aloud protocols (along with the transcriptions of the interviews and the observation check sheets) were then analysed and coded with reference to the following questions:

(1) How did the subjects write their summaries?
(2) What words did they look up?
(3) Did they search for words in the appropriate word class, and if not, why not?
(4) Did they find the word(s) they were looking for? If not, what might be the reasons for this, and how did they solve the problem?

Findings

Table 6.1 summarises the ways in which individual subjects approached the summary writing task.

It can be seen that six out of the eight subjects began looking up words whilst reading the passage for the first time. Subject 1, who was probably the least proficient PED user, read the passage word by word and looked up almost every unknown word. Only Subjects 2 and 6 started PED consultation after reading the whole passage. These were also the only two subjects to underline the words they did not know. Two subjects, 3 and 8, re-read the passage before starting to summarise it; Subject 8, who was probably the most proficient PED user, also reviewed the summary before submitting it to the researchers.

Table 6.1 Subjects' summary-writing procedures

Procedures	Subjects							
	1	2	3	4	5	6	7	8
Subjects read the whole passage first, before starting to look words up.		✓				✓		
Subjects read the passage sentence by sentence and looked up unknown words.			✓	✓	✓		✓	✓
Subjects read the passage word by word and looked up unknown words immediately.	✓							
Subjects underlined unknown words before looking them up.		✓				✓		
Subjects read the passage one more time before starting to write a summary.			✓					✓
Subjects reviewed the summary before submitting it to the researchers.								✓

Figure 6.1 shows the stages the subjects went through in order to find words in their PEDs. Stage 1 concerns the subject's choice about whether or not to consult their PED. As PED use is the focus of this study, we ignored everything that the subjects wrote that did not involve PED consultation, regardless of whether the words and phrases were used correctly or incorrectly.

The second stage concerns the appropriate identification of word class. We checked whether the words looked up belonged to the same word class as the words in the original text. For example, the word **light** in the passage functioned as part of the compound noun **light bulb**, rather than as an adjective, so we checked to see whether the subjects looked up the verb, noun or adjective entry. Failure to identify the entry for the correct word class might have been due to either of two reasons: confusion over the word form (where an inflected form in the text matches that of a word belonging to a different class), or failure to look beyond the first entry shown in the PED. For example, in *Super Smart*, there are three entries for the word **light**, listed in the following order: verb, adjective, noun. The subject might consult the verb entry simply because this is the first to appear on the PED screen.

The last stage concerns the identification of the target word in the dictionary. The PED consultation was considered successful if subjects found the word they were looking for.

A Close Look at the Use of Pocket Electronic Dictionaries 75

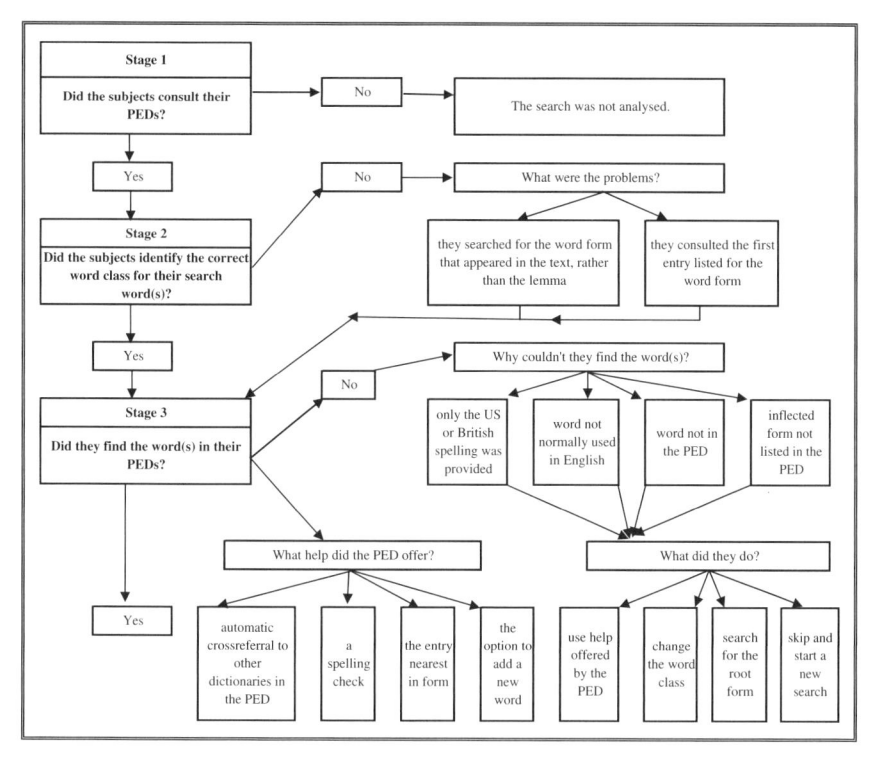

Figure 6.1 How the subjects used pocket electronic dictionaries for reception

There were four possible reasons for failing to identify the target word in a PED:

- American English or British English alternatives were not provided. For example, the British spelling of **spectre** was not included in the English-Thai dictionary in *CyberDict*.
- The target word did not exist in the PED database.
- The target word was an invented one, not in normal use in the English language.

There was one example of this: PEDs in the *TalkingDict* range indicated that the word **bulb** functioned as both a noun and a verb. (The only two verbal usages of **bulb** in the British National Corpus are very marked, from Ted Hughes' *Selected poems.*) The verb **bulb** was translated as 'งอกหัว/ngok hua/', which means 'to appear', but this is a very rare word that few native speakers of Thai would recognise out of context.

- The subjects searched for derived forms or inflected forms that were not listed in the PED. For example, instead of searching for the lemma **argue**, one subject keyed in **argues** and failed to find a corresponding entry.

If the search word was not found in the default English-Thai dictionary, the PED might provide one of the four following functions:

- an automatic cross-search to other dictionaries contained in the PED (not available in *Super Smart* and *Super Champ*);
- the nearest word in alphabetical order before or after the word the subject has searched for;
- a spelling check, which enables the subject to view possible alternatives to the word he/she has searched for;
- the option for the subject to add the word he/she has searched for, and its definition (not available in *Super Smart* and *Super Champ*).

Subjects could try to deal with the failure to locate the search word by utilising one of these functions, looking at an entry for the same word form in another word class, or removing inflections from the target word. Alternatively, they might simply start a new search.

Table 6.2 summarises the look-up behaviour of each subject, with a special focus on Stage 2, the appropriate identification of word class. As can be seen in Table 6.2, the numbers of dictionary look-ups per subject ranged from 53 (Subject 1, in 68 minutes) to 10 (Subject 6, in 35 minutes). Because subjects sometimes looked up the same word twice, often with adjustments to its morphological form, the number of words each subject looked up was slightly less than the number of look-ups each subject made. Generally speaking, the longer the subject spent on the task, the more words were looked up. These two factors did not correlate with task success, however. Subject 1, who looked up one in every four words in the English text (53 look-ups, 46 words), produced the summary that least well reflected the content of the original text, whilst Subject 8, who took the second longest amount of time (61 minutes) and made the second most frequent use of his PED (43 look-ups, 35 words) produced one of the best summaries.

The most frequent mistake was to misidentify the word class of the headword. Subjects 2 and 6 only made this mistake a few times, but the other subjects averaged six word class errors each. In total, 52 entries were consulted where the word class did not match that of the word in context. For example, subjects consulted entries for verbs when looking up **light** ('light bulb', 'the same amount of light'), **demand** ('rising energy demands'), **cost** ('rising costs') and **fuel** ('burning ever more fuel'), all of which function as nouns in the passage.

All five subjects (Subjects 1–5) who used *TalkingDict* to look up the word **bulb** found it listed as both a verb and a noun. The verb entry comes before the noun entry, and is translated as 'งอกหัว/ngok hua/',

A Close Look at the Use of Pocket Electronic Dictionaries 77

Table 6.2 A summary of look-up behaviour and word class identification

Subjects	Total minutes taken	No. of look-ups	No. of words looked up	No. of incorrect word class searches	Words placed in the wrong class
Subject 1 (*Super Smart*)	68	53	46	6	cost, dealing, bulb (2), burning, fuel, supply, demand, light, turning, less, building, wrestling
Subject 2 (*Super Smart*)	60	22	20	4	bulb, wrestling, dealing, banning
Subject 3 (*Super Champ*)	40	32	29	5	bulb, wrestling, demand, necessary, curb
Subject 4 (*Super Smart*)	42	36	29	10	light, bulb, cost, issue, fuel, supply (2), compact (2), wrestling
Subject 5 (*Super Smart*)	45	32	25	5	bulb, wrestling, cost, unnecessary, build
Subject 6 (*CyberDict3*)	35	10	9	2	wrestling, demand
Subject 7 (*CyberDict4*)	42	30	29	7	issue, compact (2), curb, wrestling, demand, building
Subject 8 (*CyberDict7*)	61	43	35	6	wrestling, rising, demand, deal, issue, curb

which makes no sense in context. In order to find the correct meaning, the subjects had to scroll down to the second entry. All five *TalkingDict* users looked first at the verb entry, but three immediately went on to successfully consult the noun entry. Subject 3 gave up the search at this point, however, and Subject 1, having looked up a number of other words, eventually returned to the verb entry to puzzle further as to its meaning.

The three *CyberDict* users, on the other hand, did not encounter this problem as the bilingual dictionary only listed **bulb** as a noun. A common cause of word class misidentification was that subjects copied the exact word form from the text to their PEDs without any adjustments to remove inflections. All eight subjects had problems with the word **wrestling** in the sentence 'Governments are wrestling with problems of rising energy demands', because they looked up **wrestling** (noun) rather than **wrestle** (verb).

Table 6.3 summarises the look-up behaviour of each subject, with a special focus on Stage 3, the identification of the target word in the dictionary. Table 6.3 indicates a widespread failure to adjust inflected forms appropriately before look-up. Subject 1, the least proficient PED user, searched unsuccessfully for **politicians**, **solved**, **cheapest**, **supplies**, **improving**, **demands** and **countries** as headwords. Other subjects who recognised that forms were inflected still failed to make appropriate adjustments: look-ups were recorded for **cheape** (adjusted from 'the cheapest way') and **bann** (from 'banning the traditional light bulb').

Some unsuccessful look-ups seem to have been due to PED content rather than the subjects' lack of skill, however. The phrases 'not so' and 'not such', searched for by Subject 8, were not listed in any of the dictionaries contained in *CyberDict* or *TalkingDict* models. Subject 3 failed to find 'win win' because it is not in any of the dictionaries in *TalkingDict* models. (Users of *CyberDict* models would have been able to find this phrase via the cross-search function if they had keyed in the hyphenated form 'win-win' rather than 'win win'.)

Although the cross-search function would sometimes have led users to entries in the *Oxford Advanced Learner's Dictionary* as one of the components of *CyberDict*, in this experiment none of the subjects ever consulted any of the monolingual dictionaries in their PEDs. The nature of the task encouraged bilingual dictionary consultation, but both the survey data and the post-task interview data suggested that most KMUTT students were unwilling to use monolingual dictionaries under any circumstances, other than in their English language classes. This raises the question of whether KMUTT English lecturers were aware of their students' normal dictionary consultation practices. They had probably observed students using monolingual dictionaries during their

A Close Look at the Use of Pocket Electronic Dictionaries 79

Table 6.3 A summary of look-up behaviour and unsuccessful searches

Subjects	No. of unsuccessful look-ups	Words not found	No. of words looked up repeatedly	Words looked up repeatedly
Subject 1 (*Super Smart*)	8	politicians, solved, cheapest, supplies, improving, demands, countries	6	demand, bulb, politician, solve (2), cheapest, supply
Subject 2 (*Super Smart*)	1	banning	1	bulb (2)
Subject 3 (*Super Champ*)	1	win win	3	demand, win, climate
Subject 4 (*Super Smart*)	0	–	4	bulb (3), fuel, supply (2), compact
Subject 5 (*Super Smart*)	3	cheapest, cheape, cheape	4	bulb (2), cost, climate (3), cheap (2)
Subject 6 (*CyberDict3*)	2	spectre, Green Room	1	climate
Subject 7 (*CyberDict4*)	0	–	2	issue, compact (2)
Subject 8 (*CyberDict7*)	5	spectre, bann, not so, not such, dealing	5	rising, demand (2), spectre, deal (2), issue, bann
Total	20	–	26	–

lessons, but may not have guessed the full extent of PED and bilingual print dictionary use outside class.

Discussion

Despite the problems reported in this study, subjects generally managed to find the entries they were looking for. In this respect, they were slightly more successful than the international students at a British university studied by Nesi and Haill (2002). In that study only two out of 77 subjects used PEDs, and the remaining 75 used conventional print dictionaries, yet 43 subjects were unsuccessful with one or more of the five dictionary consultations they were required to make; in 34 of these cases, they chose the wrong dictionary entry or subentry, and in 23 of these, the problem was due to failure to identify the word class of the look-up word.

In the Light Bulb study, students failed to find the correct entries for 20 words, after looking up 222 (a 9% failure rate), whilst the international students in Britain, using print dictionaries for the most part, failed to find the correct meanings of 65 words after making 390 consultations (a 16.4% failure rate). The two experiments are not exactly comparable, as the international students were allowed much greater freedom to choose the words they wanted to look up, but were required to prove their understanding of each look-up word, whereas in the Light Bulb experiment, correct identification of the appropriate entry was treated as proof of look-up success. Nevertheless, the Thai subjects can be regarded as relatively successful dictionary users, and this does not seem to be due to their language skills (they were much less proficient at reading in English than the advanced-level students in Nesi and Haill's study). Perhaps the speed and ease of PED consultation encouraged the Thai subjects to check the meaning of words they already knew to some extent. Our observations suggest, however, that the speed and ease of consultation more often encouraged them to persist with their searches when the first meanings they encountered did not fit the context. Most subjects who mistakenly consulted the entry for a verb rather than a noun, for example, went on to correct their mistake.

Conclusion

This chapter summarises much of what is currently known about the use of PEDs, and in so doing, highlights the fact that researchers are still tending to ignore such dictionaries as objects of study. This chapter has merely begun to examine potential lines of enquiry in PED research. Findings reported from the Light Bulb experiment seem to suggest that although the bilingual dictionaries contained within PEDs are somewhat inadequate, because of the ease and speed of PED consultation, PED users may be more likely than print dictionary users to persist with their enquiries until they reach a satisfactory outcome. The monolingual dictionary information in the PEDs tended to be ignored, but models produced by both the major brands contained monolingual English dictionaries from reputable publishing houses. The *CyberDict* models in particular had the potential to provide examples and usage information via entries from the *Oxford Advanced Learner's Dictionary* and the *Longman Dictionary of American English.* Perhaps this study will therefore go some way towards dispelling lecturers' prejudice against PEDs, and promoting their development as accessible repositories of vocabulary information. Our research carries on the tradition of electronic dictionary investigation that Paul Meara was one of the first to explore, and may also lead to better teaching and learning – the practical aim that has always motivated Meara's own work.

Chapter 7
Repeated L2 Reading With and Without a Dictionary

JIM RONALD

Introduction

Research into the effect of dictionary use on the vocabularies of second language learners is a testament to the complexities of issues associated with this field and to the efforts made by researchers to find a way through these complexities. The research described in this paper is also driven by the desire to find a workable means of addressing the challenges involved in identifying and measuring the vocabulary growth caused by dictionary use.

Much of the research into the effect of dictionary use has failed to provide convincing evidence of vocabulary growth. Three related factors may account for many of the problems encountered by researchers: the time that dictionary use requires; the consequent focus on small numbers of targeted items; and the sensitivity and reliability of the testing instruments employed. One central difficulty is the time it takes a language learner to look up a word, to identify the relevant information in the dictionary entry, and to read and understand that information. This has resulted in studies typically focusing on the learning of 12–24 targeted words. One consequence of focusing on such small numbers of words has been that words targeted from a reading passage may be grouped around just a couple of topics. Given the topic-based focus in much L2 instruction, this may mean that experimental groups' prior knowledge of the targeted items differs significantly when groups are formed from whole classes of students (e.g. Luppescu & Day, 1993; the first study reported in Aizawa, 1999) and that test-takers' selection of correct answers in a multiple-choice test may have as much to do with choosing answers related to dominant topics in the text as to actually knowing the words being tested (e.g. Knight, 1994).

A further consequence of targeting small numbers of items for testing may be that the study produces an insufficient amount of reliable data, either because language learners do not look up many of the targeted words (e.g. in Hulstijn *et al.*, 1996) or because too many of the test items are faulty (e.g. Luppescu & Day, 1993). Also, pre-tests with a small number of items may focus participants' attention on targeted items through the study and so influence learning (e.g. Laufer & Hill, 2000). Without a sufficiently sensitive testing instrument, partial or incremental changes in vocabulary knowledge may be overlooked, resulting in studies that fail to show differences between learning conditions (e.g. Fischer, 1994; Ronald & Tajino, 2005). Multiple-choice tests have been employed for their relative sensitivity, but their use has led to other problems. Among these is the difficulty of selecting effective distractors, whether in the learners' L1 (e.g. Knight, 1994) or in the target language (e.g. Luppescu & Day, 1993), and the inaccurate interpretation of data obtained through multiple-choice tests (Black, 1986). The enduring challenges of research into L2 vocabulary acquisition through dictionary use may be summarised as finding a means to substantially increase the number of targeted items and identifying a sensitive measure of dictionary users' changing vocabulary knowledge.

One possible way of increasing the number of targeted items may be found in Krantz's study (1990). His use of a long L2 text read over a few days enabled him to focus on participants' knowledge of 148 words, encountered various times within the text and either looked up or not looked up in an electronic dictionary. Through the use of longer texts, then, it becomes possible to investigate the effect of reading and dictionary use on large numbers, and types, of targeted words.

In order to measure the partial, incremental changes in a language learner's vocabulary knowledge (see, e.g. Shore & Kempe, 1999) that may take place as a result of encountering words in a text or looking them up in a dictionary, we need to consider both the choice of instrument employed and the application of the instrument chosen. Tests that presume a polar know/don't know state for word knowledge, coupled with a *pre-test – learning condition – post-test* format for experiments may fail to capture much of the vocabulary acquisition that takes place. One approach that may provide us with a fuller picture of the vocabulary acquisition that takes place through learners' dictionary use is to repeatedly test knowledge of very large numbers of items with an instrument that is capable of measuring partial, and incrementally changing, word knowledge. V_States (Meara, 2001) was chosen as the most suitable instrument, both for measuring word knowledge and producing transitional probability matrices, so that the effect of different learning conditions on one person's vocabulary could be compared (see Meara & Rodriguez Sánchez, 2001). I used V_States to measure changes in vocabulary knowledge through reading and dictionary use.

The Study

The demands made of a participant in a study involving many hours of L2 reading and testing mean that an individual case study approach is most appropriate. One intermediate-level Japanese learner of English took part in this study. Kazu was a 20-year-old third-year student majoring in English at a middle-ranking Japanese university, with little experience of language use outside formal learning contexts. His experience of extensive reading in English was limited to one graded reader almost two years previously. His knowledge of English would be rated as intermediate, and at the time of the study he had a TOEFL score close to 450. For the study, Kazu was asked to read a long English text a total of eight times. Following each reading, he rated his knowledge of a large number of lexical items drawn from the text. For the first three reading sessions, no dictionary use was permitted, but from the fourth session onwards, he was allowed to use a monolingual learner dictionary while reading.

For the study, I formulated three hypotheses:

(1) the participant would demonstrate L2 vocabulary growth as a result of repeated extensive reading;
(2) he would demonstrate L2 vocabulary growth that is attributable to dictionary use while reading beyond that attributable to reading alone;
(3) targeted items that were looked up would show greater vocabulary growth than targeted items that were not looked up.

The text used for reading and as the source for the targeted words was the children's book *The Lion, the Witch and the Wardrobe* (Lewis, 1950). This text was chosen because it would be relatively easy to read and there would also be a place for dictionary use to aid comprehension. It was a long enough text (about 40,000 tokens) to contain a sufficient number of words that would be suitable as test items (see below). In addition, the participant in an earlier study had expressed her appreciation of the book.

In order to select suitable targeted items for the study, the whole text of *The Lion, the Witch and the Wardrobe* was scanned into a computer and a concordancing programme was used to identify words that occur only once in the text. Of the over 3000 word forms, or types, occurring in the text, 1546 occur only once. Once words with other members of the same lemma or word family in the text were excluded, around 700 single-occurrence words remained. I judged that the participant would probably know about 300 of these, whether as Japanese loanwords or as words he would have encountered in his English as a foreign language (EFL) studies, leaving around 400 words suitable as task items. Words that in the pilot study had been confused with other words, such as *puddle* for *paddle*, were not used as targeted words in this study; 300 items were randomly chosen from those remaining. In addition, 20 words were selected from the third edition of the *Longman Dictionary of Contemporary*

English (henceforth LDOCE; Summers, 1995) to be control items; these were low-frequency words, beyond the 3000 most frequent words in the dictionary and judged to be unlikely to be known by the participant.

From the fourth reading onwards, Kazu was encouraged to use a monolingual EFL dictionary (LDOCE) while reading. He was lent a copy of this dictionary to use during the study, with the understanding that he would return it after the study; this was to ensure that he kept no record of words looked up in the dictionary that might affect subsequent look-up behaviour and retention of looked-up words.

Procedure

Before reading the text, Kazu rated his knowledge of the 320 items using the instrument V_States, described below. In the following week, he read the text, without referring to a dictionary of any kind. The first reading took him 7 hours to complete, over seven days. The participant then rated his knowledge of the 320 items again. This continued for two further reading and rating sessions, for which reading times were 7.5 hours and 8 hours.

From the fourth reading onwards, for five sessions, the participant was given the monolingual EFL dictionary to use. He was also given a brief guide to using the dictionary. He was advised to limit his dictionary use by aiming to keep his reading and dictionary use within the 7–8 hours that it took him to read the text on the first three readings. The participant was also instructed to affix a marker in the dictionary for each word he looked up during the reading. Each reading was followed by a V_States rating session for the 320 items. Following the final V_States rating session, the participant was given the Final Meaning Test.

Vocabulary evaluation method

The computer programme V_States (Meara, 2001) presents the targeted words, one by one, in random order and records the participant's responses. For each word that appears on the screen, the participant rates his knowledge of the word by clicking on one of four buttons 0–3 on the screen, representing the following states of word knowledge:

- **0:** I don't know what this word means.
- **1:** I'm not sure I know what this word means.
- **2:** I think I know what this word means.
- **3:** I definitely know what this word means.

The rating task averaged about 4.5 seconds per item, totalling around 25 minutes per testing session for the 320 items.

As an instrument for recording changes in vocabulary knowledge, V_States meets four important requirements of this study:

(1) It enables the rapid rating of vocabulary knowledge of large numbers of items.
(2) With four states for rating of word knowledge, it is both more sensitive and more accurate than an instrument that suggests a binary *know/don't know* representation of learners' word knowledge.
(3) It is suitable for repeated testing of knowledge of the same set of items because the use of large numbers of test items, the very rapid rating of items and the random presentation of items all reduce any possible effect that retesting itself may have on word knowledge.
(4) The repeated testing of a large number of items, in a number of states, produces data that enable the creation of transitional probability matrices. These can be used to produce projections for one learning condition (such as reading without a dictionary) to be compared with actual data for a second condition (e.g. reading with a dictionary).

A Final Meaning Test was conducted following the final V_States rating session, to check whether the participant was able to give meanings for all the words he had rated as definitely known in the final V_States session. This was done to confirm the accuracy of the participant's self-rating of targeted word knowledge.

Dictionary use

As Table 7.1 shows, Kazu looked up words in the text a total of 188 times during reading sessions 4–8, with 87 of these look-ups for targeted words.

The total of 188 look-ups was for 175 words: 162 words looked up once and 13 twice. The 87 look-ups for targeted words were for 84 words: 81 words looked up once and three words looked up twice. This left 216 targeted words which were encountered in the text but not looked up.

Table 7.1 Participant's dictionary use in reading sessions 4–8

Session	Total look-ups	Not targeted items	Targeted items
4	47	25	22
5	41	27	14
6	41	21	20
7	38	17	21
8	21	11	10
Total	188	101	87

Results

I now report data relating to the effect of L2 reading with and without a dictionary on the participant's vocabulary development. I begin with two sets of data that help establish the credibility of V_States as the main instrument used in this study: the participant's Final Meaning Test results and his V_States rating for the control items. This is followed by the results of the nine V_States rating sessions for the 300 targeted words for the pre-test. I then report the use of V_States data to obtain projections for vocabulary development in the first condition, to compare with actual data for vocabulary development in the second condition. Finally, I focus on V_States data for the 84 looked-up words.

Final Meaning Test

In the Final Meaning Test, the participant gave acceptable translation equivalents for 79% of the items that he had rated as definitely known in the final V_States session. There was some confusion with morphologically similar words, for example, mistaking *rattle* for *kettle*, some lack of semantic clarity or specificity, such as confusing *dungeon* with *cave*, and some apparent confusion with Japanese words too, giving *'ugomeku'* (wriggle) instead of *'umeku'* as the meaning of *moan*. Overall, though, this test confirmed that Kazu knew most of the meanings of the words that he had claimed to know.

Control items

Data for the 20 control items provide further confirmation of the reliability of the participant's rating of the 300 items from the text. Sixteen of the items remain 0-rated throughout the nine V_States sessions, with only one of the other four items showing any overall gain from the first session to the last. Inevitably, nine encounters with these items in the rating sessions, however brief, may increase familiarity with them. However, unless the items are onomatopoeic to some degree, or are encountered outside this study, these contextless encounters should not increase knowledge of the meanings of the items. The participant's rating of these control items appears to confirm that he was recording his knowledge of the meaning of the targeted items rather than the degree of familiarity with the word forms.

V_States sessions

There were nine V_States sessions: one session prior to reading and eight further sessions following each of the readings of the text. The results of these are shown in Table 7.2. As we can see, for 0-rated items there is a steady fall from T1 to T7, after which the numbers show signs

Table 7.2 States of targeted words for each V_States rating session

Learning condition	Session no.	State 0	State 1	State 2	State 3
Pre-test	T0	196	31	24	49
Reading, no dictionary	T1	192	14	42	52
	T2	174	34	57	35
	T3	166	31	72	31
Reading, dictionary used	T4	142	33	85	40
	T5	124	39	106	31
	T6	107	32	120	41
	T7	82	62	113	43
	T8	86	62	114	38

of levelling out. State 1-rated items are generally steady from T0 to T6, with a substantial rise for the last two sessions. The number of State 2 items rises steadily from T0 to T6, after which they start to fall for T7 and T8. Somewhat surprisingly, and requiring further investigation, the number of State 3 items starts with a drop of around 30% from T1 to T2, then remain largely unchanged from T2 to T8.

The Final Meaning Test results, the V_States figures for the control items and the lack of major changes in the number of State 3 items all alert us to two things. First, rather than overestimating his knowledge of the targeted words, the participant may have rated his word knowledge conservatively, being reluctant to rate looked-up words as State 3. Second, we are reminded that if we expect incremental vocabulary growth to take place through the learning conditions under inspection, we should expect to find greatest evidence of this growth in states of vocabulary knowledge other than 'definitely known'. This expectation is confirmed by the substantial, and steady, fall in the number of State 0 items and the rise in the number of State 1 and 2 items over the nine sessions.

Projections of vocabulary development

We will now investigate the use of V_States data to create transitional probability matrices by means of which projections of vocabulary development in one condition may be compared with the actual vocabulary development in a second condition: in this study, the comparison of projected figures for reading without a dictionary with actual figures for reading with a dictionary. The figures for the projected scores are arrived at by making projections based on the proportions of items that leave and enter each state between two adjacent V_States sessions. If we have 100 test items and ask a language learner within a given learning condition to rate knowledge of each as State 0, 1, 2 or 3, the results at two times, T1 and T2, might be as follows:

State	0	1	2	3
T1	50	20	20	10
T2	37	25	19	19

The numbers of items that stay in the same state or move to any other state will give us an indication, provided the learning condition remains constant, of the proportions of items that are likely to remain in the same state or move to other states at subsequent times. This movement, expressed in terms of proportions, is shown in Table 7.3. The proportions can, then, be used as a transitional probability matrix to predict the numbers of items in each state at subsequent times.

To return to our results, although vocabulary growth or development is typically represented as an increase in the number of items that are fully or definitely known, we can see that data for items rated State 3 do not reflect this. We could look at combined figures for States 1 to 3 (i.e. words that are at least partially known), but a more straightforward approach is to focus on falls in unknown, State 0, items over the nine V_States sessions. Actual and projected numbers of items in State 0 are shown in Figure 7.1.

Projected figures for continued reading without dictionary use, based on the movement of items between T2 and T3 (shown by the line with squares), show a rapid slowdown in the fall in numbers of State 0 items; fewer and fewer words would become known in subsequent sessions, to the point that beyond session T9 we may expect no further drop in numbers of 0-rated items. This contrasts strongly with the continued steady fall in 0-rated items from T3 for the new learning condition of

Table 7.3 Deriving a transitional probability matrix

| State | T1 | \multicolumn{4}{c|}{Proportions moving to these states at T2} | T2 |
		0	1	2	3	
0	50	0.6	0.2	0.1	0.1	37
1	20	0.2	0.5	0.2	0.1	25
2	20	0.1	0.2	0.5	0.2	21
3	10	0.1	0.1	0.2	0.6	17

[Chart showing actual numbers of State 0 items, projected scores for reading w/out dictionary use, and scores projected from T4:T5, across T0 to T9]

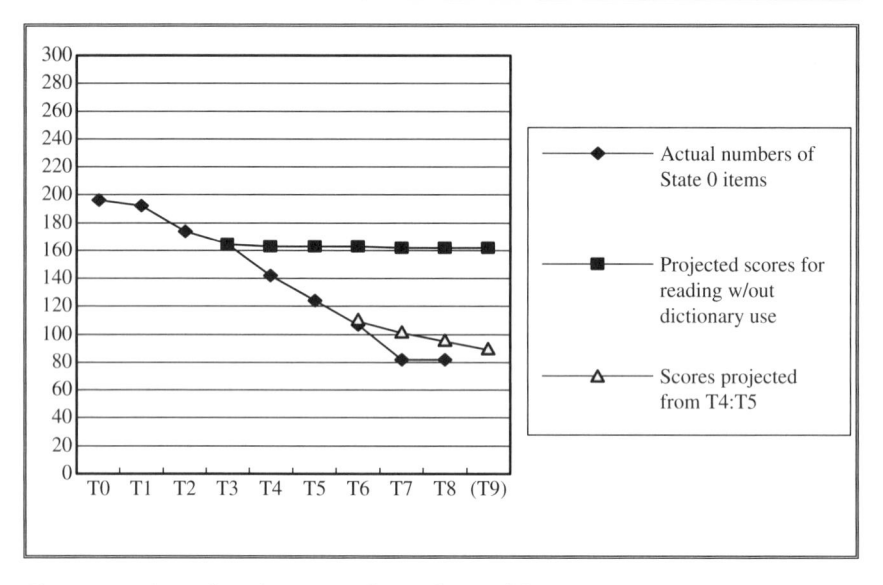

Figure 7.1 Actual and projected numbers of State 0 items

reading with a dictionary (the line with diamonds), with substantial numbers of items becoming at least partly known until T7. The projection based on T4:T5 (the line with triangles), by which we may compare real and projected figures for the same condition of reading with dictionary use, was made to confirm the accuracy of the predictive power of these V_States-generated matrices. Although actual changes from session to session are inevitably less regular than the projected figures, we can see that by T8 the projected and real figures for this condition are very close and are set to become closer. This seems to confirm the reliability of projected data obtained using V_States.

The effect of dictionary use on word state

Tables 7.2 to 7.3 and the graph provide a description of changes to the vocabulary states for the 300 items from the text. Within this set of targeted items, however, there are two distinct sets of words: words that were looked up and words that were not. We will now look at vocabulary development recorded through V_States for these sets of words.

Table 7.4 shows the effect that dictionary use while reading had on the 84 targeted words that were looked up. Four of the words were looked up twice, so in total there were 88 look-ups for these items. The column labelled 'Prior state' shows how the word was rated in the V_States session immediately prior to the reading during which the item was

Table 7.4 The effect of look-up on word state

Prior state	No. of look-ups	State following look-up				Total gain
		0	1	2	3	
0	67	22	17	24	4	77
1	16	3	0	11	2	12
2	4	0	0	2	2	2
3	1	0	0	0	1	0
Total	88	25	17	37	9	91

looked up; the four columns labelled 'State following look-up' show how the items were rated in the V_States session following the reading in which the word was looked up; and the column labelled 'Total gain' shows the total number of states by which items in each prior state rose in the V_States sessions following being looked up. So, for the 67 State 0 items that are looked up, 22 remain 0-rated, 17 move to State 1 (a gain of 17 states), 24 to State 2 (a gain of 48 states), and 4 to State 3 (a gain of 12 states), with a total gain of 77 states.

As the 'Prior state' column shows, the vast majority of items that the participant looked up were previously State 0-rated: not, as far as he could judge, even partially known to him. Much fewer State 1-rated words were looked up, while the two higher States 2 and 3 accounted for only about 6% of the total looked-up targeted words.

As we consider the effect that looking up a word had on its retention, at least as rated in the V_States session following look-up, we can see that for initially 0-rated items, there was an average rise per item of a little over one state. For 1-rated words, the average gain is a little under one state per item. As for State 2, the average gain is of half a state per item.

Looked-up words versus not looked-up words

Although the above set of data is of interest in itself, it becomes more meaningful when we compare data for looked-up words with data for targeted words that were not looked up. This allows us to address the third hypothesis: that there would be a clear effect for looked-up targeted words. In order to compare like with like, I will focus only on words which the participant consistently rated as unknown for the first four sessions. Table 7.5 shows the number of these items in each state together with the state given for these items in the final V_States rating session. Figures are also given for the control items.

Table 7.5 Development of looked-up, non-looked-up and control items

	0-rated for T0-T3	State following look-up				Total gain
		0	1	2	3	
Looked-up words	69	18	18	31	2	86
Not looked-up words	84	60	10	13	1	39
Control items	18	17	1	0	0	1

Of the 153 targeted words that were 0-rated for the first four V_States sessions, 69 were subsequently looked up and 84 were not. Only 26% of the words that were looked up remained in State 0, while over 70% of targeted words that were not looked up were still 0-rated in the final V_States session. There was an average gain for looked-up words of 1.2 states, with the largest number of these items ending rated as State 2 and very few reaching State 3. The gain for words that were not looked up averaged under 0.5. It is also worth noting the difference between final scores for the control items (neither encountered in the text nor looked up), and for the targeted words from the text that were not looked up. While 17 of the 18 control items that were 0-rated for the first four V_States sessions remained 0-rated throughout, over one quarter of targeted words that were not looked up showed some gain.

Discussion

We set out with three hypotheses proposed with regard to this study, with two general hypotheses regarding anticipated vocabulary development in the two main learning conditions under investigation. The first is that the participant would demonstrate L2 vocabulary growth attributable to repeated extensive reading. The study's findings supported this hypothesis for reading both with and without dictionary use. For the first of the three reading sessions for which dictionary use was not allowed, considerable vocabulary growth was recorded, with most of the word knowledge gains partial and for items previously rated as unknown. A possible explanation for this is that words that were encountered in isolation in the first V_States session and rated as unknown may have been subsequently recognised as known words in the context of the reading text. Alternatively, the reading text may have provided a context in which previously unknown words' meanings could be at least partially understood. Regarding reading with dictionary use, vocabulary growth was sustained for the first four sessions and, again, most word knowledge gains were partial and for items that were previously rated as unknown.

The second general hypothesis was that there would be a clear benefit in terms of L2 vocabulary growth attributable to dictionary use while reading beyond that attained through reading without the aid of a dictionary. This, too, was confirmed, as shown in Figure 7.1. Just as the benefit of repeated extensive reading without a dictionary was waning, the introduction of permitted dictionary use had the effect of accelerating vocabulary acquisition once more; half of the items that were 0-rated at this point rose above this level by the final V_States session. Unlike the low level of return in terms of vocabulary development of repeated reading alone, the rate of vocabulary growth through reading with dictionary use was largely sustained over the five reading with dictionary use sessions. It should be pointed out, however, that these gains cannot be attributed to dictionary use alone, but to the attention given to the written context for the word in the text and the information contained within the dictionary entry.

The third hypothesis was that looked-up targeted words would show greater growth than targeted words that were not looked up. As Table 7.4 and Table 7.5 show, most looked-up words were previously rated as unknown, and knowledge of previously unknown targeted words that were looked up typically rose by one or two states. This compares with an average growth rate of less than half this amount for initially unknown targeted words that were not looked up. While just over 25% of previously 0-rated items that were looked up remained 0-rated, for the words that were not looked up this figure is close to 75%.

For this learner at least, it appears that encountering a word in a long text may reactivate forgotten word knowledge; however, beyond the first couple of readings, there is relatively little further increase in knowledge of words initially rated as unknown. The results showed that some words in the textual vicinity of looked-up words in the text became better known, but that more typically unknown words that were not looked up remained unknown to the end; for many words, a single context gave too few clues to allow confident understanding of the words.

The participant seemed, usually, to need confirmation of word meaning through dictionary use before he felt that he knew the word better than he did prior to encountering it in this study. This, and the largely unchanged number of State 3 items through the study, suggests that there is a relationship between confidence about the accuracy of word knowledge gained for a given source and the extent of word knowledge growth that results. Consciously or not, a learner may invest more effort in committing to memory a word where they have become sure of its meaning. For language learners with little experience of extensive L2 reading or of monolingual learner dictionary use, there may be a hierarchy for L2 vocabulary learning resources both in terms of learner confidence and, consequently, in actual rates of acquisition. The guessing of word meaning from context may inspire least confidence about that meaning, followed by monolingual dictionary use, with mother tongue equivalents in bilingual dictionaries giving the learner the greatest confidence. This factor of learner confidence may help explain why the participant in this study rated very few words as definitely known after looking them up in the monolingual dictionary. He may, unconsciously, have equated 'definitely known' with seeing the equivalent of the word in his mother tongue.

Conclusion

V_States, the main instrument employed in this study, was of central importance to the achievement of the aims of this research. It made possible both the repeated rating of very large numbers of items and the sensitive and accurate rating of partial vocabulary knowledge, both within a reasonable time period and without apparent retesting effects. Crucially, V_States offered a means, using transitional probability matrices, of comparing the two learning conditions under investigation, and provided substantial reliable evidence of the effect on a language learner's vocabulary of monolingual dictionary use during reading.

During the eight-week study, the participant read almost 1000 pages of English, looked up 188 words and rated his knowledge of targeted and control items a total of 2880 times. The abundant data provided various insights into L2 vocabulary development through reading. One important insight is how through reading the learner recognised words that he had previously rated as unknown. A further observation was of the very limited benefit to vocabulary of subsequent readings of the same text. In contrast, the study revealed clear and continued benefits for the learner in building his knowledge of words looked up in a monolingual learner dictionary during repeated reading. Finally, the study showed that the participant rated few of the words he looked up as definitely known.

The large amount of data from this study only relates to a single language learner; further studies are needed to determine the extent to which retention is affected by differing abilities to guess from context or confidence in using a monolingual dictionary. This study has, however, demonstrated a viable means of measuring and comparing the effect on L2 vocabulary acquisition of reading without and with a learner dictionary.

Chapter 8
Exploring Productive L2 Collocation Knowledge

ANDY BARFIELD

Introduction

With corpus and concordance so strongly associated with collocation, it is not surprising that corpus analysis has been the method of choice for many L2 collocation researchers (e.g. Chi *et al.*, 1994; Gitsaki, 1999; Granger, 1998; Howarth, 1998; Hsu, 2007; Nesselhauf, 2003; Revier & Henriksen, 2006; Zhang, 1993). At the same time, others have used translation and/or cloze tests (e.g. Bahns & Eldaw, 1993; Biskup, 1992; Bonk, 2000a; Farghal & Obiedat, 1995; Huang, 2001; Webb & Kagimoto, 2007) or carried out assessment/experimental studies (e.g. Barfield, 2006; Gyllstad, 2005; Mochizuki, 2002; Schmitt, 1999). The general consensus across all of these different investigations is that learners face many difficulties in building their L2 collocation knowledge. Despite this common ground, many previous L2 collocation studies have been weakened by the small number of collocations they were able to elicit from different individual learners. Bahns and Eldaw's 1993 paper, which is one of the more widely cited investigations into L2 collocation knowledge, bases its claims on just 15 verb + noun combinations. While corpus-based measures have allowed for more instances of particular types of collocation to be recovered, they have tended to focus on standard collocation errors for a specific group of learners. Nesselhauf (2003), for instance, used a corpus consisting of 32 essays totalling 16,000 words to look at the collocation production of advanced German users of English, but there were on average fewer than two examples per essay of restricted verb + noun miscollocation. Other inquiries have similarly supported the general claim that collocation is 'an advanced type of vocabulary knowledge' (Schmitt, 2000: 89). This may be because previous research has often exclusively used advanced learners and found their collocation knowledge to be wanting. Yet, by focusing on the inaccurate production of a small number of specific surface lexico-grammatical patterns, the benchmark for productive L2 collocation knowledge has, in a sense, been set rather high. As Paul Meara has noted (Meara, 1997: 110), such a lack of generalisability in L2 lexical studies is not unusual. In fact, in the case of L2 collocation research, it is entirely normal because of the predominant focus on error analysis, surface forms and advanced learners.

If we are to arrive at some kind of more generalisable model of productive L2 collocation knowledge, we may need to approach things in a different way. It is clear that we would need to address two basic methodological questions: How can we elicit a relatively large number of collocations from individual learners in a time-efficient manner? How can we analyse collocation productions in ways that do not privilege error analysis? One way to tackle these questions may lie in adapting a measure from L2 word association studies. In many such studies, single prompt words are used, and subjects are required to produce one or more responses that they associate with the prompt word. Responses are then often judged against adult native speaker norms (e.g. Schmitt, 1998b; Schmitt & Meara, 1997; Söderman, 1993a; Wolter, 2002). Not all studies using word association as an elicitation tool have taken such an approach, however. Meara and Fitzpatrick (2000) used a 30-item word association task to elicit three or four responses to each stimulus word. The items in their test were highly frequent (within the first 1000 most frequent words of English) and chosen for their characteristic of generating nonfrequent responses. The data were first lemmatised, and, regardless of the stimulus word, responses were lexically profiled for frequency, with one point given to each infrequent word (i.e. outside the 1K band). The researchers used the lexical profiling results to provide a 'practical index of productive vocabulary' (Meara & Fitzpatrick, 2000: 26) for each individual. The study is simple in its design, produces reasonable data sets and offers an adaptable scoring procedure.

Using a similar instrument to explore productive L2 collocation knowledge would mean interpreting such knowledge differently from how it has been framed in many previous studies. The construct becomes operationalised as the ability to produce single-word appropriate collocates in response to a stimulus word:

| decision | 1. _____ | 2. _____ | 3. _____ |

Such a measure completely disregards the learner's colligational control of grammatical and syntactic features that a concern with 'holistic collocation knowledge' (Revier & Henriksen, 2006) would value. It also eschews any kind of contextual prompt to elicit the production of L2 collocation knowledge that some previous research has attempted (Schmitt, 1999). This simpler view of collocation strips away grammatical, syntactic and contextual features, and reduces the measure of learners' productive L2 collocation knowledge to a basic lexical task of producing appropriate collocates. This lexical combination task makes it possible to address the problem of the relatively limited number of items that previous studies of productive L2 collocation knowledge have based their findings on. With a 30-item test, the maximum number of responses possible per individual is 90. The measure also lets us move beyond a preoccupation with specific miscollocations, and, by its simplicity, opens the door to collecting data from both advanced and less proficient learners, too. Were we then to profile individuals' complete sets of collocate responses as lexically frequent or infrequent and to analyse the word classes chosen (i.e. adjectival, verbal, nominal), we would, moreover, be able to start raising questions about how the development of L2 collocation knowledge may be related to general changes in the overall organisation of the L2 lexicon at different levels of proficiency. This alternative approach might, in other words, let us begin to sketch out some kind of predictive model of L2 collocation knowledge and lexical (re)organisation for future research to investigate further.

Keeping these goals in mind, in this chapter I explore the following questions:

(1) What do the lexical frequency profiles of less proficient learners' collocation productions look like?
(2) Are the lexical frequency profiles of advanced learners' collocation productions different to those of less proficient learners? If different, does the difference lie in the frequent and/or infrequent subprofile?
(3) What word classes do less proficient learners tend to produce as collocates?
(4) Do advanced learners make different word class choices from less proficient learners in their collocation productions? If different, what word class choices distinguish advanced learners' L2 collocation ability?
(5) What nouns are easy or difficult for learners to collocate? How can such collocation ease or difficulty be explained?

Method, Design and Piloting

The first stage in the development of a 30-item stimulus-response collocation test was to pilot 50 highly frequent nouns from a lemmatised list of the 500 most frequent items in the British National Corpus (Kilgarriff, 1996) and to select appropriate test items. Thirty nouns that differentiated well between the responses of a group of 35 British English native speakers and 35 highly proficient Japanese users of English were chosen for use in the collocation test (see Table 8.1).

The second stage involved establishing a database of possible collocates for each target noun. Here I used *Collins Wordbanks Online* (HarperCollins, 2004) and the *Oxford Collocations Dictionary* (OUP, 2002). Collocates from both sources were combined to create a unified set of

Table 8.1 Thirty nouns selected from native speaker and non-native speaker piloting

body	example	house	police	role
car	experience	interest	power	support
child	family	issue	problem	value
country	friend	law	question	voice
death	government	life	reason	war
decision	health	paper	research	work

collocates for each noun, and the 30 collocate sets were then lexically profiled and subdivided into frequent and infrequent collocates. Frequent collocates consisted of 1K and 2K items (i.e. within the 2000 most common words of English), whereas infrequent collocates involved the Academic Word List (Coxhead, 2000) as well as off-list items. This division between frequent and infrequent is illustrated in Table 8.2 with the example collocate data set for **work**.

What is striking here (and completely typical for the collocate data sets of the other stimulus nouns) is that the great majority of collocates are frequent. Both the frequent and infrequent collocates were used for scoring the results from the collocation test (referred to as *LexCombi* from here on).

Test Procedure, Scoring and Analytical Approach

Two different pencil-and-paper forms of the same 30-item test were prepared, with items randomly jumbled in either form for counterbalancing. After a brief explanation and guided practice with three additional items (**holiday, letter** and **university**), the 89 test-takers were asked to write down three collocates for each of the 30 nouns. They had 30 seconds for each item before they were instructed to move to the next one in the test. With about five minutes for the guided practice, test administration lasted approximately 20 minutes in total. The students' L1 was Japanese, and they belonged to different first-, second- and third-year undergraduate Faculty of Law English classes, ranging in proficiency from low-intermediate through to advanced. Their Test of English for International Communication (TOEIC) scores from the institutional placement test at the start of the academic year was used as an independent indicator of their overall English ability.

The data were entered into the computer, with misspellings corrected. In the few cases where multiword combinations occurred, they were reduced to the main lexical element (e.g. **take care of** became **care**), and

Table 8.2 Collocate data set for WORK

Lexical profile (total)	Collocates
Frequent	
K1 (94)	able actually agency all alone amount and art artists as at away back began building can carried choose closely completed continue day did do effectively experience find for force full get go going hard her his home hours how I in independently make more much my nature not of on or our out own paid part people permit piece properly refuse return round school seem social some started students the their they this through time to together towards training trying used way we well went who whose will with women work would you your
K2 (10)	clock dirty lot perfectly practical practice prefer satisfactory smoothly steadily
Infrequent	
AWL (6)	enable involved motivate project undertaken voluntary
Off-list (3)	charity collaboratively efficiently

phrasal verbs were scored for the base verb (for instance, **come** for **come up with**). Uninflected base verb responses were accepted where the database indicated participle forms only. For example, **lose** and **love** were scored as appropriate collocates for **friend**, although the database included only **lost** and **loved**, and **help** was accepted for **police** (database: **helping**). These minor adjustments were made so that subject responses could be treated at a lexical rather than grammatical level of appropriacy.

The subjects' responses were initially scored as 1 or 0, according to whether they matched the collocate database for each stimulus word. This first scoring procedure produced a total for appropriate collocate responses, with a maximum of 90 possible. The students with the 20 highest and 20 lowest TOEIC scores were used to form two groups, one high and the other low. The low group's TOEIC scores ranged from 325 to 430 (mean: 389), and the high group's TOEIC scores ranged from 680 to 900 (mean: 787). In the next stage of the analysis, each individual's collocate responses were lexically profiled and categorised as frequent or infrequent, with blank responses treated as frequent in order to maintain intact data sets. Appropriate collocate responses were then separated into frequent and infrequent, and two further individual scores – appropriate frequent collocate responses and appropriate infrequent collocate responses – were derived for each of the 40 subjects. Table 8.3 shows two examples of how the scoring applied to two subjects' responses for the test item **decision**. Both subjects, Ayumi and Bitto, produced three responses. All three responses from Ayumi were frequent, of which only two were appropriate (= hits): **important** and **make**. Two of Bitto's responses were frequent and one infrequent (**final**), and all three were appropriate (= hits).

In order to gain insights into group-based performance and item difficulty, two different types of analysis were carried out. First, I ran a series of *t*-tests to compare the performance of the high and low groups. This let me explore between-group differences for productive collocation knowledge overall, as well as establish some useful comparisons between the two groups' lexical frequency profiles and word class choices for the collocates that they produced. I also used Rasch Analysis (see Shillaw, this volume) to get a clear sense of item difficulty. As this analytical approach is not that common in L2 lexical studies, I will briefly summarise certain features of Rasch Analysis relevant to the present study (for detailed explanations see McNamara [1996] and Bond and Fox [2001]). Rasch measurement works by estimating subjects' performance on a test and calculating 'from the data the chances of a candidate of a given ability achieving a certain score on an item of a given difficulty' (McNamara, 1996: 152). This analysis produces a scale to represent the relationship between person ability and item difficulty, where item difficulty is conventionally set at 0, so that items of 'above-average difficulty will be positive in sign, those of below-average difficulty negative in sign' (McNamara, 1996: 165–166). The relationship between person ability and item difficulty can also be shown in a person-item map. This is a particularly useful feature of Rasch Analysis as it provides a very clear overview of how well individuals' abilities match items along a scale of difficulty from below-average difficulty (items with negative values) to average difficulty (items with zero value) and above-average difficulty (items with positive values).

Other useful information generated by Rasch Analysis includes different infit and outfit values. These can help identify extreme items or extreme performances by individuals outside an acceptable range. The Rasch model also provides two general indices of reliability, the person reliability index and the item reliability index. The person reliability index produces a value indicating how well the test differentiates subjects according to their ability. This index will have a value that is practically the same as that produced by classical reliability measures such as Cronbach alpha. The item reliability index, on the other hand, gives a value for how well the items on the test can be

Exploring Productive L2 Collocation Knowledge 101

Table 8.3 Example responses and scoring for DECISION

Subject	Item	Responses	Frequent responses	Infrequent responses	Frequent hits	Infrequent hits
Ayumi	decision	important make my	important make my	–	important make	–
Bitto	decision	final make reach	make reach	final	make reach	final

differentiated from each other according to their difficulty. For both reliability indices, the closer the value is to 1.0, the less we need to be concerned about measurement error. The final point to note is that I used the partial credit Rasch model in the analysis of *LexCombi*. This model lets us assume that every appropriate response is at a constant distance from all other appropriate responses for each item. With large collocate data sets of sometimes over 100 possible appropriate responses, there are many possible responses for each stimulus item in *LexCombi*. The assumption of constant distance between appropriate responses simply means that any appropriate response is considered as likely as another.

Results

I report the main findings in two stages. First, I use conventional statistical analysis to look at results for the whole population, as well as the significant differences between the low and high groups. This includes the results from the lexical frequency profiling of appropriate collocates and lets us identify some interesting differences in L2 collocation knowledge for learners of different overall English proficiency (i.e. research questions 1–4). In the second stage, I present further insights from the Rasch Analysis to examine the relationship between person ability and item difficulty so that we can identify which words are easy or difficult for learners to collocate (i.e. research question 5).

Descriptive statistics for collocation appropriacy

The descriptive statistics for collocation appropriacy (i.e. score out of 90) for the whole population ($n = 89$) are shown in Table 8.4.

The reliability of the test proved to be moderately high (Cronbach $\alpha = 0.78$). Pearson correlation analysis showed a significant correlation between general English proficiency and productive L2 collocation knowledge ($r = 0.569$, $p < 0.001$).

Table 8.4 Collocation appropriacy for all subjects

	Result
n	89
Minimum	17
Maximum	61
Mean	37.93
SD	9.74

Exploring Productive L2 Collocation Knowledge 103

Table 8.5 Low and high group appropriate collocate scores

	Low	High
Mean	30.65	46.45
SD	10.20	7.14

High and low group appropriate collocation scores

The collocation responses for the low and high groups were analysed in order to get an overall picture of differences in their appropriate collocate production. An independent samples *t*-test confirmed a significant difference between the two groups for appropriate collocate responses ($t = 5.673$, df 38, $p < 0.001$), as shown in Table 8.5.

As we might expect, advanced learners produce more appropriate collocates than less proficient learners. Whether this difference between the two groups is simply one of number rather than kind becomes clearer as we look at other results.

High and low group lexical profiles for appropriate collocates

To examine differences in the lexical profiles of the two groups of learners (research questions 1 and 2), their appropriate collocate scores ('hits') were divided into frequent and infrequent items (see Table 8.6), and further *t*-tests were run on the scores for frequent and infrequent hits.

The results of the *t*-tests confirmed a significant difference between the two groups for both appropriate frequent collocation responses ($t = 4.783$, df 38, $p < 0.001$) and appropriate infrequent collocation responses ($t = 4.844$, df 38, $p < 0.001$). The high group produces a much greater average number of frequent appropriate collocates than the low group. The low SD value for the high group suggests limited variability in performance within the high group for frequent appropriate collocate

Table 8.6 Lexical profile of appropriate collocate responses

Lexical profile	Low	High
Frequent		
Mean	29.4	42.35
SD	10.02	6.8
Infrequent		
Mean	1.25	4.1
SD	1.12	2.38

production, whereas the remarkably high SD for the low group suggests huge variability in individuals' productive L2 collocation knowledge for such collocates. In contrast, the mean scores for infrequent appropriate collocates are extremely low for both groups, and the SD values are high in both cases. Here, we can infer strong variability in individual production of appropriate infrequent collocates for low-intermediate and advanced learners.

Differences between high and low group collocates

To understand whether advanced learners and low-intermediate learners differ in the word class choices they make for collocates (research question 3), I carried out two further analyses. The first involved subdividing all appropriate collocates by word class into *adjectival, nominal, verbal, nominal-verbal* (i.e. homonyms such as **answer** and **play**) and *other* (mainly prepositions and adverbials). A *t*-test was then run to determine the difference between the high and low groups for each of these word classes. As the low group did not produce enough infrequent appropriate collocates to warrant a further comparison, I present the results for frequent appropriate collocates only (see Table 8.7).

Overall, the two groups showed significant differences in frequent nominal, verbal and nominal-verbal collocates, but no difference in adjectival collocates (research question 4). The development of productive L2 collocation knowledge seems particularly marked by the high group's significantly greater production of verbal collocates. This between-group difference becomes clearer if we take the example of **problem** (an item that Rasch Analysis shows to be within the person ability of nearly all of the population – see Figure 8.1). Tables 8.8 and 8.9 show the appropriate collocates that each group produced for **problem**.

There is little difference between the number and type of adjectival collocates that either group produces (as predicted by Table 8.7). However, for the verbal collocates, the high group starts to diversify its

Table 8.7 Comparison of high and low group by word class for frequent appropriate collocates

Word class	Low	High	Sig
Adjectival	14.15	14.80	–
Nominal	5.60	7.60	$p < 0.01$
Verbal	5.95	12.45	$p < 0.01$
Nominal-verbal	2.25	4.50	$p < 0.001$
Other	1.55	2.35	–

Exploring Productive L2 Collocation Knowledge

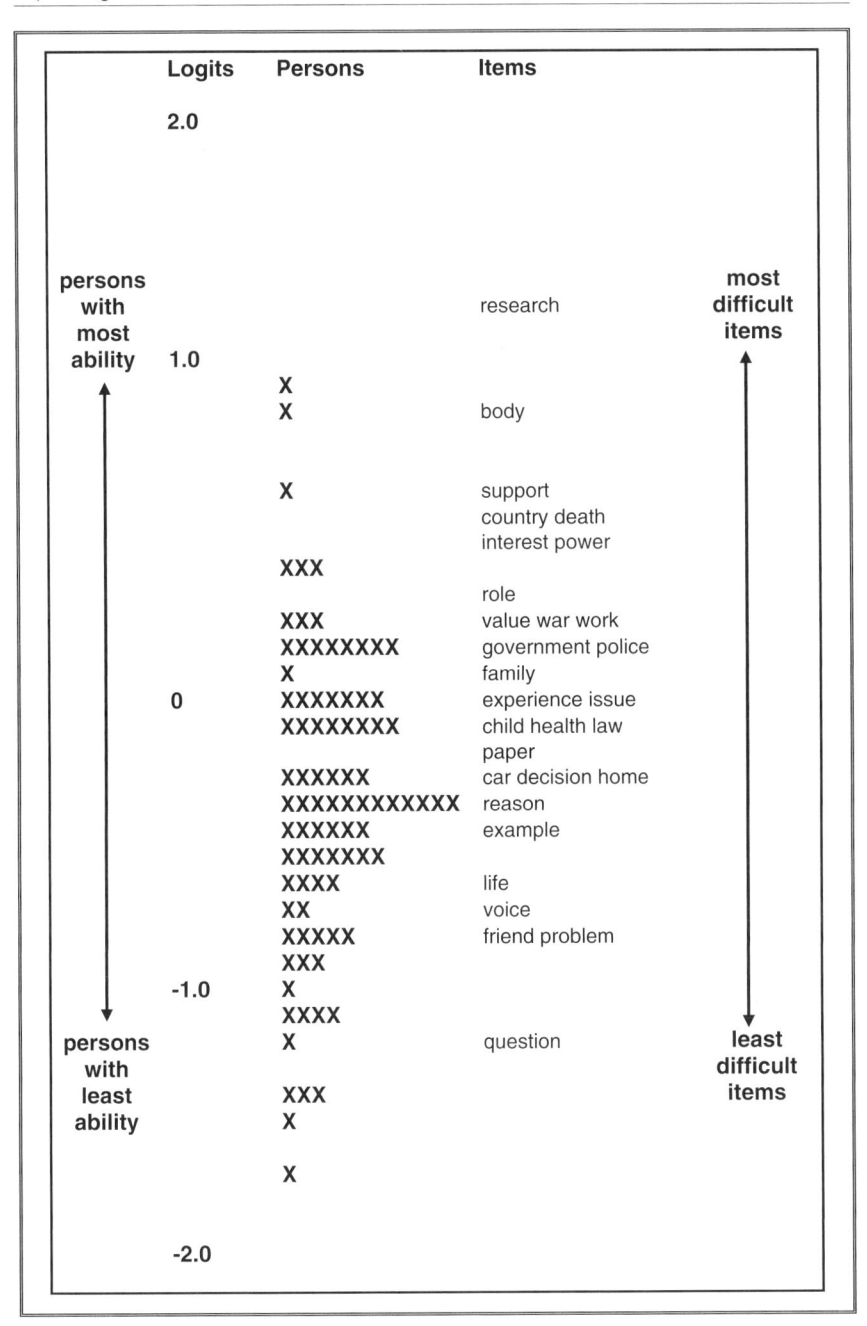

Logits	Persons	Items
2.0		
		research — most difficult items
1.0	X	
	X	body
	X	support
		country death
		interest power
	XXX	
		role
	XXX	value war work
	XXXXXXXX	government police
	X	family
0	XXXXXXX	experience issue
	XXXXXXXX	child health law
		paper
	XXXXXX	car decision home
	XXXXXXXXXXXX	reason
	XXXXXX	example
	XXXXXXX	
	XXXX	life
	XX	voice
	XXXXX	friend problem
	XXX	
-1.0	X	
	XXXX	
	X	question — least difficult items
	XXX	
	X	
	X	
-2.0		

persons with most ability ↑ / persons with least ability ↓

Figure 1 Person-item map for *LexCombi*

Table 8.8 Low group appropriate collocate choice by word class for PROBLEM (hits)

Group	Adjectival	Verbal	Other	Total
Low	easy (1), no (2), big (3), difficult (3), serious (3)	consider (1), have (2), solve (3)	solution (2)	
Total	12	6	2	20

Table 8.9 High group appropriate collocate choice by word class for PROBLEM (hits)

Group	Adjectival	Verbal	Other	Total
High	easy (1), hard (1), big (3), serious (4), difficult (7)	consider (1), deal (1), find (1), occur (1), have (3), resolve[a] (3), solve (11)	answer (1), cause (1), solution (1), health (2)	
Total	14	21	5	40

[a]**resolve** is the only infrequent appropriate collocate produced.

range; more importantly, they generate over three times as many appropriate verbal combinations for **problem**.

Rasch Analysis results

We move now to the Rasch Analysis results to consider the relationship between item difficulty and person ability (research question 5). The results showed that the person reliability index for *LexCombi* was 0.77. As mentioned earlier, this index is very close to Cronbach alpha (0.78). Person misfit (i.e. 'extreme' responses by particular subjects) involved seven individuals, which comes to 8% of the whole population of 89 – higher than the particularly strict 2% benchmark given by McNamara as the upper limit for the level of person misfit (McNamara, 1996: 178), but nonetheless acceptable for this kind of low-stakes exploratory research. Although *LexCombi* has moderately high person reliability, the item reliability index is 0.93, showing that there is a very good spread of items from difficult to easy. Indeed, results indicated that all items have acceptable fit values.

The person-item map in Figure 8.1 shows that all items fall between +2 (above average difficulty) and −2 (below average difficulty). In Figure 8.1, each X represents one learner. Items nearer to the top are more difficult to collocate, and items closer to the bottom are easier to collocate. The figure shows that **research** turns out to be the most difficult word to collocate: it lies just outside person ability, suggesting that only a few learners in this population may have some sense of how to collocate **research**. In contrast, **question** is the easiest word to collocate. We can describe it as lying within person ability, as there are five learners on the scale below **question**. The person-item map indicates that this small group of learners may have a very limited ability to produce any appropriate collocates at all for the items on *LexCombi*.

Other relatively difficult items are **body**, **support**, **country**, **death**, **interest** and **power**. These form a small group of words that a few learners are able to produce appropriate collocates for. Two items, **experience** and **issue**, prove to be of medium difficulty to collocate: a person of average ability has a 50% chance of being able to collocate **experience** and **issue**. This more or less holds for the bulk of items clustering closely above and below 0 on the scale (i.e. **role**, **value**, **war**, **work**, **government**, **police**, **family**, **child**, **health**, **law**, **paper**, **car**, **decision**, **home**, **reason** and **example**). This constitutes a large group of nouns that is within the ability of learners with intermediate collocation proficiency, but beyond that of the least collocationally proficient for the most part. The bottom of Figure 8.1 shows us that **life**, **voice**, **friend** and **problem** prove to be more or less easy to collocate for nearly the whole population (hence the choice of **problem** for analysis and commentary in Tables 8.8 and 8.9).

Discussion

In this study, I set out to explore productive L2 collocation knowledge in a way that would not be limited to error analysis. My aim was to use a measure that would enable the collection of a considerable number of collocations by individuals and be sensitive enough to allow comparison of both low-intermediate and advanced learners. I also wanted to get some sense of item difficulty and see which nouns were easy or difficult for learners to collocate. By eliciting a maximum of three collocates per stimulus over 30 items, the stimulus-response instrument provided large individual collocate data sets for analysis. The comparison of the high and low groups enabled us to examine lexical frequency profiles and to establish that more collocationally competent learners produce significantly more infrequent *and* frequent collocates. If we make the assumption that the difference in TOEIC scores between the two groups provides an indirect measure of vocabulary size, we may claim that not only are advanced learners' L2 lexicons bigger, but core items such as the 30 nouns used in the test also appear to be more readily linkable with other highly frequent lexical items, as well as with infrequent vocabulary. There is evidence, then, that the lexicons of more collocationally proficient learners are distinguishable along two dimensions, those of size and organisation (cf. Meara, 1996).

The second insight that the results from this study offer is that adjectival links form a major type of collocation production for both groups of learners; however, we also have some evidence that, in later stages of collocation development, adjectival links remain frequent, but are also complemented by nominal and verbal, as well as nominal-verbal links (see Tables 8.7, 8.8 and 8.9). In particular, the marked increase in verbal collocates for the high group points to a major area of development in productive L2 collocation knowledge. Advanced learners still produce adjectival collocation links, but appear to diversify these with other types of word class connections in the collocations that they produce. We may infer that adjective + noun collocations are the foundation of L2 collocation knowledge. Assuming that learners initially tend to opt for two-word collocations, it seems that verb + noun collocations may be the next common type of lexical combination to be frequently produced, and that such collocations may then be followed by more complex three-word combinations such as verb + adjective + noun. The results from this study begin to point to such an order of development, but further research is needed to explore whether L2 phraseological performance can be so clearly differentiated (cf. Hsu, 2007).

As noted in the Introduction, L2 collocation knowledge is generally thought to be an advanced type of lexical knowledge, but the results from this study suggest otherwise. *LexCombi* shows that the development of L2 collocation knowledge can be tracked at both low-intermediate and advanced levels of proficiency. Part of the reason for this is that the test uses individual nouns to elicit L2 collocation knowledge, but unlike previous studies of L2 collocation knowledge (cf. Schmitt, 1999), the test does not analyse the results in terms of 'depth of knowledge' of the particular stimulus word. Rather, both the lexical frequency profiling and word class analysis of appropriate collocate responses provide representative samplings that shed light on a more general understanding of the L2 lexicon. The findings from the present study let us see that L2 collocation development is a function not just of growth in terms of vocabulary size, but also of ongoing L2 lexical reorganisation through the establishment of:

- greater links between frequent lexis;
- greater links between frequent and infrequent lexis;
- word-class diversification/an increase in polysemous links.

Although our conclusions remain cautious, it nevertheless is of interest that a small group of five learners could not produce appropriate collocates for the easiest item on the test, **question**. It is perhaps also surprising that **question** proved to be the easiest item, unless we consider how often most learners of English will have translated, read, heard and used that word in their classroom-based English education.

Future versions of this kind of test might need to include more 'easy' nouns that are part of learners' everyday lives as university students, if we are to use similar populations to explore further low proficiency learners' productive collocation knowledge. Some candidate items might include: **advice**, **book**, **computer**, **environment**, **exam**, **job**, **language**, **money**, **party**, **photo**, **report**, **seminar**, **sports**, **story** and **trip**. At the same time, the analysis of the collocates produced by both groups for **problem** seems to indicate that particular collocations will remain favoured choices for advanced and low-intermediate learners. Thus, **easy**, **serious**, **difficult** and **solve** were produced by both groups and provide some evidence of a 'safe bet' strategy (Granger, 1998: 148): learners may tend to know and produce a few established frequent collocations repeatedly rather than vary their collocate choices. In a sense, they may resist diversifying their L2 collocation links and prefer to stay with what they know to be certain (cf. Wray, 2002: 206–212). Our further understanding of this tension between certainty, creativity and conventionality is limited by the number of items in *LexCombi*, as mentioned above, and by the relatively small population ($n = 89$). McNamara, for example, notes that recommended sample sizes should comprise 100 subjects minimum, although he adds that smaller groups can be used 'if the size of the error term is not an imperative consideration' (McNamara, 1996: 163). A population of 89 would seem to be just about the lower limit for this exploratory study. However, understanding that tension is not just a quantitative issue; in the end, we need qualitative insights to guide us, too.

Conclusion

This study has let us begin to identify some possible directions for drawing out an alternative model of the development of productive L2 collocation knowledge. The question now is what do we want to do next. Would it be useful to look more closely at the lexical frequency and word class patterns in appropriate collocate responses across all items for the high and low groups? Should we run this measure with a greater number of items and larger populations? Or perhaps we should be content with what this kind of small-scale exploratory study has suggested, and move on? My own judgment is that it is critically important to understand how learners address the challenge of improving their L2 collocation knowledge in practice (see Barfield, 2009). Longitudinal qualitative studies, rare indeed within the field of L2 vocabulary studies, are also needed so that we can develop a real sense of the processes that learners use (and why), and what problems they face and decisions they make, in becoming more L2 collocationally competent. Do learners themselves see their L2 vocabulary and collocation development in terms of frequent and infrequent vocabulary? Are they conscious of word class choices that they can make in developing their collocation ability? What criteria do learners use for selecting words for collocation learning and using? What stages of development do they see themselves going through, and how do they go through them? These are some of the different questions that we might beneficially address in further exploring how learners deal with the difficulties that they face in building their L2 collocation knowledge.

Chapter 9
The Messy Little Details: A Longitudinal Case Study of the Emerging Lexicon

HUW BELL

Introduction

This paper is a case study of change in one productive lexicon over 16 months, analysed through 28 pieces of writing in one genre. I focus on the use of a limited range of lexical items that are used repeatedly, and examine their use in a variety of single-word and multiword instances. I take the view that the lexicon is a dynamic subsystem within the larger linguistic system, and that the behaviour of lexical items shows characteristics of larger systems. The analysis of the individual lexicon is accompanied by measurements of other aspects of linguistic development, and the relationship between them is discussed. I chart the complicated relationship between single item lexical units and prefabricated formulaic structures in order to show how they are related to the developing control of syntactic patterns, and highlight the emergence of lexical structures over time.

The study investigates the role of formulaic lexical structures in building one language system, and the ways in which the structures themselves are related. It is informed in spirit by insights and themes from Dynamic Systems Theory (DST) and Chaos Theory (Larsen-Freeman, 1997, 2002, 2007). These themes are *inter alia* the interconnectedness of linguistic systems and subsystems; the fluctuating and nonlinear nature of growth; the emergence of states of (sub)systemic stability (so-called 'attractor' states and their converse, 'repeller' or nonpreferred states); and the dynamism and change that permeate all levels (De Bot *et al.*, 2007: 8). I have also been influenced by word-centred accounts of language structure, such as those of Hoey (2005) and Hudson (e.g. 2007).

Longitudinal studies tend to have a fairly small number of data points (e.g. Robinson & Mervis's [1998] FLA study, although Churchill [2008] is a counterexample). For very good theory-building reasons, also, much work in this area is either theoretical (e.g. Meara 2004, 2006) or based on large data sets. There have been calls for 'case studies to discover relevant sub-systems ... [I]f we really want to know what happens in the actual process of language acquisition, we should also look at the messy little details, the first attempts [and], the degree of variation at a developmental stage' (De Bot *et al.*, 2007: 19). I supply such a close-up view of some aspects of lexical development, using a DST perspective informally and analogously (Van Geert, 2007: 47). Specifically, I investigate how far patterns of growth and interconnectedness are visible at the level of individual lexical items and routines within a larger subsystem (the lexicon), and how far these can be related to other subsystems such as grammar.

Experimental Study

The subject, K, is a Korean male in his mid-20s who studied in the UK for 16 months. His English proficiency ranged from intermediate at the beginning of the study towards upper-intermediate at the end. He achieved grade C in the Cambridge First Certificate in English (FCE) after five months in the UK, and International English Language Testing System (IELTS) composite grades of 5.5 after 11 months, and 7 one month after leaving the UK. Neither grades nor examiners' guidelines give any specifically lexical insight, but one might expect K's improved grades to reflect improved lexical abilities, and the growth of lexical output to be considerable in this stage of learning. K was highly motivated, and his language learning training led him to place great emphasis on vocabulary. During his stay in the UK, he reported that his habits of finding, recording and learning new words improved, and claimed to be systematically recording and attempting to learn between 15 and 60 new items a week culled from lessons, contact with native speakers (he was resident with a local family), newspapers and course materials.

In 16 months, K wrote 28 discursive essays totalling around 6500 words, and a smaller number of descriptive and narrative pieces. Only the former are analysed here because they were typically longer, and because their genre similarity allows us to view them to some extent as repeated tasks rather than a series of different tasks. They were written on a range of topics under semi-exam conditions in 30–40 minutes and without access to spellcheckers, dictionaries or previous essays, and can thus be taken as representative of his productive ability.

Overview of the data: Developing fluency and complexity

To give an impression of the change in K's output, it is worth examining one early and one late essay, of approximately equal length but with considerable differences in grammatical control, text structure and use of formulae.

Month 1

These days many young people don't think what is right what is wrong in their life. I am going to say the problems of young people. The young are getting selfish. They just think themselves. They want to get a high position as stepping over other people. They don't care what happens to their friends or family. Succeeding is goal for them. In addition, relaxing and comfortable is also their goal. They don't want to effort to do something. Every day they make a party, drinking and just enjoy their life without producing. They don't realise what is right. Murder, drug and rob are serious problem. Young people are doing these criminal without hesitation. They think it is pleasure and play. A plenty of scholars and educator suggest the solution is parents suppose to educated their children correctly and strictly. So the making their children realise the correct way of life.

Month 16

It is certainly true that the role of parents for children is very important for this reason: educate children, bring them up and helping them set up values. It seems to me that all parents need is experience. Therefore older parents can be more helpful for children than young parents, for a number of reasons. To start with, the first point to be made is that children can learn many practical life skills through older parents. For example, children, see their parents talk with other people almost everyday, and they learn parents' behaviour and speaking. This will be useful for their interpersonal relationships. Moreover, it is said that parents can help children other practical skills – cooking, fixing, home management, because they are experienced. Another point is that it is widely believed that older parents give a sense of stability to children...

To help define some of the differences between the essays, and to give an overview of some of the performance changes in systems, I use certain basic metrics to describe productiveness, fluency, grammatical complexity and vocabulary difficulty. As an indication of increasing fluency and confidence, raw essay length and mean sentence length per essay are shown in Figures 9.1 and 9.2, respectively (following Larsen-Freeman, 2006). As a further measure of fluency, I calculated the mean number of words per t-unit, where a t-unit is a main clause plus all its dependent clauses (Ellis & Barkhuizen, 2005), and this is shown in Figure 9.3. To measure syntactic complexity, the mean number of clauses per t-unit was calculated and is shown in Figure 9.4. Despite the interdependence of these last two measures, and some outstanding methodological problems,

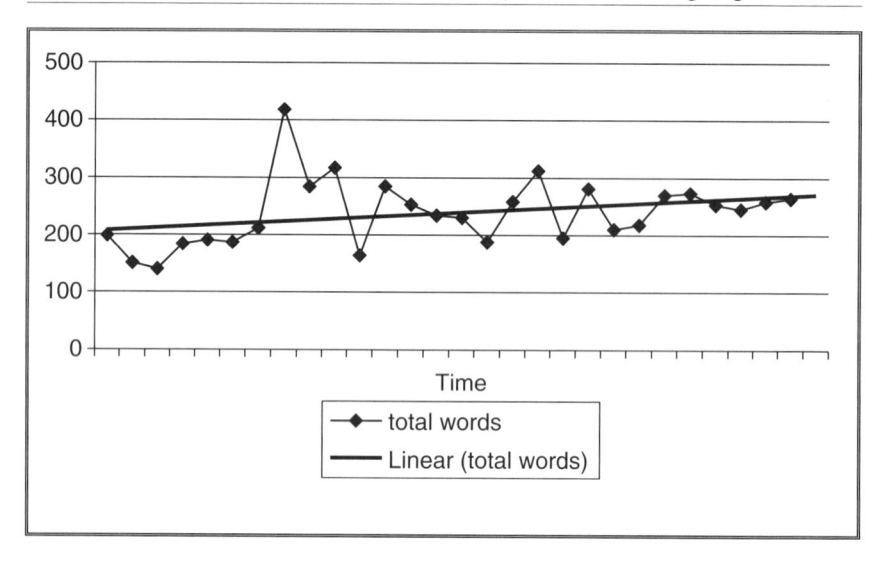

Figure 9.1 Essay length in words

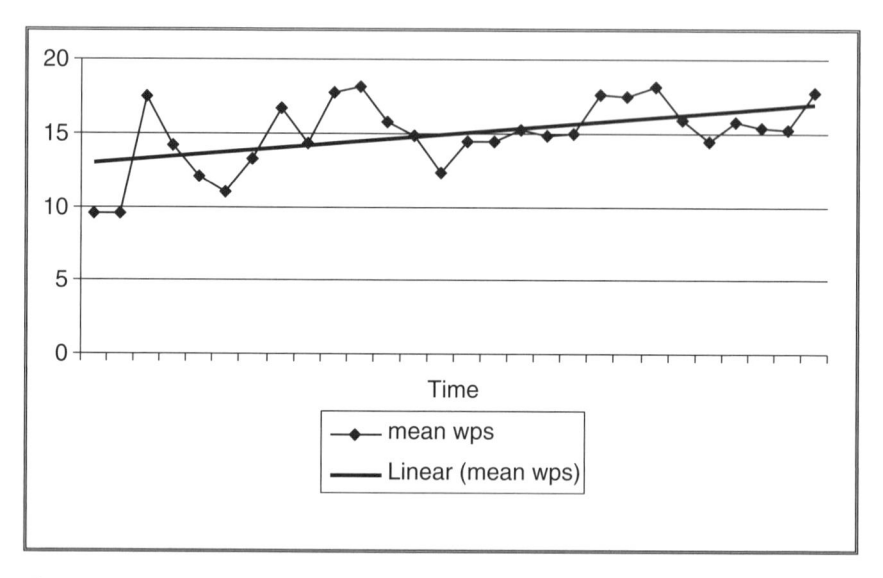

Figure 9.2 Mean words per sentence

they serve as an approximate guide to developing fluency and complexity. To measure one aspect of developing vocabulary output, specifically the use of 'rare' vocabulary, I used P_Lex v2.0, an established measure of 'rare' words (Meara & Bell, 2001); results are shown in Figure 9.5.

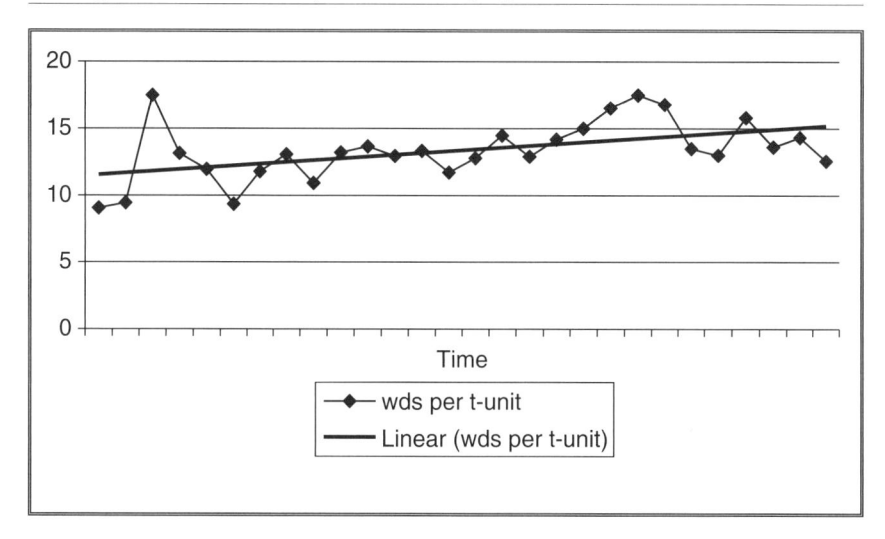

A Longitudinal Case Study of the Emerging Lexicon

Figure 9.3 Mean number of words per t-unit

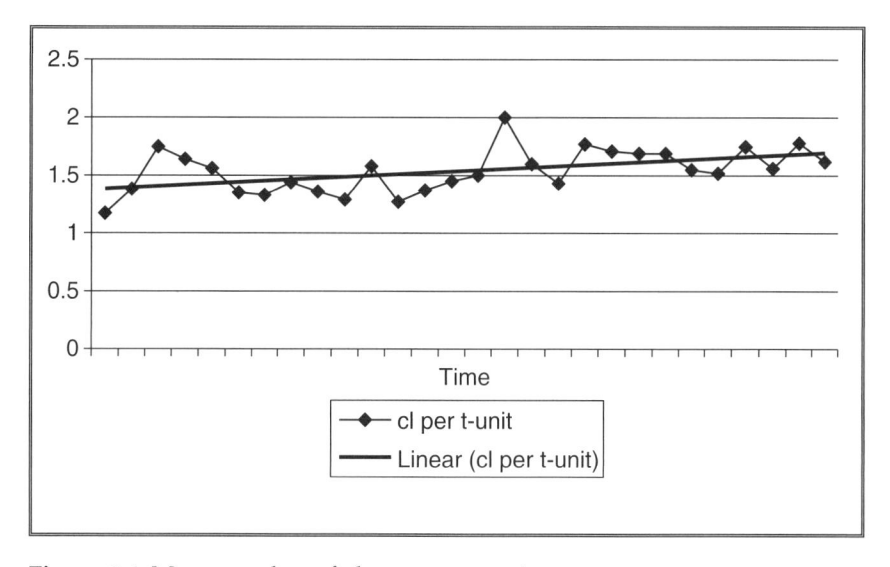

Figure 9.4 Mean number of clauses per t-unit

All measures show a slight though jagged development overall. By the end of the series, K was able to produce longer essays with longer sentences within the time limit, suggesting increased fluency. Increased sentence length is not simply a feature of chaining main clauses together; the t-units themselves are getting longer, which confirms the impression of increasing fluency. Figure 9.4 shows a slight increase in grammatical

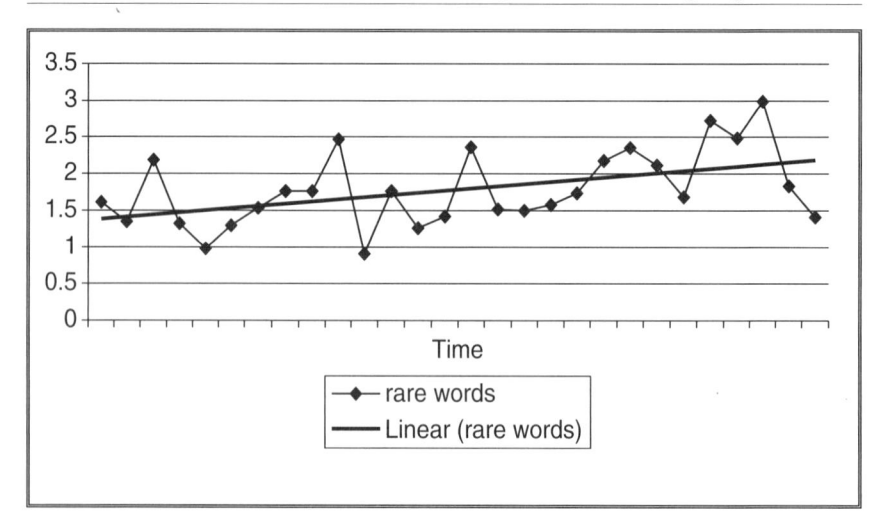

Figure 9.5 P_Lex scores

complexity, in that the mean number of clauses per t-unit steadily increases overall. Figure 9.5 shows an overall increase in the use of 'rare' words (here defined essentially as words falling outside the 2000 most frequent band).

Analysis and Results

As Figure 9.1–9.5 suggest, change is constant and scores vary considerably. The fact that all measures show this variability means it must be considered a natural reflection of the changing nature of interlanguage and of the natural variability of even same-genre productions rather than a deficiency in measurement. One interesting area in which subsystems appear to merge is in the use of lexical formulae.

Initial sequential reading of the essays suggested that some formulae declined in frequency, or 'came apart' from their initial formulaicity; others ('growers') became more frequent, and often became more stable in structure; and still others remained comparatively stable or fluctuated around a number of related patterns. The 'growers' included phrases centred around the words *reason, positive, negative, aspect, start, case, point, seem, say, number* and *believe*. The major items in decline appeared to be based on *advantage, disadvantage* and some patterns with *reason*. Fluctuating across the output were phrases based on *start, hand, addition* and *conclusion*.

There are multiple names for and definitions of formulaic items (Wray, 2002: 9, 22–28), and in this paper I use a variety of terms to avoid aligning myself with any one theoretical perspective. My starting point is formulaic sequences containing at least one lexical item that occur three or more times in K's work (e.g. *the point is*; I do not include functor-only sequences

A Longitudinal Case Study of the Emerging Lexicon   117

such as *am going to*). The analysis also covers other occurrences of the central lexical item, as well as 'near-misses', which do not necessarily occur three times. The study yielded very rich data, and here I present some of the most interesting patterns of distribution, structure and collocation, and compare them with other words or formulae that fulfil similar functions. Figures in square brackets are essay numbers.

Frequency and stability in decline

Advantage, disadvantage

    An *advantage* cluster is apparent early on, but appears to move out of favour over the series. *Advantage* occurs 12 times in a sentence without *disadvantage*, and *disadvantage* five times in a sentence without *advantage*. In four cases they co-occur as *advantages and disadvantages*. In early essays, the appearance of either *advantage* or *disadvantage* implies the existence of the other, but by the end of the series, the words are only occurring singly. The meaning remains stable throughout. The contextual structural variation is fairly complex, but centres around two main types – describing advantages and disadvantages in general (an introductory function), and describing a specific instance. The distribution of the different structures is shown in Table 9.1.

    Advantage and *disadvantage* initially show clear-cut patterns of collocation and formulaicity. They occur together as a phrase four times, but only in the first five essays. In three of these four occurrences, they are part of a

Table 9.1 Structural distribution of *advantage, disadvantage*

	Example structure	Distribution	Total
1	There are adv~s of VB-ing	[4] [5] [6] [12]	4
2	NP has both its adv~s and its dis~s	[4] [5] [6]	3
3	The adv~ is (that) + SENTENCE	[4] [5]	2
4	There are some adv~s of NP	[6] [26]	2
5	NP has adv~s.	[6] [10]	2
6	There are some adv~s and dis~s in NP	[1]	1
7	A further adv~ is VB-ing	[5]	1
8	The main adv~ of NP + SENTENCE	[20]	1
9	... think whether the journey is adv~ to them or dreadful.	[26]	1
10	[They] should ask themselves are there any dis~ ... ?	[27]	1

longer sequence, *it has both its advantages and disadvantages.* When *disadvantage* recurs at the end of the series, it has lost its formulaic pattern and its similarity to native-speaker constructions. *Benefit* has semantic overlaps with both the *advantage* cluster and *positive/negative* (see below). It occurs five times from [14] on, and in [26] and [27] is a substitute for *advantage* balanced against *disadvantage*. Interestingly, *drawback*, a near-synonym of *disadvantage*, occurs three times in the first essay, and then not at all, even where *disadvantage* does occur. Each occurrence uses a different sentence pattern, although all are essentially correctly used.

A similar pattern of decline is seen with certain structures focused on *reason* (see Table 9.2), particularly *the/a reason (why +SENTENCE) is NP*. This pattern comes to prominence in the middle of the series, occurring nine times correctly, but then disappears entirely.

Frequency and stability in growth

Reason, positive, negative

Reason(s), always a noun, does not occur until the eighth essay. It occurs in a wide variety of sentence patterns, not all of which are fully controlled. Table 9.2 shows its distribution across K's work in each of these forms (numbers in round brackets show repeated uses in one essay).

Table 9.2 Structural distribution of *reason*

	Example structure	*Distribution (essays)*	*Total*
1	The reason is (that) + SENTENCE	[11] [15] [16(3)] [17] [18] [19(2)] [23] [27] [28]	12
2	The reason (why) + SENTENCE is NP	[8] [9] [15(2)] [17]	5
3	A further reason is NP	[9] [13] [18(2)]	4
4	SENTENCE + for a number of reasons	[23] [24] [28]	3
5	A further reason is (for) VB-ing	[17] [18]	2
6	There are reasons (why) + SENTENCE	[16] [20]	2
7	This is for ADJ reasons.	[27]	1
8	Because of those reasons + SENTENCE	[12]	1
9	NP can be one of reason	[13]	1
10	The other reasons is what NP is	[19]	1
11	SENTENCE for the reason of VB-ing	[20]	1
12	SENTENCE for the reason this	[26]	1
13	SENTENCE this reason: VB-inf	[28]	1

The two preferred *reason*-structures account for almost half the total, and are well distributed. The next most frequent, *the reason is NP*, occurs only around the middle third of the essays. Sentence-final adverbial *for a number of reasons* doesn't appear until the end of the series, and when it does it is as a fully formed, identically structured sequence. Seven of the patterns only occur once, and of these perhaps five are poorly formed.

Second, as soon as *reason* starts to occur it does so in 18 of the remaining 21 essays, and frequently appears twice or three times (once four times). The function of *reason* is ASSIGNING OR EXPLAINING CAUSALITY, and K also uses *because* 14 times to deal with this function. *Because* is well distributed, and the growing use of *reason* does not seem to be at the expense of *because*. Finally, there are established collocations with *reason*: *a further reason is* (5 times), *for a number of reasons* (3), *one reason for this is* (3) and *a second reason is* (2). Table 9.3 shows their distribution and the strong cluster effect.

Positive, negative

Positive and *negative* have semantic/functional similarities with *advantage*. However, their distribution over time is very different: where *advantage* and *disadvantage* occur most frequently early on, *positive* and *negative* only occur at all in the last six essays. The pattern of collocation is also revealing. The routine *[this] has both positive and negative aspects* occurs twice; *positive aspects* and *positive way* both occur twice; and *in a negative way* occurs three times, and *negative factors* twice. The routine *negative way* only occurs as part of a longer sequence with the verb *influence*, in the structure 'SUBJ influences OBJ in a negative way' (see Table 9.4).

Factor, aspect, number

Factor, aspect and *number* occur less frequently overall than *reason*, but form important networks of reciprocal collocation both with each other and with *reason, advantage* and *positive*. They also show considerable growth.

Factor occurs nine times, and has clear semantic affinities with *reason*. Like *reason*, it does not occur at all until the eighth essay, but its distribution is very uneven: it occurs five times in the last three essays, and four of these are within just one essay. *Negative factor* appears twice in consecutive essays; in four other cases, it is used in proximity to near-synonyms of *negative* – once each with *harmful, problem, trouble* and *difficulties*. *A number of factors* appears once in [27].

K's use of *aspect* is always with the related meanings 'distinct feature' or 'perspective on a situation'. It is interesting that although it is used once early on, it clearly becomes preferred towards the end of the series. When it does start to appear regularly, it is part of a preferred unit based on the verb *have* with an evaluative adjective; a typical example is *this*

Table 9.3 Collocation with *reason*

	Essays [1]–[9]	Essays [10]–[18]	Essays [19]–[28]
further ~			
for a number of ~s			
one ~ for this is			
a second ~ is			

Table 9.4 Collocation with *positive* and *negative*

	Essays [1]–[9]	Essays [10]–[18]	Essays [19]–[28]
has p~/n~ aspects			
in a p~ way			
influence in a n~ way			

system has both positive and negative aspects. Of eight occurrences, five are with either *positive* or *negative*, and one is with *bad*.

Number occurs nine times, three times in [7] and [10], then seven times from [21] on. It occurs twice as *the number of* and seven times as *a number of*. From the outset it is formulaic, but it is suggestive that *a number of reasons* occurs three times, and *a number of points* and *a number of factors* once, all in the last third of the essays. There appears to be a convergence between *number* and *reasons*.

Fluctuation and variability

Several items exhibit a fluctuating pattern of use; they may appear intermittently, with or without internal consistency, or they may exhibit a change in nature as the series progresses. The most salient are *start, point, case, seem, say, conclusion, hand* and *believe*.

Start

Start occurs 17 times, 16 of which are in the correctly formed routine *to start with* in sentence-initial position. Its textual function makes it a very likely candidate for all the essays, and it occurs early on. However, after the first usage there is a gap followed by a reappearance (see Table 9.5), and this sequence is repeated. In the essays where *to start with* is not used, alternatives are used. In [21], [27] and [28] the conjoined formulaic sequences *to start with* + *the first point to be made* occurs, which accounts for the overlap towards the end of the series. Table 9.5 shows the distribution.

Point

Point is used once with reference to scores or grades; once in the phrase *at this point*; once in *there are points that need improvement* [5]; but nine times meaning 'part of an argument'. It therefore shows a marked developing pattern of preference. The nine occurrences argument-*point* all occur in the last third of the essays. In addition, there is a developing collocation with *made* in variants of the phrase *make a point*. Five of the nine argument-*points* contain the sequence 'point(s) to be made'. (*Made* itself only occurs three times outside this sequence.) *Point* shows sharp growth of one usage coupled with formulaic hardening of the lexical environment.

Conclusion

Conclusion is well distributed and appears 11 times. However, until [15], the basic pattern is a sentence-initial adverbial *in conclusion*; after this point, all instances are in the pattern 'the/my conclusion is that + S', and five of these six are *the unavoidable conclusion*.

Hand

Hand occurs only once outside the sequence *on the other hand* (in *hand sth down*). It occurs four times in the first 10 essays and six

Table 9.5 Distribution of *to start with* and *first*-variants

	Essays [1]–[9]	Essays [10]–[18]	Essays [19]–[28]
to start with			
first, first of all, firstly			

times in the last eight, but is absent from the middle period. It is entirely structurally correct except for two cases of *in other hand* in [4] and [6].

Case

Case does not appear until almost halfway through the series. In seven out of its eight occurrences, it is used as part of the sequences *in (the) case of* or *in NP's case*, both used for instantiation. The first, second and fifth occurrences of *in the case of* are realised wrongly as *in case of*, and the full correct form appears at the third, fourth and sixth attempts. The other *case*-structure is *it is this case with many issues* [22].

Seem

Seem occurs 11 times, nine of which are in the last third of the series. All the occurrences indicate stance to some extent, but the structures harden after the first two appearances, where *seem* is the main verb ('TV seems to be ... precious' and 'the Olympic games seem to have a ... role'). In later essays, two fairly fixed structures dominate: *it seems to me that* (six times) and *it seems more likely that* (three times). The function, DESCRIBING THE AUTHOR'S STANCE, is also realised by *in my opinion,* which occurs in a wider distribution (Table 9.6).

Say

Say appears 10 times, twice early on as a reporting verb. In the other cases it is becoming formulaic: the three uses in [16] and [27] are of the form PERSPRON *can(not) say whether +S*, but the remaining five are identical: *it may indeed be true to say that*. Again, as with *point* and *case*, there is a distinct move towards fixedness. *True*, incidentally, appears five further times, four of which are in *it is certainly true that*.

Believe

Believe occurs nine times, almost exclusively in the latter third of the series. In six of these instances an identical phrase – *it is widely believed that +S* – is used, and the final example uses the same structure with *commonly*. Here too we sense growing formulaicity, an impression confirmed by co-occurrence with *to start with* (2) and *another point is that* (2).

Discussion

In the following discussion, I describe patterns underlying K's use of formulaic items and regular lexical groupings, and relate them to the themes of growth and decline, combination, and grammatical–lexical interaction. The following generalisations can be made.

Items move in and out of prominence

We see that *positive, negative* and *aspect*, as well as *believe* (in a different context) all appear in the last third of the essays – none occur in any form before, then there is an explosion of use in most of the remaining essays.

Table 9.6 Distribution of *it seems (to me) that* and *in my opinion*

	Essays [1]–[9]	Essays [10]–[18]	Essays [19]–[28]
it seems (to me) that			
in my opinion			

This dramatic effect strongly suggests that the items have moved into prominence in the writer's lexicon, assuming a 'first-choice' position. They sometimes fulfil a textual function that was earlier fulfilled by other means, and sometimes represent a comparatively under-represented function. So, for example, the phrase *it is widely believed* has as precursors and co-occurers a number of active voice realisations using SUBJ + *suggest, say, maintain, insist* and *think*. The function of GENERALISING EXTERNAL OPINION/BELIEF is well represented, appearing overtly marked in 20 essays overall, but appears to harden towards the formulaic *it is widely believed that*, which takes over by the end of the series. It also seems that prominence can approach overdependence, with certain items, such as *factor*, appearing perhaps too frequently within one essay.

Disappearance is seen in the case of the *advantage* cluster and one or two of the *reason*-structures. Stable and well-used routines suddenly vanish. The routine *advantages and disadvantages* disappears entirely after the sixth essay, along with the fully formed pattern *[this] has both its advantages and disadvantages*. In the same way, *one reason for this* and *a second/further reason for this* vanish after a burst of frequency towards the end of the middle period.

Why do these routines appear and disappear? After successful usage, there is no reason to suppose that the ability to produce a piece of language disappears. Nor does functional necessity provide an obvious answer, as the function often appears differently realised in other essays. The answer may lie partly in feedback – 'this worked last time, it will work again' – and partly in the displacement of existing routines by new ones (but these explanations work in opposition; one cannot simultaneously apply both). We can take it as evidence that these formulaic items reach a state of stability, and that from then on, the state can either remain stable or become less stable and less likely to be invoked. The factors that decide how this might work in practice are not clear. A further potentially fruitful explanation is that the learner's interlanguage idiolect, just like the native speaker's, contains favourites – 'safe' items in Altenberg and Granger's (2001) terms. We could also invoke a type of priming effect (cf. Hoey [2005] who uses the term in a slightly different sense), where the use of any item makes it more likely that it will occur again soon (this also works against displacement); metaphorically, 'customers who bought this book also bought this book'.

Lexical systems interact with grammar systems

Overall, it is quite clear that K is 'chunking chunks' (Ellis, 2003: 76). *To start with* begins to occur immediately preceding *one of the first points to be made is that*; in two later essays ([22] and [28]) *on the other hand* is immediately followed by *it may indeed be true to say that*. Other combined pairs include: *in summary* with *the unavoidable conclusion is that* (four occurrences, three consecutive; *I would like to suggest that* also occurs twice with the *conclusion* routine); *on the other hand* with *it may indeed be true to say that* (two occurrences) and *there are certain disadvantages* (two occurrences). K is developing systematic textual or discourse understanding, and to an extent the growing and/or declining use of certain phrases, and their combination, exemplifies his control of functional discourse units (Stubbs, 2001: 112). One result of chaining formulaic structures is increasing grammatical complexity: these phrases bring with them a grammatical pattern, especially in combination, and these are one form of evidence of the interplay between grammatical and lexical complexity. Further evidence comes from the grammatical demands made by certain formulaic items: of eight passive form occurrences of *to be*, for example, four involve *make a point*, typically in the phrase *the first point that needs to be made*. Grammatical complexity can be fast-forwarded by lexical formulae such as *it seems that* followed by an embedded sentence. This has undoubtedly contributed to the growing rate of t-units per sentence in K's work; for example, in [23], the initial formulaic structure embeds one structure inside another: *The first point to be made here is that the academic studies are much more serious.* Phraseology also affects the distribution of grammatical features: the growth of passive *it is believed that* at the expense of active-voice representations of outside opinion/belief. A key question is whether and how far the developing lexicon can push structural development, or whether grammatical control pushes lexis. I suggest that the two systems are intertwined and that the answer depends on the actual structural/lexical item in question; it can work both ways.

There are intermediate structures

Over time, we also see the development of intermediate structures: *it is this case with many issues* appears to conflate two sequences that do not appear in the texts: 'in this case as in many others' and 'as is the case with many issues'. With *reason*, the dominant, favoured varieties are accompanied by a pair of near-misses: SENTENCE +*for the reason this*, and *(this) is very important this reason: educate children.* These might also be evidence that K is moving towards structures such as 'for the reason that/ for this reason'. Similarly, *the main advantage of art gives us a sense of stability* appears to be an intermediate pattern somewhere between *the advantage of NP is NP* and *the advantage of NP is that it +S*. We have also seen how structures such as *in the case of* evolve nonlinearly, with two early near-misses followed by two correct uses, followed by another near-miss and then a final reversion to the correct form (in this instance, almost certainly because of the existence of *in case of* as in *in case of fire*). The phrase *in other hand* similarly occurs twice in a run of perfectly formed *on the other hand* routines; these ill-formed versions may have suffered degradation as a result of analytical processing subsequent to the initial acquisition of the form (Wray, 2002). Overall, there is some evidence that progress towards fully controlled use of a particular lexical item or routine is nonlinear and is accompanied by false starts and misaligned attempts; these incompletely controlled lexical items can be used productively.

Conclusion

The discussion above highlights key points about some of the emerging features of K's lexicon, and in particular about his developing control of single items and formulaic sequences. These move in discernable ways, sometimes moving into prominence, sometimes fading from use, and sometimes showing productive use of intermediate 'self-built' constructions. Increasing effort is put into converting individual lexical items into routines, then building these routines into longer routines, in ways that both affect and are affected by developing grammatical control. One cannot easily see progress through repeated measurement of one linguistic phenomenon (Figure 9.1–9.5), because no one measure is a 'magic window' that reveals progress in a directly linear fashion. But close up, I contend, patterns are visible that support a broad dynamic systems interpretation of K's developing interlanguage. One of these shows the ongoing interplay between lexical and grammatical subsystems. Another pattern can be seen in the behaviour of lexical items (whether single item or part of a routine), which distinctly resemble those of the larger dynamic systems of which they are a part. Complex lexical networks involving preferred structures and collocations show both movement (growth and decline) and stability as K's language systems evolve during the period of the study. The patterns visible at the start of this sequence of essays probably predate it; but it also needs to be emphasised that the sequence of development need not stop at the end of the study – there is every reason to suppose that the lexical flux we observe in the series would continue in a similar vein after it, provided language learning does not cease, and that similar patterns of interacting development would be visible in different lexical instances.

This study only reveals a snippet of the full developmental sequence, and the remainder is forever outside our view. Further, the essentially noncommunicative and repetitive nature of the task produces language that resembles experimental data; the study also lacks any worthwhile insight into K's input. Future work should start from the beginning of the L2 acquisition process, and would benefit from studying a greater variety of genres and obtaining insight into the processes that motivate the changes in output. Given these changes, single-subject case studies can have an important role to play in illustrating some of the processes of development of lexical and structural systems.

Chapter 10
Meaning-Last Vocabulary Acquisition and Collocational Productivity

BRENT WOLTER

Introduction

Over the past few decades, we have made remarkable strides in understanding issues related to lexical acquisition and processing. This has allowed us to establish some important beliefs regarding how vocabulary is acquired in a second language. At this point, for instance, few people would claim that learning a word consists of simply gaining an understanding of that word's definition. Thanks to the work of researchers such as Nation (1990, 2001) and Richards (1976), it is now widely acknowledged that 'knowing' a word also involves knowledge of a number of characteristics linked to the word outside of the traditional notion of semantic meaning. Related to this multifaceted view of word knowledge is the idea that vocabulary acquisition is, in many cases, not an 'either/or' situation (Meara, 1999b). Partial (and sometimes fossilized) acquisition of words is a common outcome, and at any given time a speaker of a language, regardless of their status as native or non-native, will possess varying degrees of mastery over the store of words they know.

This view of vocabulary knowledge has often been linked, either implicitly or explicitly, with the idea that words follow a predictable route from a state of being unknown to a state of being systematically linked to other words in the mental lexicon. Aitchison (1994) has described this process in terms of three basic steps that a child native speaker travels through en route to fully acquiring knowledge of a word. The first step is labeling, which refers to the process of mapping meaning onto form. The next step is packaging, which describes how the semantic 'boundaries' of words come to be realized. The last step is network-formation, which involves linking newly acquired words with other words in the lexical network. Even though Aitchison was referring specifically to first language acquisition, her description has achieved widespread acceptance in adult learner, L2 research circles. Henriksen (1999), Nation (2001) and Schmitt (2000), for example, all incorporate Aitchison's ideas into their own accounts of vocabulary description and acquisition. Naturally, there is good reason for this. Intuitively speaking, the process laid out by Aitchison makes good sense, and it is not hard to find real-life examples from both L1 and L2 speakers that conform to this general sequence.

A potential conflict arises, however, when we note the fact that a good deal of our vocabulary learning appears to take place incidentally. Encountering a new word in a naturally occurring context is not an event that would usually lead us to the first two steps of labeling and packaging, both requiring a decent grasp of the word's definitional meaning. Instead, a learner who encounters a new word usually does so in a situation where the cotextual information is available, but the definitional meaning is often not directly ascertainable. Researchers who have investigated incidental vocabulary acquisition, and its natural counterpart lexical inferencing, have typically circumvented this issue by assuming that the first, essential step for incidental acquisition (aside from recognizing that the phonological or orthographic form is unfamiliar) is the act of deducing meaning from the contextual clues. Pulido (2007: 157) provides us with a typical description of this process:

> Vocabulary development through reading... first involves noticing that particular word forms are unfamiliar and that there exist gaps in one's knowledge. Then, in the absence of dictionaries or human assistance, it requires inferring meaning from context (lexical inferencing) using linguistic and extralinguistic knowledge.

Similar beliefs, which might be labeled as 'meaning-first' accounts of lexical acquisition, can be found in the descriptions of other vocabulary researchers as well (see, e.g. Schmitt, 2000: 117–118). I would suggest, however, that this entire line of reasoning (and the meaning-first account that is associated with it) is predicated upon three interconnected assumptions that may be somewhat oversimplified. The first assumption is that words are consistently interpreted and treated by language users as discrete, isolatable units of meaning. The second is that the leap from cotextual clues to acquisition of definitional meaning is straightforward and unproblematic. The third assumption involves the idea that when there is a connection between cotextual information and a new word, the learner uniformly uses the cotextual information to infer meaning of the new word rather than using the new word to infuse meaning into the larger stretch of language in which it is embedded.

While such assumptions are subtle, I would argue that they underlie an approach to vocabulary acquisition that is, in some important respects, irreconcilable with the reality of how a good portion of our vocabulary comes to be acquired. Instead, there seems to be reason to believe that some of our vocabulary acquisition occurs in a process that is diametrically opposed to the meaning-first process. In this chapter, I will present this opposing view of vocabulary acquisition, a process I call 'meaning-last acquisition'. After this, I will introduce and discuss the issue of 'collocational productivity', which I feel is of central importance in helping us understand how language users make use of language input for developing lexical knowledge. I will then take a look at the implications of meaning-last acquisition and collocational productivity for two perennial issues in second language vocabulary acquisition, namely the aforementioned incidental vocabulary acquisition and the distinction commonly drawn between receptive and productive vocabulary. Finally, I will suggest a simple corpus-based method that can be used for quantifying collocational productivity.

Meaning-last Acquisition

The basic idea behind meaning-last acquisition rests in the assumption that functional vocabulary knowledge (like many other types of language knowledge) consists of a careful balance between knowledge of abstract rules and knowledge of how the words are used in predictable but often limited lexical environments. Although this distinction is similar in form to the difference noted by Sinclair (1991) between the 'open-choice principle' and 'the idiom principle', it is also different in some important respects. For Sinclair, rule-based knowledge would be drawn upon for the generation of novel syntactic structures, while pattern-based knowledge would be used for reproducing language structures that are lexically and grammatically patterned. For meaning-last acquisition, however, I am suggesting that rule-based knowledge aligns with definitional knowledge of a word, while pattern-based knowledge corresponds with knowing the lexical environments in which the word commonly occurs coupled with an idea of what the word contributes to the overall meaning (or perhaps more precisely the nuance) of the larger stretch of language in which the word appears (cf. Sinclair's [2004] notion of semantic prosody). Meaning-last acquisition, then, assumes that vocabulary acquisition often starts from a state of recognition for this combination of pattern-based and prosodic knowledge and moves to a state in which the word's isolatable, definitional meaning is finally understood. In short, the pattern described by Aitchison is more or less reversed. As with any description of vocabulary acquisition, however, meaning-last acquisition continues to assume that partial acquisition is a very real (and not uncommon) outcome. When this occurs for meaning-last acquisition, though, the result will be words that are understood in predictable lexical environments, but not actually known once these environments are changed or removed.

An example of this type of acquisition comes from my own experience with encountering the word *frumpy* in an unfamiliar lexical environment. While reading a review of a car several years ago, I was struck by the author's use of the word *frumpy* in describing the steering wheel. What surprised me about this was the fact that I suddenly had a hard time understanding what *frumpy* meant, even though I had previously never remembered having any trouble with the word. After querying half a dozen native-speaker colleagues about the word, I found that their knowledge was quite similar to mine. We all knew that the word was typically used to describe someone's dress, and that it was always loaded with negative connotation. When pressed, however, we all struggled to come up with a precise definition. What was even more interesting is that some of my colleagues were able to provide a good synonym for *frumpy* (specifically *dowdy*), but were still unable to define *frumpy* with any degree of accuracy. It appeared, then, that the knowledge we had acquired about *frumpy* was incomplete. We all had a good idea of the situations in which we could use *frumpy*, what things were typically described as *frumpy*, and the effect the word had on the surrounding words in the immediate lexical environment, but we lacked knowledge of definitional meaning. Nonetheless, this partial knowledge seemed to be pragmatically sufficient for our communicative needs. As we had only encountered *frumpy* in a limited set of cotextual environments, we had no pressing need to develop a rich understanding of the definitional meaning. In short, our knowledge was definitionally incomplete, but functionally sufficient.

The above example illustrates that vocabulary can be acquired via meaning-last routes, but it is also worth noting that *frumpy* is probably not a 'normal' word. It occurs in a very narrow range of restricted lexical environments, and in this sense it is akin to other words that occur in similarly restricted environments. Examples include words like *moot*, which almost always appears in *moot point*, and *kindred*, which is usually found in *kindred spirit(s)*. Researchers such as Wray (2002) would argue that the highly restricted environments in which these words occur lead native speakers to acquire them as unanalyzed chunks; chunks that are only subsequently broken down into constituent parts when necessary. Wray's view reflects developments in corpus linguistics, which have shown us that language can best be described as a combination of rule-generated and (more or less) prefabricated chunks (cf. Sinclair's afore-mentioned distinction between the open-choice and idiomatic principles). From a language-processing perspective, there is even evidence which suggests that this description of language closely matches how we perceive and store language at a psychological level (see, e.g. Hoey, 2005; Pawley & Syder, 1983). In short, our internalized language knowledge seems to rely heavily on the ability to recognize and process predictable patterns in language, the pervasiveness and utility of which cannot be adequately accounted for by purely syntactic accounts of language alone.

Where this line of inquiry starts to become intriguing for vocabulary acquisition is when we start to consider the effect patterning in the lexical environment might have on the acquisition of *all* the words we know. Corpus linguistics has shown us quite convincingly that words exert a nonrandom influence on their lexical environments. Sinclair (2004: 30) argued this point when he stated that 'words cannot remain perpetually independent in their patterning unless they are either very rare or specially protected'. The extent of this influence, however, varies considerably. While some words will occur only in highly restricted lexical environments, some words will tend to collocate quite strongly with a wide variety of other words. Many others will lie somewhere between these two extremes. The key question that arises here, then, is how this variability in collocational proclivity relates to the way words are eventually acquired. I will deal with this issue next.

Collocational Productivity and Vocabulary Acquisition
Basic assumptions

So far, I have made two main assumptions regarding meaning-last acquisition. The first assumption is simply that it represents a viable description for how words can be acquired through incidental encounters. The second assumption is that vocabulary acquisition can fossilize prior to the acquisition of definitional meaning, in which case we would be left with lexical knowledge that is functional only when the lexical environment is sufficiently predictable. However, at this point we still have no way of knowing what would lead us to continue acquiring certain words until definitional meaning is realized, and what would cause us to stop short of definitional meaning for other words. I would argue that the answer to this lies in collocational productivity. Collocational productivity refers to the ease with which words enter into collocational relationships with a wide variety of other words. A word with high collocational productivity enters into collocational relationships with a large number of words, while a word with low productivity does so with only a handful of words.

In relating this notion of collocational productivity to lexical acquisition (and lexical fossilization), it is important to bear in mind the widely accepted idea that language acquisition is ultimately a pragmatic and needs-based activity: an activity that is geared towards maximizing efficiency by reducing cognitive load. This is why, it would seem, native speakers rarely develop explicit knowledge for (say) morphological or syntactic rules in their L1. In specific reference to collocational productivity and lexical fossilization, it seems reasonable to suggest that we would only acquire definitional meaning when necessary, and what seems to lead to this necessity is the likelihood that we are going to encounter a particular word in a wide and diverse range of lexical environments. In other words, if we can make do with only recognizing a word in a fairly small range of lexical environments, we can dispense with the inconvenience of deciphering what the word means as an isolated unit. It is simply more efficient this way. When a word starts to appear in a wide array of varied lexical environments, however, this strategy starts to become less effective. At this point, we may start to subconsciously recognize that the most pragmatic knowledge for the word in question is acquisition of isolated meaning, as this will increase the likelihood that we will be able to decipher meaning in future encounters in unpredictable lexical environments. In short, then, preisolated meaning fossilization is the default mode for incidental acquisition, and isolated meaning acquisition occurs when this default ultimately proves inefficient for our language-processing needs. In the next section, I will explore some of the implications this has for differences in L1 and L2 vocabulary acquisition.

Differences between L1 and L2 vocabulary acquisition

It may seem somewhat odd that in a book dedicated to second language vocabulary processing, I have yet to mention anything directly about L2 learners. In this section, I will address this issue in an effort to show how meaning-last acquisition and collocational productivity might allow us to gain some new perspectives on important differences in L1 and L2 vocabulary development. The question here is whether or not L2 learners are as 'good' as native speakers at acquiring vocabulary via meaning-last routes. In exploring this, it is useful to note that it is practically impossible for L2 learners to replicate the sheer volume of language exposure that L1 speakers receive. In addition, it has been repeatedly demonstrated in much of the research literature on noticing (see, e.g. Schmidt, 2001) that L2 learners' conscious attention to form is very important for transferring language input into potential language uptake. Thus, unless a learner is carefully tuned in to the vocabulary input that they are encountering, they might not be receptive to the fact that they are hearing a new word, much less pick up on some of the subtleties of nuance implied through things like semantic prosody. Finally, as has been observed throughout the history of second language acquisition research, L2 learners bring with them massive amounts of L1 knowledge. This knowledge will sometimes help them and sometimes hinder them when learning the L2, but in either case it is extremely difficult, if not impossible, for adult learners to completely disregard this wealth of information. It informs them about how language works.

These differences between learners and native speakers have mostly been drawn upon in helping us understand how learners acquire L2 grammar. They have received far less attention when it comes to L2 vocabulary acquisition. When we turn the focus back to the claims I made earlier in this paper regarding vocabulary knowledge as a careful balance of rule-based and pattern-based knowledge, however, we can start to see how differences in language experiences might limit a learner's ability to acquire vocabulary through meaning-last routes. To begin with, most adult learners need to start their learning with some sort of grounding in rule-based knowledge. Despite our best efforts, few of us will be able to pick up and fully acquire knowledge of a language through exposure alone. Where this relates to vocabulary acquisition is in respect to the perceived need for some sort of definitional meaning as a starting point for understanding a word. As much as teachers might encourage their students to avoid immediately reaching for their dictionaries upon encountering new words, for many of us it seems to be a necessary first step to understanding. As Wray (2002) has suggested, learners (often by necessity) tend to be more analytical than native speakers in their approach to language learning, and this might force them to focus on isolated aspects of meaning over holistic aspects. Clearly, this would not completely inhibit learners from making observations regarding things like lexical environments and semantic prosody for particular words, but it would certainly make this a less viable strategy when we reintroduce the idea that language acquisition proceeds in a manner that is, above all, pragmatic. Finally, if a learner is first coming to grips with L2 words through a method that encourages translation with lexical equivalents in the L1, she/he is obviously going to proceed with vocabulary acquisition in a way that strongly favors meaning-first acquisition.

When we take these considerations into account, it leads us to some potentially interesting questions for understanding differences between native speakers and L2 learners; questions which, as far as I know, have not really been addressed so far in the L2 vocabulary acquisition research literature. For example, if we have a learner whose vocabulary is roughly the same size as a native speaker, is the main difference going to be one of qualitative differences? Would the learner have a better idea of the isolated meaning of the words, while the native speaker has a better understanding of how the words function in particular contexts? Furthermore, is there a point at which learners can move from a meaning-first approach to a meaning-last approach? If so, is there some sort of threshold level at which the learner is able to make the shift from mostly meaning-first to mostly meaning-last for words with low collocational productivity? Or will they forever be forced to acquire vocabulary via meaning-first routes?

Limitations of current research agendas

These are intriguing questions that could have some important implications for how we understand second language vocabulary acquisition and processing. Unfortunately, however, our current research agendas in L2 vocabulary study do not seem well equipped to deal with such issues. As noted at the outset of this paper, incidental vocabulary acquisition (for instance) has tended to assume that when new words are encountered in texts, the learner's primary goal in acquisition must be one of inferring meaning for the atomistic (the word) from the holistic (the cotext) rather than inferring what the word might contribute to the meaning or nuance of the cotext. Approaching vocabulary from this perspective almost assures us that any gains that are observed in empirical studies are going to occur in terms of inferring meaning, rather than inferring the less obvious aspects of semantic prosody and lexical environments, and this may be one reason why both native speakers and learners seem so poor at inferring meaning from context (see Nagy [1997] for a summary). Fortunately, some recent research has broken away from this approach to show us that understanding of incidental vocabulary can be partial when different aspects of meaning are taken into consideration (see Webb, 2007). However, this still stops short of assuming that the route of acquisition might actually be reversed, and the associated belief that fossilization occurs prior to acquisition of definitional meaning rather than integration into the lexical network.

Another prominent area of research that seems positioned against the exploration of meaning-last acquisition is the division between receptive and productive vocabulary knowledge. Although some researchers have suggested that the distinction between receptive and productive vocabulary is not as clear as it might appear at first glance (see, e.g. Meara, 1997; Melka, 1997; Melka Teichroew, 1982), there does seem to be something of a general consensus that for most words receptive knowledge precedes productive knowledge. Henriksen (1999), for example, identifies this distinction between receptive and productive as one of her three 'dimensions' of vocabulary development, a description she has offered up as a standard for other researchers to work from.

If we assume, however, that quite a number of words can be acquired via meaning-last routes, then the distinction between receptive and productive becomes far less important than whether or not our knowledge of the words has reached a level of definitional meaning that would permit us to extract the word from the lexical environments we are familiar with and successfully place it into other environments. To refer back to the example of my encounter with *frumpy* mentioned above, my failure to comprehend *frumpy* in reference to a steering wheel had far more to do with a combination of my lack of knowledge of definitional meaning and the fact that the word was in an unfamiliar lexical environment than it did with any distinction that could be reasonably described in reference to receptive and productive knowledge. As long as I was using the word *frumpy* in lexical environments that I felt comfortable with, my knowledge of the word's semantic prosody was sufficient for me to use the word with precise receptive and productive accuracy. It was only when the lexical environment shifted to the unfamiliar that I was at a loss, but this was not intrinsically linked to my ability to access the receptive over the productive (I was at a loss for both).

Quantifying Collocational Productivity

If it is true that collocational productivity can help us explain whether or not a word is acquired via meaning-last vocabulary acquisition routes, then it stands to reason that we should want to find a straightforward and unbiased way of operationalizing it. For this reason, I will conclude this chapter by proposing a system for quantifying collocational productivity in the hope that the system can eventually be used to test issues related to meaning-last acquisition. The most obvious place to begin is by consulting a corpus. Through the use of scores designed to estimate the strength of collocation between words (such as mutual information and *t*-scores), we can begin to understand how much a word influences its lexical environment. Traditionally, these scores have been used to make observations about the strength of the connection between a target word and particular collocates, but the scores can also be used to gain an understanding of the extensiveness of the target word's influence on its lexical environment in terms of how many words the target word collocates with. As *t*-scores are adjusted to take into account the relative frequency of the words involved (Hunston, 2002), they seem particularly well suited for this task. In order to derive a figure for collocational productivity, we need to determine at what point the *t*-scores for a particular word begin to reach levels that are near what would be predicted by random chance. Hunston (2002: 72) has suggested that a *t*-score value of 2 or higher is generally viewed as significant (i.e. non-random), so it seems reasonable to set our threshold at this value. The next step is relatively straightforward. We simply need to obtain a list of collocates for a node word we are interested in, and determine how many of these collocates have a *t*-score of more than 2. The higher the number of collocates, the greater the collocational productivity of the target word. This gives us an objective way to quantify collocational productivity.

Using *t*-score data from the 450-million word Bank of English corpus created by COBUILD at Birmingham University, I calculated collocational productivity scores for the previous examples of *frumpy*, *moot* and *kindred*. These turned out to be 23, 30 and 24, respectively. At first glance, given the nature of these words, these collocational productivity scores may appear high, but it is important to note that the list of significant collocates includes grammatical as well as lexical words, and that the default range for estimating collocation scores in the Bank of English is plus or minus four words from the target word. More importantly, however, is the fact that these numbers will pale in comparison to words that we know are much more productive. For illustrative purposes, let's take the two words *strong* and *powerful*, which Halliday (1966) used quite some time ago to show how near synonyms can be similar in meaning, but distinct in terms of lexical patterning (e.g. *strong man*, *powerful man*; **strong car*, *powerful car*; *strong tea*, *?powerful tea*). My intuition would lead me to estimate that *strong* is slightly more productive than *powerful*, and the *t*-score data tend to support this. The collocational productivity score for *strong* is 1895, while the score for *powerful* is 1418, meaning that *strong* exerts more of an influence on its lexical environment than *powerful* does. Both words, however, have much greater productivity than the three words reviewed above.

One problem with this procedure, however, arises from the fact that the Bank of English provides collocation scores only for the 2000 most common collocates, and some words will still be collocating with other words well above the threshold figure of 2 once the 2000th most common collocate is reached. The 2000th collocate for the word *high*, for example, has a *t*-score of 3.17. In addition, the rate at which the collocations are decreasing is leveling off, suggesting that the difference in the strength of collocations is becoming less pronounced as we move further away from the strongest collocations. This can be seen in Figure 10.1, which shows the collocation plots (ordered from highest to lowest *t*-scores) for *strong*, *powerful* and *high*.

Fortunately, however, the data for all of these words are clearly arranged in a Poisson distribution, and as such they are easily amenable to curve-fitting procedures, in particular procedures that generate an equation based on a power law. Using the curve-fitting function standard in any modern spreadsheet software, we can derive an equation from a word's data, and then use this equation to extrapolate beyond the 2000th strongest collocation. When the data for *high* are submitted to such curve fitting, the resulting equation is $y = 319.35x^{-0.5993}$ with an *R*-squared value of just under 0.99 (indicating that the equation can account for around 99% of the variation in the data). Once the equation has been generated, it is simply a matter of setting the value of the *y*-axis at 2 (representing the point at which the *t*-scores reach the established

[Figure: Comparison of t-score profiles for strong, powerful and high]

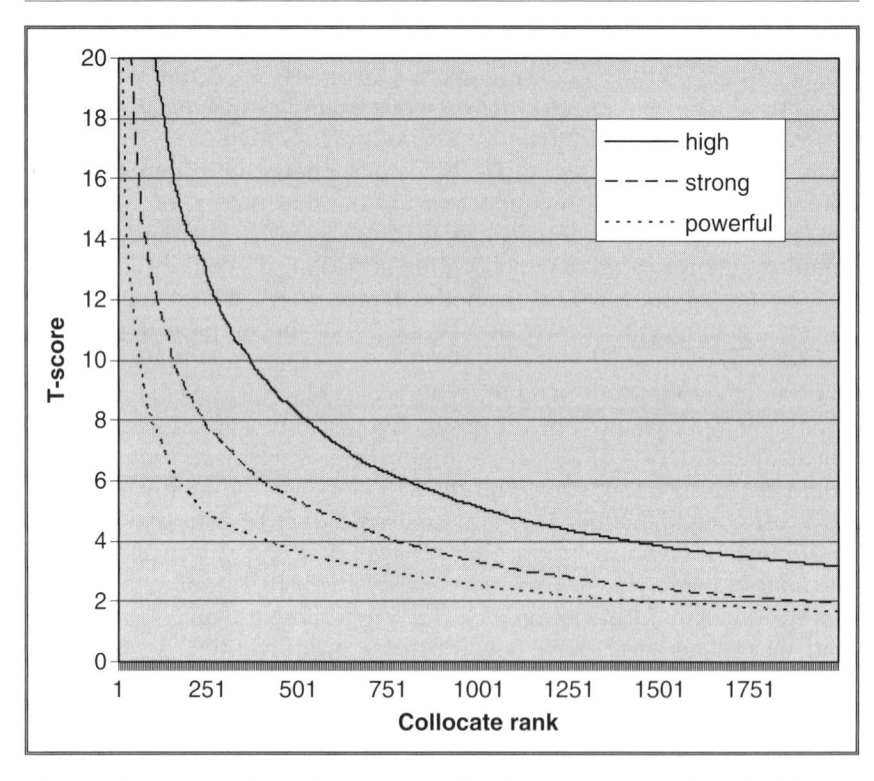

Figure 10.1 Comparison of *t*-score profiles for *strong, powerful* and *high*. (Note: *t*-scores over 20 have been truncated.)

threshold level) and working out the value for *x*, which will give us our collocational productivity score. In the case of *high*, this turns out to be around 4746, indicating that *high* has a much stronger influence on its lexical environment than either *strong* or *powerful*. In short, it is more collocationally productive.

Of course, quantifiable collocational productivity scores are only of value if they ultimately allow us to make predictions about how words might be acquired. If the assumptions I laid out earlier are correct, then we would expect words with low productivity to be more susceptible to acquisition via meaning-less routes than words with high productivity. In order to give an initial indication of whether or not this seems to work intuitively, I would like to take a look at the adjective *logical*, which I have chosen at random from the JACET 8000 word frequency list (Ishikawa *et al.*, 2003). Figure 10.2 shows a list of concordance lines for *logical* generated using the Bank of English. As we can see from this example, *logical* appears with quite a large number of words. However, when we look at the concepts underlying these words, we can soon find a fairly

```
          film are, and so on. Nevertheless there are  logical  decisions that can be made about when to
[p] The cookers from Parkinson Cowan come in a       logical  range of sizes so that you can choose the
       put my EDD back by four weeks, which wasn't   logical  because then I would have been only one week
    simply humans under pressure taking the next    logical  step. There are flaws-the ethnic characters
       stop horses. [p] At Aintree, one of only two  logical  places is the first fence after they have
           nuclear artillery shells from Europe is the  logical  next step after the decision not to
      about these problems there are two or three   logical  avenues of approach. So they say, LOGAN:
         answer is that she loves him. If I may draw a  logical  conclusion from that, you wouldn't stand for
     with a consequent reluctance to take a bold,   logical  grasp of the immense possibilities of the
             heavy industrialization, that is, the `logical" move after ISI, was given its justification
      Given the previous arguments, it might seem  logical  to dismiss the idea of reincarnation
   does not follow his explanation through to its    logical  and obvious conclusion. If almost everybody
          of fairness, there might be curious but  logical  reversals. Tribespeople in the African
   War, including safari clients, found that the     logical  answer to problems caused by the people
    CIA, were also involved. It might have seemed  logical  for Fearey to be the `keynote" witness, but
        tradition critical of religion. The deeper   logical  inconsistency between the claim that culture
    of facts, of concepts, or of mathematical or    logical  operations I believe that this understanding
    conclusion. For me, I found that the habit of   logical  thought abdicated with hardly a struggle and
     followed from San Benito. It seemed the only   logical  reason to explain why Dennison would have
           cure. `There is a science to this. It is  logical. It looks peculiar but it's not." [p] The
      illustration of the law's frequent evasion of  logical  development. [p] During the past three
       be jailed for life anyway. [p] Taken to its    logical  conclusion, this line of argument suggests
          said. [p] Lord Donoughue said that it was a `logical  extension" of the Lords decision on the
           as possible [p] [h] Todd left to draw    logical  conclusion;Football [/h] [b] Keith Pike [/b]
   president-elect of Leicester, said: `The only   logical  step in the Carling affair is a vote of no
        must be some sort of explanation. Something  logical," he added without much conviction. [p]
     and cannot ask too much of any comrade. It's  logical, isn't it? The Party is conducting this
         trying to get a sense of its shape, of the  logical  groupings within it. A brass quintet wearing
       to adults, they apparently appear perfectly   logical  to many teens, which is one reason they have
        Goodman, `like the others, was arguing from  logical  extrapolation, rather than factual
         forms that they have not heard but that are  logical  within their current grammar. Complex
     his jaw, spoke sternly, adopting a minister's  logical, reasoning tones. Shawnee Ray doesn't `
       s radical economic reforms, said it is a    logical  outcome of the federation's crisis.
      and Middle School pupils to demonstrate a   logical  approach to problem solving. The playing
    double room [F05] Yes. [M01] that seems quite  logical  [F05] [ZGY] yes. [M01] but I can't
    from a completely different direction for no   logical  reason. I think [ZF1] that [ZF0] that thing
    difference. [M01] [ZG1] I see. [ZG0] It's a   logical  test [ZF1] I've been do [ZF0] I've been
         the way MX would do it because he's such a  logical  guy will be to run bits off-line with P G N
   mean it sounds you know kind of you know very   logical  and sensible [ZGY] suppose you know if you'
        Mm [M01] earlier [F01] Mm [M01] but it is a  logical  extension in the winter season of ninety-six
```

Figure 10.2 Collins Bank of English concordance lines for the word *logical*. (Reprinted by permission of HarperCollins Publishers Ltd)

small set of central themes underpinning these, the majority of which seem linked to polysemous extensions of what might be considered the less commonly represented core meaning. For example, the use of *logical* in several of these lines seems to be linked with either the notion of *progression* (either in respect to a series of happenings or a process of decision making) or the notion of *reasoning/thinking*. Thus, although *logical* is clearly more productive than examples like *moot* and *kindred*, it is still fairly limited in terms of how it interacts in different lexical environments.

The question here, however, is whether or not this characteristic of *logical* is likely to be revealed through its productivity score. The collocational productivity score is 342, which is far less than adjectives like *strong* and *powerful*, but it is still considerably more than the highly restricted adjectives like *moot* and *frumpy*. Using the assumptions listed above regarding the link between lexical productivity and the pragmatic nature of language acquisition, it would appear that *logical* could be acquired through the meaning-last route. It seems restricted enough that we might expect a language user with repeated exposure to the word to acquire recognition of the typical lexical environments in which *logical* occurs, which would lead them to develop an understanding of the semantic prosody of *logical*. This foundation would then allow them to use it with semantic accuracy, even without an understanding of definitional meaning. This does not, of course, mean that knowledge of the word would necessarily become permanently fossilized before understanding of definitional meaning occurred. Ideally, a partial understanding devoid of definitional meaning could serve as an intermediary step towards full acquisition. If fossilization were to occur, however, it would likely happen at the expense of definitional meaning rather than integration in commonly occurring lexical environments.

Conclusion

In this chapter, I have described an alternative route for vocabulary acquisition (meaning-last acquisition) that challenges long-standing assumptions regarding how new words come to be integrated into the lexicon of language users. I have also proposed the idea of collocational productivity, which is a characteristic of individual words that can be used to explain fossilization within this description. Furthermore, I have provided a practical description for how collocational productivity might usefully be operationalized through the use of a corpus. Finally, I have suggested that viewing vocabulary acquisition from a meaning-last perspective might lead us to rather different conclusions regarding incidental vocabulary acquisition, differences between L1 and L2 vocabulary acquisition and the distinction between receptive and productive vocabulary. It remains to be seen whether or not the ideas I have put forth in this chapter provide us with any sort of explanatory power for describing the many mysteries underlying vocabulary acquisition in a second language. At the very least, however, I hope that by approaching vocabulary acquisition from this new perspective, we will be able to determine whether or not our current approaches are in need of revision.

Chapter 11
Acting on a Hunch: Can L1 Reading Instruction Affect L2 Listening Ability?

RICHARD PEMBERTON

In this chapter, I tell a seven-year (and ongoing) story of how a hunch has led me to start investigating the unlikely possibility that the way someone is taught to read their first language might affect their ability to listen in a second language. I have used a chronological timeline (structured around excerpts from my notes) to tell the story as a way of showing that research is not always the smooth, logical, step-by-step process it appears in neatly constructed journal articles. That, at any rate, is the case here. I suspect – and hope – it is the case elsewhere too!

The Germs of an Idea

> *Jan 2001*
> *N.B. 'abducted' transcribed as 'of doctors'. HK students have difficulty catching the ends of words – why? Possible influence of lack of IPA teaching in HK. Situation different in mainland China??*

The problem

In a series of six experimental studies (Pemberton, 2003), I was surprised to find that intermediate-level Hong Kong learners consistently recognised at most only three out of every four of the 1000 most frequent words of English when listening to connected English speech – words that they knew very well in written form. Equally surprising was the fact that recognition rates for frequent content words (e.g. *lights*, *red*, *shot*, *turned*, *wave*) were no higher than for grammatical words (e.g. *and*, *have*, *of*). As recognition rates were lower for less frequent words, the result was that Hong Kong learners were recognising fewer than two out of every three words when listening to BBC news items. At this level of word recognition, as research by Bonk (2000b) involving recognition rates of less than 80% has indicated, comprehension is likely to be severely compromised.

Why were the results surprising? Because most of my research participants had undergone 12–15 years of English-medium education, were attending an English-medium university, were encountering spoken English on a daily basis and were familiar with the 1000 most frequent words of English that were the focus of my studies. Although listening to a news item is no easy task for a learner at intermediate level, I had not expected learners with this length of exposure to English to experience such problems in recognising the most common words of English.

However, on greater reflection, there were several factors likely to contribute to the recognition rates that Hong Kong learners of English were displaying. In the first place, features such as linking, weak forms and assimilation make connected English speech difficult for learners to catch. Secondly, although English content words are frequently added into informal Cantonese conversations in Hong Kong, the majority of the population have much less exposure to spoken English than might be expected. There is little social mixing between the majority local Chinese population and the small English-speaking community; as Lin (1996: 62) put it: 'The majority of Chinese children in Hong Kong live in a lifeworld where it is impossible and unnatural to use English'. Thirdly, research has consistently shown that the amount of English spoken by teachers and pupils in so-called English-medium schools has varied considerably and has, in some cases, been minimal (e.g. Johnson, 1983; Johnson *et al.*, 1991; Littlewood & Liu, 1996). Finally, Hong Kong students at upper-secondary level are typically given practice listening tests to prepare for exams, but are not actually taught how to improve their listening performance (Tauroza, 1997).

The hunch

Initially, it did not occur to me that one of the solutions to the listening problems Hong Kong students were facing might lie just over the border, in mainland China. However, as time went by, a paradoxical idea started to germinate and take root in my mind. Could the listening performance of Hong Kong students in these experiments have been influenced by the way they had been taught to *read*? The participants in my studies, like pupils in most schools in Hong Kong, would have learnt to read English using what has been characterised as a 'look and say' approach, with no systematic teaching of phonics (McBride-Chang *et al.*, 2005). As a result, many Hong Kong students have difficulty in reading aloud words that they know only in written form or have never seen before. What if this 'look and say' approach to reading had an effect on listening as well as on reading aloud?

I recalled that when confronted by a fragment of speech, such as /ˈdʌktɪd/, and being unable to find a match in their lexicon, some participants had overlooked or failed to recognise the word-final morpheme – ed. Would, I wondered, a more phonics-based approach to reading instruction help Hong Kong students to recognise that the unknown item *abducted* would be likely to be a verb form, and therefore avoid wild guesses such as *of doctor*? Would instruction that focused on the phonemes of English help second language learners to match sounds to spelling and approximate native-English-speaker ability to backtrack and identify words, often on the basis of word-final information alone (Nooteboom, 1981; Salasoo & Pisoni, 1985)? In other words, can reading instruction affect listening ability?

In fact, I had no direct evidence of the extent to which phonics was or was not taught in Hong Kong schools, beyond anecdotal evidence from teachers, generalisations about Hong Kong schools (e.g. McBride-Chang *et al.*, 2005) and statements referring to particular kindergartens and schools (e.g. Ho & Bryant, 1997). Nor did I have evidence to show whether phonics were or were not taught in mainland China.

However, I was aware of two key ways in which reading instruction in Hong Kong and mainland China differ and which, to my mind, make a difference in approach to phonics training more likely too. The first is that whereas Hong Kong children learn to read Chinese using a logographic (or more properly, morphosyllabic) system, with each syllable or morpheme represented by a Chinese character, their mainland counterparts are introduced to an alphabetic system in the first 10 weeks of primary school before they are formally taught to read and write characters (Wang & Geva, 2003). In the Chinese morphosyllabic script, characters do not convey phonemic information at the subsyllabic level (although many characters contain phonetic information at the syllabic level). In contrast, in the Romanised pinyin system to which mainland Chinese children are introduced, letters or digraphs represent the phonemes of Beijing-based Putonghua (standardised spoken Chinese, literally 'common speech') in a one-to-one correspondence.

The second key difference is that the International Phonetic Alphabet (IPA) is introduced throughout mainland China at the beginning of junior-middle school (when pupils are aged 12–13). This helps students to learn the phonemes of English, recognise particular sound – spelling correspondences (e.g. that /ɜː/ is spelled 'er', 'ir' or 'ur') and pronounce words that they look up in their dictionary. In Hong Kong, by contrast, systematic teaching of IPA is limited to a few elite schools, and where it is introduced into mainstream schools, it is often 'covered' in one or two lessons only. As a result, few Hong Kong students are aware of the symbols when they reach university, and those that have previously been introduced to them have often forgotten them.

Together, these two known differences and the third assumed difference (the lack or presence of phonics training) suggested to me that two research questions were worth investigating:

(1) Are mainland Chinese schoolchildren better than their Hong Kong counterparts at breaking up words (in both Chinese and English) into their constituent phonemes?
(2) If so, are they also better at spoken-English word recognition?

At this point, my ideas were nothing more than a hunch. I did not expect to find these assumptions confirmed in the literature. However, one day I came across an article by Holm and Dodd (1996) and I realised that I was on the right track.

> October 2002
> Fascinating paper by Holm & Dodd: big differences in phonological awareness between HK+mainland students – ascribed to pinyin instruction in mainland. Follow up – this could be key.

Previous Research into Phonological Awareness and *Reading* Ability in Hong Kong and Mainland Chinese Learners of English

Phonological awareness refers to awareness of the sounds of speech – the ability to perceive, analyse and manipulate the sounds that make up spoken words. In tests of phonological awareness, participants have been asked to carry out a variety of tasks (deleting, counting, blending, etc.) at a variety of levels (phoneme, rhyme, syllable) and with a variety of word-types (words, pseudowords and nonwords). One common task-type, however, is matching of sounds at the subsyllabic level. Typically, this might involve:

- matching the initial phoneme (or onset) of a word – e.g. which of 'cow', 'dog' and 'town' has the same beginning sound as 'cat'?
- matching rhymes – e.g. which of 'car', 'hat' and 'fun' rhymes with 'cat'?
- matching the final phoneme (or coda) of a word – e.g. which of 'can', 'red' and 'sit' ends with the same sound as 'cat'?

There are two strands in phonological awareness research. The first, inspired by studies such as Bradley and Bryant (1983), has investigated the relationship between phonological awareness and reading ability, a relationship that a recent review paper (Castles & Coltheart, 2004: 79) describes as 'undisputed'. In an attempt to determine whether the link is causal, researchers have investigated the effect of rhyme and phoneme training given to preschool readers of alphabetic scripts on later ability to read words aloud.

The second strand has investigated the relationship in the opposite direction. Rather than seek to determine the effect of phonological awareness on reading, this strand has examined the effect of reading an alphabetic script on phonological awareness. This is the strand that I will be discussing here.

First impressions

In the first paper that I came across, Holm and Dodd (1996) presented a battery of phonological awareness, reading and spelling tasks to 40 students at an Australian university — 10 each from Australia, mainland China, Hong Kong and Vietnam. Some of the tasks appear unnatural and/or difficult (e.g. spelling nonwords such as /ʃepɑːtəʊ/ and 'spoonerising' /tʃɪp ʃɒp/ to form *ship chop*) and the number of students involved was small. Nevertheless, the results are intriguing: the Hong Kong students were markedly weaker than the other groups on all the phonological tasks and on the reading of pseudowords (e.g. *tain*); by contrast, the mainland Chinese students did quite well. This is despite the fact that the Hong Kong students on average had five more years of English and three more years of residence in Australia than the mainland Chinese group. Holm and Dodd argue that the mainland Chinese students had been able to transfer phonological skills that they had developed when learning to read their L1 to their learning of English, whereas the Hong Kong students relied on a visual strategy, and would have difficulties in recognising 'known' words presented orally for the first time.

If the results are valid, they suggest that the effect of learning to read pinyin not only lasted for 25 years (the average age of the mainland group was 32) but also transferred to the L2.

Following up on Holm and Dodd's paper, I read a paper by Bertelson *et al.* (1997), comparing the phonological awareness of three groups of Chinese students: 24 first-year university students each from Beijing, Taiwan and Hong Kong. Target syllables were presented in Chinese characters according to the testees' L1 (Cantonese or Mandarin). When the task involved matching whole rhymes (final vowel e.g. *tai*, or vowel + consonant e.g. *lin*), the Hong Kong students were only slightly weaker than the others. However, when they had to match the final consonant (coda) of the target syllable, the Hong Kong students performed much more poorly than the Beijing students. Broadly speaking, the ranking in terms of scores was as follows: Beijing students > Taiwan students > Hong Kong students.

Like Holm and Dodd, Bertelson *et al.* attribute the difference in the scores between mainland and Hong Kong Chinese students to the fact that the mainland group had been exposed to an alphabetic script whereas the Hong Kong group had not. Similarly, they attribute the intermediate scores of the Taiwan group to the fact that they had been exposed to a writing system (Zhuyin Fuhao) that is largely phonemic, but (unlike pinyin) does not have a completely 1:1 correspondence between sounds and letters. Overall, their findings confirm the results of an earlier study in Beijing (Read *et al.*, 1986), in which adults who had learned to read using pinyin were significantly better at adding or deleting consonants in spoken-Chinese words than adults who had learned to read just before the pinyin system was introduced.

The third paper I read (Cheung *et al.*, 2001) investigated the effect of reading experience on children rather than adults. Three groups of children were compared: one of native-English-speakers from New Zealand and two groups of native-Cantonese-speakers (60 from Hong Kong and 60 from Guangzhou in mainland China). Half of each group were roughly four years old (classified as prereaders) and half were roughly seven years old (readers). The Cantonese-speaking children had to match L1 syllables, onsets, rhymes and codas. At the pre-reader stage, Hong Kong children performed well. However, when the readers were tested, the Guangzhou children performed significantly better than the Hong Kong children at matching onsets and codas (initial and final phonemes), though not rhymes. Again, Cheung *et al.* ascribe this difference to the fact that the mainland children had learned to read Chinese using pinyin.

Taken together, the three studies suggested to me that because Hong Kong students did not learn to read Chinese through an alphabetic script, they were likely to have difficulties in analysing and matching sound units at the phonemic level – and that this would hold true for both Chinese and English, and for both children and adults. Given the well-established relationship between phonological awareness and learning to read successfully, I assumed that these difficulties in phonological processing would make it difficult for them to read English words that they had not encountered before. And I further hypothesised that the lack of instruction in pinyin might also make it difficult for them to process words they had not heard before or stretches of speech they could not match with words in the mental lexicon when listening to English. By contrast, the three studies suggested to me that learning to read their L1 through an alphabetic system would help mainland Chinese students not only to read English, but also to listen to English effectively.

Second thoughts

> September 2007
> How come there's been no replication of Holm & Dodd?

However, when I came back to the topic five years later and started to read more widely, I gradually realised that the picture was not nearly as simple as I had imagined.

In the first place, reading experience is not the only influence on phonological awareness. Walley (1993) has shown that with L1 English-speaking children, vocabulary size also plays an important role: as the child's English vocabulary expands, so the phonemic specification for words (especially for words that have many phonologically similar neighbours – e.g. *cat, pat, bat, cap, gap, tap*) becomes more precise. This increased awareness of differences between words at the phonemic level develops through exposure to spoken English. Similarly, Cheung *et al.*'s (2001) study found that the preliterate New Zealand children outscored the Hong Kong and Guangzhou prereaders on tests of L1 phonological awareness (onset, rhyme and coda matching), due to their exposure to a spoken language (English) that has a more complex syllable structure than Cantonese, with consonant clusters common at the beginning and end of syllables.

Secondly, as far as I am aware, no study has tested Holm and Dodd's (1996) finding that learning to read an L1 (Chinese) through an alphabetic system benefits phonological awareness in an L2 (English). I know of only one other study that has compared the L2 ability of Chinese students with different orthographic backgrounds and this focused on English reading ability rather than phonological awareness. Jackson *et al.* (1999) compared the ability of students from Hong Kong (10), Taiwan (48), Korea (28) and the USA (40) to read English texts silently and aloud. Unlike Holm and Dodd, they found no advantage for those learning to read their L1 using an alphabetic system (the Koreans and Taiwanese) over the Hong Kong students. The Hong Kong students performed similarly to the native-speaker groups in terms of silent-reading speed (outperforming the other L2 groups) and Jackson *et al.* ascribe the differences in L2 group performance to the length of time the students had been exposed to English rather than to L1 reading experience.

Altogether, the lack of corroboration to date means that we have to treat Holm and Dodd's findings with some caution.

Nevertheless, despite these second thoughts, I still had a gut feeling that there might be something in Holm and Dodd's findings. The three studies that I read first of all (together with Read *et al.*, 1986) suggest that learning to read Chinese through pinyin helps students to match sounds to phonemes and that this skill lasts into adulthood. And although no study had replicated Holm and Dodd's findings and shown that alphabetic instruction leads to phonological awareness (let alone to listening ability) in the L2, equally, there had been no evidence in the opposite direction. My hunch that different reading experiences might lead to different listening abilities could still turn out to be accurate. So, I began an investigation into the relationship between the two.

Investigating Reading Instruction and Listening Ability Among Mainland and Hong Kong Chinese Learners of English

The study I report here used a spoken-word recognition test to compare the ability of Hong Kong and mainland Chinese students to recognise common English words when spoken in isolation (as in most of the phonological awareness research) as opposed to being spoken in context (as in the six studies reported in Pemberton [2003]). Testing adults on their ability to recognise decontextualised words does not mirror the sort of listening task they generally face in their everyday life. Nevertheless, by removing the influence of contextual factors that aid or hinder word recognition in the messiness of connected speech, it allows the researcher to state whether words are known in their spoken form. In a previous study (Pemberton, 2003), I found that Hong Kong students had experienced some difficulty in recognising certain common English words when spoken in isolation (particularly those beginning or ending with plosives), and I was interested to see whether mainland Chinese students exhibited similar patterns.

The participants were nine Hong Kong and 11 mainland students, all postgraduates at the University of Nottingham. The Hong Kong group had all started to learn English at kindergarten, whereas the mainland group began to learn English at junior secondary school (apart from two who started in the third grade of primary school). The Hong Kong group had higher International English Language Testing System (IELTS) listening scores than the mainland group (a mean of 7.7 as opposed to 6.6).

In the test, I read aloud 100 single words taken from the 1000, 2000 and 3000 frequency levels that were likely to be known by the students, and asked the participants to write down what they heard. I gave 1 point for each correct spelling.

The average mean scores for the two groups were very similar (85.3 for the Hong Kong group and 85.8 for the mainland group – although the latter group's scores ranged from 66 to 96 as opposed to a much narrower range of 81–92 for the Hong Kong group), but interestingly, the groups differed in the 'errors' they made. Although the sample of errors is small, it is noticeable that in only one case did a Hong Kong student produce a transcription that was incorrect orthographically but correct phonologically (i.e. it accurately represented the way the word is pronounced). When they were wrong, the Hong Kong students were unable to represent accurately the sound of the word they had heard, although they were often able to represent the vowel sound correctly. By contrast, as Table 11.1 shows, many of the mainland Chinese students were able to represent the sound of the whole word (onset, rhyme and coda), if not consistently.

If we look more closely at the ability of the two groups to recognise different parts of the target syllables (the onset, rhyme and coda), further differences appear. As Table 11.2 shows, although there is little difference between the groups when it comes to rhyme recognition (e.g. recognising the /eʃ/ in *flesh*, the /əʊst/ in *most* or the /eə(r)/ in *scare*), the mainland students are noticeably better at recognising onsets and codas – the single consonants or consonant clusters at the beginning and end of syllables. For example, while five of the nine Hong Kong students failed to recognise the 'f' onset at the beginning of *fold*, none of the mainland students did so (see Table 11.1). Similarly, five of the Hong Kong group failed to identify the /ts/ coda at the end of *lights*, but none of the mainland group did.

The results here suggest that the mainland students are outperforming their Hong Kong counterparts when it comes to onset and coda recognition, despite having had seven years less exposure to English language teaching and scoring slightly less on tests of written vocabulary knowledge. If this is true, it would imply major benefits for alphabetic L1 reading instruction. As Cohort Theory (Marslen-Wilson & Tyler, 1981; Marslen-Wilson, 1987) suggests, it is vital to identify word onsets correctly in order to activate the appropriate word candidates so that the correct word is accessed during online processing. Unlike reading, listening is a linear process with little opportunity to backtrack. Perceiving /fl/,/fr/,/θ/,/θr/or/v/ instead of /f/ as the word *fold* is heard, immediately takes the listener down the wrong path and leads to the wrong word being identified.

However, the numbers of students and errors involved are small, and further research is needed to see whether these differences are found over larger populations and data sets. At the same time, this study revealed that there was a range of recognition scores among the mainland Chinese students (with one student recognising only 66% of the words). This suggests that the listening ability of mainland Chinese students may vary widely and that future studies should explore the degree of homogeneity in recognition performance of learners from mainland China.

Table 11.1 Cases where mistranscriptions in single-word recognition test were phonologically accurate (phonologically accurate mistranscriptions in bold italics; inaccurate ones asterisked)

Target word	Mistranscriptions	
	Hong Kong students (n=9)	Mainland Chinese students (n=11)
bake		***baik***, *back, *beack
days/daze		***dayze***, *death
mate	*made	***mait***, *maits, *mates
nail		***nale***, *knell, *nill
phrase	*pharse, *phase, *frace, *flace	***fraze*** (×2), *freeze, *frace
scale		***scail***, *skell, *skill
his		***hiz***
burst	***birst***, *burse, *brust, *breast, *brused	***birst*** (×2), *bourst, *bust
urge	*earch, *eage	***earge*** (×2), *age
her		***hur***
palm	*paml, *pump, *parb	***parm***, *pam, *pum, *pulm (×2)
climb		***clime***, *clim, *claim
fold	*float, *thoat, *throw, *vote, *frost	***fould***, *ford (×2), *fords, *fault (×2), *fort
No. of phonologically accurate mistranscriptions	1	16
No. of students producing phonologically accurate mistranscriptions	1	7

The story so far

So far, my small-scale investigation into possible links between reading instruction and listening ability has shown some differences between Hong Kong and mainland Chinese learners of English. However, the variability of the mainland Chinese learners' performance on the recognition test, taken in conjunction with the evident complexity of the issues and lack of research support, was prompting me to have

Can L1 Reading Instruction Affect L2 Listening Ability?

Table 11.2 Number of cases where participants failed to recognise phonemes in target words, by syllable part

		Hong Kong group (n = 9)	Mainland group (n = 11)
Onsets (k = 89)	Per person	4.2	1.1
	Per item	0.05	0.01
Rhymes (k = 100)	Per person	12.7	12.2
	Per item	0.13	0.12
Codas (k = 79)	Per person	8.22	5.55
	Per item	0.10	0.07

serious doubts about my hunch at this point. Just as I was about to give up, though, I came across some research findings that I had not expected at all.

Previous Research into Phonological Awareness and Listening Ability in Hong Kong and Mainland Chinese Learners of English

> *February 2008*
> *Have found further articles on phonological awareness of Hong Kong and mainland students (Cheung & Chen 2004; Cheung, 2007) that relate phonological awareness to speech processing. Really interesting: Cheung & Chen suggest that for Hong Kong Chinese + perhaps Zhuyin Fuhao-reading Taiwanese, speech processing might not operate at phonemic level (not fine-tuned by L1 alphabetic literacy). First time I've seen PA linked to listening! Wish I'd seen this earlier!*

Cheung and Chen (2004) compared Cantonese-speaking undergraduates from Guangzhou and Hong Kong, and found, as Cheung *et al.* (2001) had discovered with young children, that the pinyin-reading mainland Chinese group (n = 36) significantly outperformed the Hong Kong group (n = 30) at matching onsets and codas in Cantonese syllables. More interestingly, they also found differences in the way that the two groups processed speech. In a primed shadowing task, participants heard a prime syllable, and then, 100 milliseconds later, the target syllable, and had to repeat the target syllable aloud as soon as they could. Target syllables had the same lexical tone as the prime syllables. The Guangzhou (pinyin-reading) group reacted significantly more slowly to primes that were phonologically similar to the target syllable (e.g. *gok*) – whether at onset (e.g. *gyun*), rhyme (e.g. *pok*) or coda (e.g. *haak*) – than to unrelated primes (e.g. *baan*). With Hong Kong undergraduates, reactions to related primes were actually slightly faster than they were to unrelated primes, though not significantly so. Cheung and Chen (2004: 17) conclude that those who use an alphabetic system to read their first language 'listen to speech in a generally more "analytical" fashion' than those who do not.

In a follow-up study, Cheung (2007) explored the relationships between phonological awareness, phonological processing of speech, listening comprehension, reading comprehension and reading aloud. In a second primed shadowing experiment, he found that undergraduates from New Zealand reacted significantly faster in related than in unrelated conditions, indicating a facilitatory priming effect with native English-speakers in contrast to the inhibitory effect found with native Cantonese-speakers from Guangzhou. The processing of primed syllables was also found to correlate with the ability to read passages aloud (scored according to speed and accuracy). And in a series of English language tasks conducted with 60 native Cantonese-speaking undergraduates in Hong Kong, Cheung found that the ability to read passages aloud correlated with phonological awareness (here, the ability to delete and count phonemes) and phoneme discrimination (here, the ability to identify matching syllables when presented in background noise) – but not with listening comprehension.

These two studies restored my belief in my original hunch. If learning to read using an alphabetic system is related to phonological awareness, and if phonological awareness is related to the ability to perceive phonemes in speech, then it remains possible that pinyin-reading mainland Chinese students may have an advantage over their Hong Kong counterparts when it comes to perceiving – though not necessarily comprehending – spoken English.

Conclusion

In this chapter, I have told the story of the first stages of an ongoing research investigation. I hope this story has been able to convey the hunch-led, stop-start, evolving nature of the research process in this case. I have shown that the Hong Kong and mainland Chinese learners of English I studied did differ in their ability to recognise spoken-English phonemes and syllables, and that my original and unlikely hunch – that alphabetic L1 reading instruction may have a beneficial effect on the ability to listen to English as an L2 – is worth investigating further.

I suspect, though, that in the findings of the small-scale study reported here, are the seeds of another hunch that will demand investigation. As well as the between-group variation, a degree of within-group variation has emerged. The picture within such a vast country as China is certainly likely to be far from uniform, and potentially will become more varied as control over syllabi is relaxed. For example, with the teaching of pinyin, a whole-syllable approach exists alongside synthetic phoneme-by-phoneme approaches, and currently some schools are starting to teach characters for the first few weeks of primary school, before pinyin is introduced (Chen, 2008, personal communication). Similarly, when children are taught to read English, whole-word approaches exist alongside phonics-based approaches (Mellen, 2002) and there is an increasing range of textbooks being developed (Lam, 2005).

Future research that compares the reading ability of Hong Kong and mainland Chinese students will need to investigate students' educational experiences rather than assuming that they have followed a particular pattern. For this to happen, we will need longitudinal in-school studies alongside the snapshot experimental studies that tend to characterise the cognitive psychology literature. If the Chinese educational experience is becoming more diverse, as appears to be the case, then this type of research will be increasingly important, especially with the generation that has started school in the 21st century.

At the same time, there will continue to be a place for research that attempts to compare the reading ability, speech processing and phonological awareness of those who have, and have not, been exposed to an alphabetic reading system in the L1 and phoneme-focused instruction in the L2. As Paul Meara reminded me in the early years of my PhD when I was hung up on listing particular words that were known at particular levels: 'It's not about the words, Richard, it's about the learners. Learners have patterns – words don't'.

Acknowledgement

My thanks go to the editors for their wonderfully patient and constructive support during the gestation of this chapter.

Chapter 12
Taking Stock

ANDY BARFIELD and TESS FITZPATRICK

As researchers into the many facets of lexical acquisition, we are long past the days when we could justify/introduce our latest work with a version of Meara's oft-quoted 'vocabulary: a neglected aspect of language learning' (1980). By the mid-1990s, when most of the authors in this volume were beginning their research activities, the importance of vocabulary studies was well established, not only by insightful, detailed, experimental investigations – many of which are cited in this volume – but also by books accessible to a readership beyond the immediate research community. Perhaps the most influential of these, in terms of raising awareness, were, from an applied point of view, Paul Nation's *Teaching and Learning Vocabulary* (1990) and, from a more theoretical psycholinguistic perspective, Jean Aitchison's *Words in the Mind* (1987). The generation of researchers represented here, then, no longer had to fight for vocabulary research to be recognised as a valid area of investigation, but rather take up the challenges posed by the work of the previous decade or so.

This volume, then, can perhaps be seen as exemplifying the work of a second generation of lexical researchers: there is certainly a strong sense in these chapters of the importance of grounding new research and building on questions raised by previous studies. There is a tension here, too, between acknowledgement of valuable existing contributions to our knowledge base, and a reluctance to accept earlier findings at face value. By definition, the authors here have been influenced by the work of Paul Meara, and many refer explicitly to particular studies of his that have inspired their own work. However, there are also instances of direct and indirect challenges to findings and conclusions central to Meara's work. Shillaw, for example, places the Yes/No test format in a historical context so that we can understand how the test has evolved from being used to evaluate the relationship between vocabulary and reading ability, to becoming a freestanding measure of vocabulary size of learners of English as a foreign language. Having established this, though, Shillaw's chapter goes on to unpick the fundamental construct of the Yes/No tests, challenging the inclusion of what until now has been regarded as an essential – though problematic – component: the nonwords. Fitzpatrick, in revisiting previous interpretations of word association responses, challenges Meara's own early conclusions about the pattern of development of L2 word associations. Her emphasis on the bilingual dimension, and on consistency of individual response behaviour across two languages, is perhaps a sign of more studies to come that will explore lexical processing from the perspective of the L2 *and* the L1 – an area which Meara has not yet fully engaged with himself.

Most, if not all, of the lexical issues addressed in this volume were initially explored using quantitative data from multisubject experimental studies. Indeed, the authors themselves were all trained to some degree in this sort of experimental approach. Many of the chapters here, though, represent a shift away from the search for clear statistically significant patterns, towards exploring the immensely rich data that can be gathered by looking at the behaviour of individual subjects, in depth, over time. Wilks, building on a previous study that used 84 participants, here investigates questions which arose from that study, with a very detailed examination of the word association behaviour of just six informants, allowing for semistructured post-task interviews and analyses of individuals' behaviour. There is a clear recognition here of the need for qualitative indepth understanding of individuals as a useful basis for refining and developing our knowledge. Bell and Ronald, though focusing on very different aspects of lexical development – the changing selections and contextualisations of lexical items, on the one hand, and the developing receptive knowledge of individual words, on the other – also source their very rich data sets from single participants. This is still a relatively uncommon approach in L2 lexical studies, though it is the accepted norm in most areas of L1 acquisition research. These longitudinal case studies offer a new approach to developing lexical measurements too. Extrinsic 'norms' in the form of proficiency measures, frequency lists, corpus evidence, etc., are increasingly seen as problematic, necessitating questions about which skills and what kind of knowledge we are measuring 'proficiency' in, and which output genres our frequency lists are gleaned from. Longitudinal case studies allow intrinsic measures to be used, with the subjects' performances measured not against their peers or other so-called 'norms', but against their own previous performances. This kind of approach creates spaces for the sort of matrix model predictions used in Ronald's study, and the identification of individual trends seen in Wilks' chapter. The case study approach also takes us away from the relatively secure environment of statistical significance and identification of (sometimes superficial) patterns. Instead, the researcher is confronted with, as Bell quotes, the 'messy little details', which, ironically, as Wilks observes, produce the 'classically "messy" data that... Meara has rightly cautioned generations of research students about'.

Of course, there are other methodological choices to be made than the quantitative/qualitative decision. Treating lexical items in a contextualised or decontextualised mode is one of the great tensions in doing L2 vocabulary research. In this volume, Barfield, Fitzpatrick, Pemberton, Shillaw and Wilks use decontextualised measures, which have the advantage of stripping down the language output (or input) so that we can look with a higher degree of certainty at patterns in the data. The downside of this approach is the loss of the obvious relationship between how a construct is measured experimentally and the reality of how people actually use that construct in real time for real communicative purpose. The 2005 debate between Meara and Laufer in *Applied Linguistics* (Laufer, 2005; Meara, 2005a) addresses the potential in taking this decontextualisation a step further, so that the data are simulated rather than produced by real learners. Chapelle (1998) has been critical of the language-out-of-context focus, which is often seen as typifying Meara's work, arguing that the backwash effect of such measures sees learners *acquiring* language out of context and neglecting 'the interactional abilities that are no less essential for communicative development' (Chapelle, 1998: 63). The authors who use these techniques, though, would argue that it is as essential to focus on the structure of a precise component of the linguistic system as it is to analyse the operation of that system, in part or in whole, so long as we realise that one approach informs the other, and we remain wary of unfounded extrapolations and assumptions. Barfield, in particular, is very clear about this, presenting in his chapter a 'simpler view of collocation (which) strips away grammatical, syntactical and contextual features and reduces the measure of learners' productive L2 collocation knowledge to a basic level task of producing appropriate collocates'. Barfield's study also exemplifies how the decontextualisation process allows for analysis of productive vocabulary in a way that is relatively unmuddied by consideration of receptive knowledge.

Many of the chapters, though, focus very much on language in use. Bell, Ronald and Nesi and Boonmoh ask their learners to participate in realistic, contextualised tasks, but the distinctions between realistic data, contrived data and modelled data still aren't at all clear – Bell's subject produces a 'messy' profile, Nesi and Boonmoh find that researchers, teachers and students do not concur in their assessment of PEDs, while Ronald shows how his real, contextualised data can be used to produce some pretty accurate matrix models. Shillaw's study gives us a further insight into the issue of context in vocabulary testing. He points out that while the simplicity of the no-context Yes/No test allows learners to make snap decisions, when they do the same test with minimal contextualisation in a sentence, there seems to be a greater sense of confusion or uncertainty. Contextualisation muddies the water in that it probably activates more lexical knowledge and makes it difficult for learners to be certain sometimes about judging their knowledge in absolute terms. This points to the primacy of partial lexical knowledge as being critical, and lets us see the need for instruments that track states of partial knowledge, such as the kind of knowledge ranking used in Ronald's study, or the developmental analysis of an individual corpus established over time, such as Bell's.

A number of the chapters (most notably Horst and Wilks) present studies that are similar in design to ones previously published. This partial replication is far removed from slavish imitation; it represents a critical perspective on the shortcomings of different measures, rather than a simple assumption that they work. Through partial replication, or development of methodology and analysis, a number of additional insights can be gained. Shillaw's chapter exposes the fact – also recognised by Meara – that the simplicity of the Yes/No test format is itself deceptive. His study demonstrates how difficult it is to develop a problem-free measure of a particular aspect of vocabulary knowledge. Wilks shows that, having identified certain data patterns (in this case in word associations), we can use think-aloud techniques or post-task interviews to get subject feedback. These protocols tend to provide interesting information where there is room for doubt, and where knowledge is partial, allowing insights into the processing systems that underlie test performance. The belief in the importance of replication is not only evident in these experiments that have been based on earlier studies – all the studies in this volume are themselves essentially replicable. Work is presented in such a way that others can understand the decision making, the strengths and weaknesses, and see clearly how – and why – the study might be modified and tried again.

The chapters by Pemberton and Wolter further exemplify the sort of extended critical reflections that come to the researcher who has completed a body of research, and has an overview of findings that are related but usually do not straightforwardly tell the same story. It is the researcher's fate at this stage to notice interesting phenomena, become intrigued by new questions and read related research. At this point, the researcher might try some quick and dirty experiments, formulate hypotheses and present ideas or arguments for discussion – and out of this, over time, particular new positions and questions evolve. The message here is that it is OK to start with a small question and take it further, and that it is OK to travel in the wrong direction from time to time because the experience will always provide new perspectives and realisations (see Barfield [2005] and Ronald and Tajino [2005] for examples of such 'germination' studies where a new approach was first tried, but needed time to be improved on). In the 'second wave' of investigations that follow such reflection, we often see unexpected tools applied imaginatively to more finely honed research questions. Examples of this are the use of Rasch Analysis in Barfield's collocation study and the use of the V_States tool by Ronald in his dictionary study. Horst, recognising the constraints of using published frequency lists in the assessment of learner vocabulary in her study, similarly creates her own bespoke intrinsic measure of 'words the exposure to which is frequent *to these learners*'.

Perhaps the strongest thread running through the studies in this volume is the willingness to ask uncomfortable questions and to question comfortable assumptions. Wolter's 'meaning-last acquisition' proposition flies in the face of the fundamental principles of the communicative language teaching generation. After so much vocabulary research – including work by the authors here – has been built on the construct of generic lexical frequency measures (using bands such as those in Nation's Range programme, the JACET 8000 lists and the BNC lists), Horst questions whether these lists are appropriate to her subjects' language exposure, and presents an alternative intrinsic frequency measure. Pemberton raises the complex issue of methodological washback on vocabulary processing, which is difficult to unpick as the teaching methods in question are not vocabulary-specific, and their effect is only revealed in specific language-culture comparisons such as the Hong Kong-mainland China context. Nesi and Boonmoh address the explosion in learners' use of PEDs, recognising that, despite the fact that they are imperfect language tools, disliked by teachers and largely ignored by researchers, they are now a pervasive component of language learning in many cultural contexts. These studies represent a shift in emphasis from what we think learners should do (according to our theories of acquisition or teaching), to the observation and analysis of what they actually do. Add to this Bell's and, to a lesser extent, Ronald's observation of nonlinear, lexical development, Fitzpatrick's and Wilks' suggestions that different individuals' lexicons might not be organised or accessed in the same ways, and Shillaw and Barfield's acknowledgement that item difficulty must be accounted for in even the most apparently simple test formats, and we are obliged to admit that any worthwhile study of lexical processing will produce inconvenient, awkward and often contradictory findings.

We know that vocabulary acquisition research is no longer being neglected. The challenge now is to identify, in the interesting diversity of our findings, those aspects of vocabulary research that must be pursued and unpacked in order to maintain the momentum that Meara and his associates and colleagues have pioneered. We hope this volume, written in honour of Paul Meara's work, does some initial justice to that challenge.

References

Aitchison, J. (1994) *Words in the Mind* (2nd edn). Oxford: Blackwell.
Aizawa, K. (1999) A study of incidental vocabulary learning through reading by Japanese EFL learners. PhD thesis, Tokyo Gakugei University.
Alderson, J.C. (2005) *Diagnosing Foreign Language Proficiency*. London: Continuum.
Alderson, J.C. and Huhta, A. (2005) The development of a suite of computer-based diagnostic tests based on the Common European Framework. *Language Testing* 22 (3), 301–320.
Altenberg, B. and Granger, S. (2001) The grammatical and lexical patterning of MAKE in native and non-native student writing. *Applied Linguistics* 22 (2), 173–195.
Anderson, R.C. and Freebody, P. (1981) Vocabulary knowledge. In J.T. Guthrie (ed.) *Comprehension and Teaching: Research Reviews* (pp. 77–117). Newark, NJ: International Reading Association.
Anderson, R.C. and Freebody, P. (1983) Reading comprehension and the assessment and acquisition of word knowledge. In B. Hutson (ed.) *Advances in Reading/Language Research* (pp. 231–256). Greenwich, CT: JAI Press.
Atkins, B.T.S. and Varantola, K. (1998) Monitoring dictionary use. In B.T.S. Atkins (ed.) *Using Dictionaries: Studies of Dictionary Use by Language Learners and Translators* (pp. 83–122). Tübingen: Max Niemeyer Verlag.
Bahns, J. and Eldaw, M. (1993) Should we teach EFL students collocations? *System* 21 (1), 101–114.
Banay, R.G. (1943) Immaturity and crime. *The American Journal of Psychiatry* 100 (2), 170–177.
Barfield, A. (2005) Complications with collocations: Exploring individual variation in collocation knowledge. *JABAET Journal* 9, 85–103.
Barfield, A. (2006) An exploration of second language collocation knowledge and development. PhD thesis, University of Wales, Swansen.
Barfield, A. (2009) Following learners' L2 collocation development over time. In A. Barfield and H. Gyllstad (eds) *Researching Collocations in Another Language: Multiple Interpretations*. Basingstoke: Palgrave Macmillan.
Barfield, A. and Brown, S.H. (2007) *Reconstructing Autonomy in Language Education: Inquiry and Innovation*. Basingstoke: Palgrave Macmillan.
Barfield, A. and Gyllstad, H. (2009) *Researching Collocations in Another Language: Multiple Interpretations*. Basingstoke: Palgrave Macmillan.
Beeckmans, R., Eyckmans, J., Janssens, V., Dufranne, M. and Van de Velde, H. (2001) Examining the Yes/No vocabulary test: Some methodological issues in theory and practice. *Language Testing* 18 (3), 235–274.
Bertelson, P., Chen, H-C. and de Gelder, B. (1997) Explicit speech analysis and orthographic experience in Chinese readers. In H-C. Chen (ed.) *Cognitive Processing of Chinese and Related Asian Languages* (pp. 27–46). Hong Kong: The Chinese University Press.
Biskup, D. (1992) L1 influence on learners' renderings of English collocations: A Polish/German empirical study. In P.J.L. Arnaud and H. Béjoint (eds) *Vocabulary and Applied Linguistics* (pp. 85–93). London: Macmillan.

Black, A. (1986) The effect on comprehension and memory of providing different types of defining information for new vocabulary: A report on two experiments conducted for Longman Dictionaries and Reference Division. Unpublished internal report, Medical Research Council Applied Psychology Unit, Cambridge.
Bogaards, P. (2000) Testing L2 vocabulary knowledge at a high level: The case of the Euralex French Tests. *Applied Linguistics* 21 (4), 490–516.
Bond, T.G. and Fox, C.M. (2001) *Applying the Rasch Model: Fundamental Measurement in the Human Sciences*. Mahwah, NJ: Lawrence Erlbaum.
Bonk, W.J. (2000a) Testing ESL learners' knowledge of collocations. Educational Resources Information Center Research Report ED 442 309.
Bonk, W.J. (2000b) Second language lexical knowledge and listening comprehension. *International Journal of Listening* 14, 14–31.
Boonmoh, A. and Nesi, H. (2008) A survey of dictionary use by Thai university staff and students, with special reference to pocket electronic dictionaries. *Horizontes de Lingüística Aplicada* 6 (2), 80–90.
Bradley, L. and Bryant, P. (1983) Categorizing sounds and learning to read – a causal connection. *Nature* 301, 419–421.
Castles, A. and Coltheart, M. (2004) Is there a causal link from phonological awareness to success in learning to read? *Cognition* 91 (1), 77–111.
Chapelle, C.A. (1998) Construct definition and validity enquiry in SLA research. In L.F. Bachman and A.D. Cohen (eds) *Interfaces Between Second Language Acquisition and Language Testing Research* (pp. 32–70). Cambridge: Cambridge University Press.
Cheung, H. (2007) The role of phonological awareness in mediating between reading and listening to speech. *Language and Cognitive Processes* 22 (1), 130–154.
Cheung, H. and Chen, H-C. (2004) Early orthographic experience modifies both phonological awareness and on-line speech processing. *Language and Cognitive Processes* 19 (1), 1–28.
Cheung, H., Chen, H-C., Lai, C.Y., Wong, O.C. and Hills, M. (2001) The development of phonological awareness: Effects of spoken language experiences and orthography. *Cognition* 81 (3), 227–241.
Chi Man-Lai, A., Wong Pui-Yiu, K. and Wong Chau-Ping, M. (1994) Collocational problems amongst ESL learners: A corpus-based study. In L. Flowerdew and A.K.K. Tong (eds) *Entering Text* (pp. 157–163). Hong Kong: Hong Kong University of Science and Technology Language Centre.
Churchill, E. (2008) A dynamic systems account of learning a word: From ecology to form relations. *Applied Linguistics* 29 (3), 339–358.
Cobb, T. (2000) The Compleat Lexical Tutor (website). On WWW at http://www.lextutor.ca.
Collins, L. and White, J. (2005) *Closing the Gap: The Effects of Concentrated Instructional Time on Language Learning Outcomes*. London, Ontario: Canadian Association of Applied Linguistics (CAAL).
Collins, L., White, J., Cardoso, W., Horst, M. and Trofimovich, P. (2007) When comprehensible input isn't comprehensive input: A multi-dimensional analysis of past tense in classroom input. Paper presented at the American Association of Applied Linguistics Conference, Costa Mesa, CA.
Coxhead, A. (2000) A new academic wordlist. *TESOL Quarterly* 34 (2), 213–238.
De Bot, K., Lowie, W. and Verspoor, M. (2007) A dynamic systems approach to second language acquisition. *Bilingualism: Language and Cognition* 10 (1), 7–21.

References

Deese, J. (1962a) Form class and the determinants of association. *Journal of Verbal Learning and Verbal Behavior* 1, 79–84.

Deese, J. (1962b) On the structure of associative meaning. *Psychological Review* 69, 161–175.

Deese, J. (1965) *The Structure of Associations in Language and Thought*. Baltimore, MD: Johns Hopkins University Press.

Deng, Y.P. (2005) A survey of college students' skills and strategies of dictionary use in English learning. *CELEA Journal* 28 (4), 73–77.

Ellis, N. (2003) Constructions, chunking and connectionism: The emergence of second language structure. In C. Doughty and M. Long (eds) *Handbook of Second Language Acquisition* (pp. 33–68). Oxford: Blackwell.

Ellis, R. and Barkhuizen, G. (2005) *Analysing Learner Language*. Oxford: Oxford University Press.

Entwisle, D.R. (1966) *Word Associations of Young Children*. Baltimore, MD: Johns Hopkins University Press.

Ervin, S.M. (1961) Changes with age in the verbal determinants of word association. *American Journal of Psychology* 74, 361–372.

Eyckmans, J. (2004) *Measuring Receptive Vocabulary Size*. Utrecht: LOT. On WWW at http://webdoc.ubn.kun.nl/mono/e/eyckmans_j/measrevos.pdf.

Eyckmans, J., Van de Velde, H., Van Hout, R. and Boers, F. (2007) Learners' response behaviour in Yes/No vocabulary tests. In H. Daller, J. Milton and J. Treffers-Daller (eds) *Modelling and Assessing Vocabulary Knowledge* (pp. 59–76). Cambridge: Cambridge University Press.

Farghal, M. and Obiedat, H. (1995) Collocations: A neglected variable in EFL. *International Review of Applied Linguistics* 33 (3), 315–331.

Fischer, U. (1994) Learning words from context and dictionaries: An experimental comparison. *Applied Psycholinguistics* 15 (4), 551–574.

Fitzpatrick, T. (2006) Habits and rabbits: Word associations and the L2 lexicon. *EUROSLA Yearbook* 6, 121–145.

Fitzpatrick, T. (2007a) Productive vocabulary tests and the search for concurrent validity. In H. Daller, J. Milton and J. Treffers-Daller (eds) *Modelling and Assessing Vocabulary Knowledge* (pp. 116–132). Cambridge: Cambridge University Press.

Fitzpatrick, T. (2007b) Word association patterns: Unpacking the assumptions. *International Journal of Applied Linguistics* 17 (3), 319–331.

Fitzpatrick, T. and Meara, P.M. (2004) Exploring the validity of a test of productive vocabulary. *Vigo International Journal of Applied Linguistics* 1, 55–74.

Gewirth, L., Shindler, A. and Hier, D. (1984) Altered patterns of word association in dementia and aphasia. *Brain and Language* 21, 307–317.

Gitsaki, C. (1999) *Second Language Lexical Acquisition: A Study of the Development of Collocational Knowledge*. San Francisco, CA: International Scholars Publications.

Glaser, B.G. and Strauss, A.L. (1967) *The Discovery of Grounded Theory: Strategies for Qualitative Research*. Chicago, IL: Aldine.

Gougenheim, G., Michea R., Rivenc, P. and Sauvageot, A. (1956) *L'élaboration du français élémentaire*. Paris: Didier.

Granger, S. (1998) Prefabricated patterns in advanced EFL writing: Collocations and formulae. In A.P. Cowie (ed.) *Phraseology: Theory, Analysis, and Applications* (pp. 145–160). Oxford: Oxford University Press.

Green, D.M. and Swets, J.A. (1966) *Signal Detection Theory and Psychophysics*. New York: Wiley.

Greidanus, T. and Nienhuis, L. (2001) Testing the quality of word knowledge in a second language by means of word associations: Types of distractors and types of associations. *The Modern Language Journal* 85 (4), 567–577.

Gyllstad, H. (2005) Words that go together well: Developing test formats for measuring learner knowledge of English collocations. *The Department of English in Lund: Working Papers in Linguistics* 5, 1–31.

Halliday, M.A.K. (1966) Lexis as a linguistic level. In C.E. Bazell, J.C. Catford, M.A.K. Halliday and R.H. Robins (eds) *In Memory of J.R. Firth* (pp. 148–162). London: Longman.

HarperCollins (2004) *Collins WordbanksOnline*. On WWW at http://www.collins.co.uk/Corpus/CorpusSearch.aspx.

Henriksen, B. (1999) Three dimensions of vocabulary development. *Studies in Second Language Acquisition* 21 (2), 303–317.

Hirsch, K.W. and Tree, J.J. (2001) Word association norms for two cohorts of British adults. *Journal of Neurolinguistics* 14 (1), 1–44.

Ho, C.S-H. and Bryant, P. (1997) Development of phonological awareness of Chinese children in Hong Kong. *Journal of Psycholinguistic Research* 26 (1), 109–126.

Hoey, M. (2005) *Lexical Priming: A New Theory of Words and Language*. Abingdon: Routledge.

Holm, A. and Dodd, B. (1996) The effect of first written language on the acquisition of English literacy. *Cognition* 59 (2), 119–147.

Horst, M., Cardoso, W., Collins, L., Trofimovich, P. and White, J. (2007) Vocabulary instruction: A word of praise for primary teachers. Paper presented at La société pour la promotion de l'anglais, langue seconde, au Québec (SPEAQ), Montreal.

Horst, M., Cobb, T. and Meara, P.M. (1998) Beyond a clockwork orange: acquiring second language vocabulary through reading. *Reading in a Foreign Language* 11 (2), 207–223.

Horst, M. and Collins, L. (2006) From 'faible' to strong: How does their vocabulary grow? In M. Horst and T. Cobb (eds). Special issue on second language vocabulary acquisition. *Canadian Modern Language Review* 63 (1), 83–106.

Howarth, P. (1998) The phraseology of learners' academic writing and second language proficiency. In A.P. Cowie (ed.) *Phraseology: Theory, Analysis, and Applications* (pp. 161–186). Oxford: Oxford University Press.

Hsu, J-Y. (2007) Lexical collocations and their relation to the online writing of Taiwanese college English majors and non-English majors. *Electronic Journal of Foreign Language Teaching* 4 (2), 192–209. On WWW at http://e-flt.nus.edu.sg/v4n22007/hsu.pdf.

Huang, Li-Szu (2001) Knowledge of English collocations: An analysis of Taiwanese EFL learners. In C. Luke and B. Rubrecht (eds) *Texas Papers in Foreign Language Education: Selected Proceedings from the Texas Foreign Language Education Conference* 6 (1), 113–132. Austin, TX: University of Texas.

Hudson, R. (2007) *Language Networks: The New Word Grammar*. Oxford: Oxford University Press.

Huibregtse, I., Admiraal, W. and Meara, P.M. (2002) Scores on a yes–no vocabulary test: Correction for guessing and response style. *Language Testing* 19 (3), 227–245.

Hulstijn, J.H., Hollander, M. and Greidanus, T. (1996) Incidental vocabulary learning by advanced foreign-language students: The influence of marginal glosses, dictionary use, and reoccurrence of unfamiliar words. *The Modern Language Journal* 80 (3), 327–339.

Hunston, S. (2002) *Corpora in Applied Linguistics*. Cambridge: Cambridge University Press.

Ishikawa, S., Uemura, T., Kaneda, M., Shimizu, S., Sugimori, N. and Tono, Y. (2003) *JACET 8000: JACET List of 8000 Basic Words*. Tokyo: JACET.

Jackson, N.E., Chen, H., Goldsberry, L., Kim, A. and Vanderwerff, C. (1999) Effects of variations in orthographic information on Asian and American readers' English text reading. *Reading and Writing* 11 (4), 345–379.

Johnson, R.K. (1983) Bilingual switching strategies: A study of the modes of teacher-talk in bilingual secondary school classrooms in Hong Kong. *Language Learning and Communication* 2 (3), 267–285.

Johnson, R.K., Shek, C.K.W and Law, E.H.F. (1991) Implementing Hong Kong's proposed language policy for secondary schools: Research and its implications. In N. Crawford and K. Hui (eds) *The Curriculum and Behaviour Problems in Schools: A Response to Education Commission Report No. 4 (Education Paper 11)* (pp. 95–109). Hong Kong: Faculty of Education, University of Hong Kong.

Kent, G.H. and Rosanoff, A.J. (1910) A study of association in insanity. *American Journal of Insanity* 67; 37–96; 317–390.

Kilgarriff, A. (1996) *BNC Database and Word Frequency Lists*. On WWW at http://www.kilgarriff.co.uk/bnc-readme.html.

Kiss, G. (1968) Words, associations and networks. *Journal of Verbal Learning and Verbal Behavior* 7, 707–713.

Knight, S. (1994) Dictionary use while reading: The effects on comprehension and vocabulary acquisition for students of different verbal abilities. *Modern Language Journal* 78 (3), 285–299.

Koren, S. (1997) Quality versus convenience: Comparison of modern dictionaries from the researcher's, teacher's and learner's points of view. *TESL-EJ* 2 (3), A-2, 1–16. On WWW at http://tesl-ej.org/ej07/a2.html.

Krantz, G. (1990) *Learning Vocabulary in a Foreign Language: A Study of Reading Strategies*. Göteborg: Acta Universitatis Gothoborgensis.

Krashen, S. (1982) *Principles and Practice in Second Language Acquisition*. Oxford: Pergamon.

Krashen, S. (1985) *The Input Hypothesis: Issues and Implications*. New York: Longman.

Kruse, H., Pankhurst, J. and Sharwood-Smith, M. (1987) A multiple word association probe in second language acquisition research. *Studies in Second Language Acquisition* 9 (2), 141–154.

Lam, A.S.L. (2005) *Language Education in China: Policy and Experience from 1949*. Hong Kong: Hong Kong University Press.

Lambert, W.E. (1972) Developmental aspects of second language acquisition. In A.S. Dil (ed.) *Language, Psychology and Culture: Essays by Wallace E. Lambert* (pp. 9–31). Palo Alto, CA: Stanford University Press.

Lambert, W.E. and Rawlings, C. (1969) Bilingual processing of mixed-language associative networks. *Journal of Verbal Learning and Verbal Behaviour* 8, 604–609.

Larsen-Freeman, D. (1997) Chaos/complexity science and second language acquisition. *Applied Linguistics* 18 (2), 141–165.

Larsen-Freeman, D. (2002) Language acquisition and language use from a chaos/complexity theory perspective. In C. Kramsch (ed.) *Language Acquisition and Language Socialization* (pp. 33–46). London: Continuum.

Larsen-Freeman, D. (2006) The emergence of complexity, fluency and accuracy in the oral and written production of five Chinese learners of English. *Applied Linguistics* 27 (4), 590–619.

Larsen-Freeman, D. (2007) On the complementarity of chaos/complexity theory and dynamic systems theory in understanding the second language acquisition process. *Bilingualism: Language and Cognition* 10 (1), 35–37.

Laufer, B. (2005) Lexical frequency profiles: From Monte Carlo to the real world. A response to Meara (2005). *Applied Linguistics* 26 (4), 582–588.

Laufer, B. and Hill, M. (2000) What lexical information do L2 learners select in a CALL dictionary and how does it affect word recognition? *Language Learning and Technology* 3 (2), 58–76.

Laufer, B. and Nation, P. (1995) Vocabulary size and use: Lexical richness in L2 written production. *Applied Linguistics* 16 (3), 307–322.

Lewis, C.S. (1950) *The Lion, the Witch and the Wardrobe*. London: Geoffrey Bles.

Lexicon (1978) *LK-3000* (pocket electronic dictionary).

Lightbown, P.M., Meara, P.M. and Halter, R. (1998) Contrasting patterns in classroom lexical environments. In D. Albrechtsen, B. Henriksen, I.M. Mees and E. Poulsen (eds) *Perspectives on Foreign and Second Language Pedagogy* (pp. 221–238). Odense, Denmark: Odense University Press.

Lin, A.M.Y. (1996) Bilingualism or linguistic segregation? Symbolic domination, resistance and code switching in Hong Kong schools. *Linguistics and Education* 8 (1), 49–84.

Littlewood, W. and Liu, N.F. (1996) *Hong Kong Students and Their English*. The LEAP Project: Learning Experience, Attitudes and Proficiency of First-Year University Students. The English Centre, University of Hong Kong/Macmillan.

Longman Dictionary of Contemporary English (2005, 4th edn) London: Longman.

Luppescu, S. and Day, R. (1993) Reading, dictionaries, and vocabulary learning. *Language Learning* 43 (2), 263–287.

McBride-Chang, C., Cho, J-R., Liu, H., Wagner, R.K., Shu, H., Zhou, A., Cheuk, C.S-M. and Muse, A. (2005) Changing models across cultures: Associations of phonological awareness and morphological structure awareness with vocabulary and word recognition in second graders from Beijing, Hong Kong, Korea, and the United States. *Journal of Experimental Child Psychology* 92 (2), 140–160.

McNamara, T. (1996) *Measuring Second Language Performance*. London: Longman.

Marslen-Wilson, W.D. (1987) Functional parallelism in spoken word recognition. *Cognition* 25 (1–2), 71–102.

Marslen-Wilson, W.D. and Tyler, L.K. (1981) Central processes in speech understanding. *Philosophical Transactions of the Royal Society of London* Series B 295 (1077), 317–332.

Meara, P.M. (1978) Learners' word associations in French. *The Interlanguage Studies Bulletin* 3 (2), 192–211.

Meara, P.M. (1980) Vocabulary acquisition: A neglected aspect of language learning. *Language Teaching and Linguistics: Abstracts* 13 (4), 221–246.

Meara, P.M. (1982a) *Vocabulary in a Second Language, Vol. 1 Specialised Bibliography 4*. London: CILT.

Meara, P.M. (1982b) Word associations in a foreign language. *Nottingham Linguistic Circular* 11 (2), 28–38.

Meara, P.M. (1984) The study of lexis in interlanguage. In A. Davies, C. Criper and A.P.R. Howatt (eds) *Interlanguage* (pp. 225–235). Edinburgh: Edinburgh University Press.

References

Meara, P.M. (1987) *Vocabulary in a Second Language, Vol. 2 Specialised Bibliography 4*. London: CILT.

Meara, P.M. (1990a) A note on passive vocabulary. *Second Language Research* 6 (2), 150–154.

Meara, P.M. (1990b) Some notes on the Eurocentre vocabulary tests. In J. Tommola (ed.) *Foreign Language Comprehension and Production* (pp. 103–113). Turku: Publications de l'Association Finlandaise de Linguistique Appliquée.

Meara, P.M. (1992a) *EFL Vocabulary Tests*. Swansea: University of Wales Swansea.

Meara, P.M. (1992b) *Euralex French Vocabulary Tests*. Swansea: University of Wales Swansea.

Meara, P.M. (1992c) Vocabulary in a second language. Vol 3. *Reading in a Foreign Language* 9 (1), 761–837.

Meara, P.M. (1992d) Network structures and vocabulary acquisition in a foreign language. In P.J.L. Arnaud and H. Bejoint (eds) *Vocabulary and Applied Linguistics* (pp. 62–70). London: Macmillan.

Meara, P.M. (1992e) New approaches to testing vocabulary knowledge. Unpublished paper. Centre for Applied Language Studies, University College Swansea, Swansea.

Meara, P.M. (1993) Tintin and the World Service: A look at lexical environments. *IATEFL Annual Conference Report*, 32–37.

Meara, P.M. (1994) The complexities of simple vocabulary tests. In F.G. Brinkman, J.A. van der Schee and M.C. Schouten van Parreren (eds) *Curriculum Research: Different Disciplines and Common Goals* (pp. 15–28). Amsterdam: Vrije Universiteit. On WWW at www.lognostics.co.uk/vlibrary/meara1994a.pdf.

Meara, P.M. (1996) The dimensions of lexical competence. In G. Brown, K. Malmkjaer and J. Williams (eds) *Performance and Competence in Second Language Acquisition* (pp. 35–53). Cambridge: Cambridge University Press.

Meara, P.M. (1997) Towards a new approach to modelling vocabulary acquisition. In N. Schmitt and M. McCarthy (eds) *Vocabulary: Description, Acquisition and Pedagogy* (pp. 109–121). Cambridge: Cambridge University Press.

Meara, P.M. (1999a) Self-organisation in bilingual lexicons. In P. Broeder and J. Murre (eds) *Language and Thought in Development* (pp. 127–144). Tubingen: Narr.

Meara, P.M. (1999b) The vocabulary knowledge framework. On WWW at http://www.lognostics.co.uk/vlibrary/meara1996c.pdf.

Meara, P.M. (2001) *V_States (version 0.3)*. On WWW at http://www.lognostics.co.uk/tools/index.htm.

Meara, P.M. (2002) The rediscovery of vocabulary. *Second Language Research* 18 (4), 393–407.

Meara, P.M. (2004) Modelling vocabulary loss. *Applied Linguistics* 25 (2), 137–155.

Meara, P.M. (2005a) Lexical frequency profiles: A Monte Carlo analysis. *Applied Linguistics* 26 (1), 32–47.

Meara, P.M. (2005b) *X_Lex: The Swansea Vocabulary Levels Test* (version 2.05). Swansea: Lognostics.

Meara, P.M. (2006) Emergent properties of multilingual lexicons. *Applied Linguistics* 27 (4), 620–644.

Meara, P.M. and Bell, H. (2001) P_Lex: A simple and effective way of describing the lexical characteristics of short texts. *Prospect* 16 (3), 5–19.

Meara, P.M. and Buxton, B. (1987) An alternative to multiple choice vocabulary tests. *Language Testing* 4 (2), 142–154.

Meara, P.M. and Fitzpatrick, T. (2000) An improved method of assessing productive vocabulary in L2. *System* 28 (1), 19–30.

Meara, P.M. and Jones, G. (1988) Vocabulary size as a placement indicator. In P. Grunwell (ed.) *Applied Linguistics in Society* (pp. 80–87). London: CILT.

Meara, P.M. and Jones, G. (1990) *Eurocentres Vocabulary Size Test. 10KA*. Zurich: Eurocentres.

Meara, P.M., Lightbown, P.M. and Halter, R.H. (1994) The effect of cognates on the applicability of YES/NO vocabulary tests. *Canadian Modern Language Review* 50 (2), 296–311.

Meara, P.M., Lightbown, P.M. and Halter, R.H. (1997) Classrooms as lexical environments. *Language Teaching Research* 1 (1), 28–47.

Meara, P.M. and Milton, J. (2005) *X_Lex: The Swansea Levels Test* (CD-ROM). Newbury, UK: Express Publishing.

Meara, P.M. and Miralpeix, I. (2006) *Y_Lex: The Swansea Advanced Vocabulary Levels Test* (version 2.05). Swansea: Lognostics.

Meara, P.M. and Rodriguez Sánchez, I. (2001) A methodology for evaluating the effectiveness of vocabulary treatments. In M. Bax and J-W. Zwart (eds) *Reflections on Language and Language Learning* (pp. 267–278). Amsterdam: John Benjamins.

Meara, P.M. and Wolter, B. (2004) V_Links: Beyond vocabulary depth. *Angles on the English Speaking World* 4, 85–97.

Melka, F. (1997) Receptive vs. productive aspects of vocabulary. In N. Schmitt and M. McCarthy (eds) *Vocabulary: Description, Acquisition and Pedagogy* (pp. 84–102). Cambridge: Cambridge University Press.

Melka Teichroew, F.J. (1982) Receptive versus productive vocabulary: A survey. *Interlanguage Studies Bulletin* 6 (2), 5–33.

Mellen, B. (2002) Teaching reading in China: Phonics versus whole word. MA dissertation, University of Hong Kong.

Merten, T. (1993) Word association responses and psychoticism. *Personality and Individual Differences* 14, 837–839.

Merten, T. (1995) Factors influencing word association responses: A reanalysis. *Creativity Research Journal* 8, 249–263.

Merten, T. and Fischer, I. (1999) Creativity, personality and word association responses: Associative behaviour in forty supposedly creative persons. *Personality and Individual Differences* 27 (5), 933–942.

Midlane, V. (2005) Students' use of portable electronic dictionaries in the EFL/ESL classroom: A survey of teacher attitudes. M.Ed dissertation, Faculty of Education, University of Manchester.

Milton, J. and Hopkins, N. (2006) Comparing phonological and orthographic vocabulary size: Do vocabulary tests underestimate the knowledge of some learners? *Canadian Modern Language Review* 63 (1), 127–147.

Milton, J. and O'Riordan, O.L. (2007) Level and script effects in the phonological and orthographic vocabulary size of Arabic and Farsi speakers. In P. Davidson, C. Coombe, D. Lloyd and D. Palfreyman (eds) *Teaching and Learning Vocabulary in Another Language* (pp. 122–133). Dubai: TESOL Arabia.

Mochida, A. and Harrington, M. (2006) The Yes/No test as a measure of receptive vocabulary knowledge. *Language Testing* 23 (1), 73–98.

Mochizuki, M. (2002) Exploration of two aspects of vocabulary knowledge: Paradigmatic and collocational. *Annual Review of English Language Education in Japan* 13, 121–129.

Nagy, W. (1997) On the role of context in first- and second-language vocabulary learning. In N. Schmitt and M. McCarthy (eds) *Vocabulary: Description, Acquisition and Pedagogy* (pp. 64–83). Cambridge: Cambridge University Press.

Nakamura, M. (2003) The use of the electronic IC dictionary in the EFL environment. In M. Murata, S. Yamada and Y. Tono (eds) *Dictionaries and Language Learning: How Can Dictionaries Help Human and Machine Learning?* (pp. 346–350). Papers submitted to the Third ASIALEX Biennial International Conference, Meikai University, Urayasu, Japan.
Nation, I.S.P. (1990) *Teaching and Learning Vocabulary.* New York: Newbury House.
Nation, I.S.P. (2001) *Learning Vocabulary in Another Language.* Cambridge: Cambridge University Press.
Nation, I.S.P. (2007) Fundamental issues in modelling and assessing vocabulary knowledge. In H. Daller, J. Milton and J. Treffers-Daller (eds) *Modelling and Assessing Vocabulary Knowledge* (pp. 35–43). Cambridge: Cambridge University Press.
Nation, I.S.P. (2008) *Teaching ESL/EFL Reading and Writing.* Abingdon: Routledge.
Nation, I.S.P. (2008) *Teaching Vocabulary: Strategies and Techniques.* Boston: Heinle Cengage Learning.
Nation, I.S.P. and Gu Yongyi, P. (2007) *Focus on Vocabulary.* Sydney: NCELTR, Macquarie University.
Nation, I.S.P. and Meara, P.M. (2002) Vocabulary. In N. Schmitt (ed.) *An Introduction to Applied Linguistics* (pp. 35–54). London: Arnold.
Nation, I.S.P. and Newton, J. (2008) *Teaching ESL/EFL Listening and Speaking.* Abingdon: Routledge.
Nesi, H. and Meara, P.M. (1991) How using dictionaries affects performance in multiple choice EFL tests. *Reading in a Foreign Language* 8 (1), 631–643.
Nesi, H. (1994) The effect of language background and culture on productive dictionary use. In W. Martin, W. Meijs, M. Moerland, E. ten Pas, P. van Sterkenburg and P. Vossen (eds) *Proceedings of the 6th Euralex International Congress* (pp. 577–585). Amsterdam: Euralex.
Nesi, H. (1996) The role of illustrative examples in productive dictionary use. *Dictionaries: The Journal of the Dictionary Society of North America* 17, 198–206.
Nesi, H. and Haill, R. (2002) A study of dictionary use by international students at a British university. *International Journal of Lexicography* 15 (4), 277–306.
Nesi, H. and Meara, P.M. (1994) Patterns of misinterpretation in the productive use of EFL dictionary definitions. *System* 22 (1), 1–15.
Nesselhauf, N. (2003) The use of collocations by advanced learners of English and some implications for teaching. *Applied Linguistics* 24 (2), 223–242.
Nissen, H.B. and Henriksen, B. (2006) Word class influence on word association test results. *International Journal of Applied Linguistics* 16 (3), 389–408.
Nooteboom, S.G. (1981) Lexical retrieval from fragments of spoken words: Beginnings vs endings. *Journal of Phonetics* 9 (4), 407–424.
Orita, M. (2002) Word associations of Japanese EFL learners and native speakers: Shifts in response type distribution and the associative development of individual words. *Annual Review of English Language Education in Japan* 13, 111–120.
Oxford Collocations Dictionary for Students of English (2002) Oxford: Oxford University Press.
Paul, P.V., Stallman, A.C. and O'Rourke, J.P. (1990) Using three test formats to assess good and poor readers' word knowledge. Technical Report No. 509. Center for the Study of Reading, University of Illinois, Urbana-Champaign, IL.
Pawley, A. and Syder, F.H. (1983) Two puzzles for linguistic theory: Nativelike selection and nativelike fluency. In J.C. Richards and R.W. Schmidt (eds) *Language and Communication* (pp. 191–225). London: Longman.

Pemberton, R. (2003) Spoken word recognition and L2 listening performance: An investigation of the ability of Hong Kong learners to recognise the most frequent words of English when listening to news broadcasts. PhD thesis, University of Wales Swansea.
Pemberton, R., Li, E., Or, W. and Pierson, H. (1996) *Taking Control: Autonomy in Language Learning*. Hong Kong: Hong Kong University Press.
Pemberton, R., Toogood, S. and Barfield, A. (2009) *Maintaining Control: Autonomy and Language Learning*. Hong Kong: Hong Kong University Press.
Politzer, R.L. (1978) Paradigmatic and syntagmatic associations of first year French students. In V. Honsa and M.J. Hardman-de-Bautista (eds) *Papers in Linguistics and Child Language: Ruth Hirsch Weir memorial volume* (pp. 203–210). The Hague: Mouton.
Pollio, H. (1963) A simple matrix analysis of associative structure. *Journal of Verbal Learning and Verbal Behavior* 2, 166–169.
Postman, L.J. and Keppel, G. (eds) (1970) *Norms of Word Association*. New York: Academic Press.
Prescott, M. (2006) Light bulbs: Not such a bright idea. On WWW at http://news.bbc.co.uk/2/hi/science/nature/4667354.stm.
Pulido, D. (2007) The relationship between text comprehension and second language incidental vocabulary acquisition: A matter of topic familiarity? *Language Learning* 57 (1), 155–199.
Qian, D. (2002) Investigating the relationship between vocabulary knowledge and academic reading performance: An assessment perspective. *Language Learning* 52 (3), 513–536.
Randall, M. (1980) Word association behaviour in learners of English as a foreign language. *Polyglot* 2.2, B4-D1.
Read, C., Zhang, Y., Nie, H. and Ding, B. (1986) The ability to manipulate speech sounds depends on knowing alphabetic writing. *Cognition* 24 (1–2), 31–44.
Read, J. (1993) The development of a new measure of L2 vocabulary knowledge. *Language Testing* 10 (3), 355–371.
Read, J. (1998) Validating a test to measure depth of vocabulary knowledge. In A.J. Kunnan (ed.) *Validation in Language Assessment* (pp. 41–60). Mahwah, NJ: Lawrence Erlbaum Associates.
Read, J. (2000) *Assessing Vocabulary*. Cambridge: Cambridge University Press.
Read, J. and Nation, P. (2006) An investigation of the lexical dimension of the IELTS speaking test. *IELTS Research Reports* (Vol. 6; pp. 207–231). Canberra: IELTS Australia.
Revier, R.L. and Henriksen, B. (2006) Teaching collocations: Pedagogical implications based on a cross-sectional study of Danish EFL learners' written production of English collocations. In M. Bendtsen, M. Björklund, C. Fant and L. Forsman (eds) *Språk, Lärende och Utbildning i Sikte: Festskrift tillägnad Professor Kaj Sjöholm* (pp. 173–189). Vasa: Pedagogiska fakulteten Åbo Akademi.
Richards, J. (1976) The role of vocabulary teaching. *TESOL Quarterly* 10 (1), 77–89.
Riegel, K. (1968) Some theoretical considerations of bilingual development. *Psychological Bulletin* 70 (6), 647–670.
Riegel, K., Ramsey, R.M. and Riegel, R.M. (1967) A comparison of the first and second languages of American and Spanish students. *Journal of Verbal Learning and Verbal Behaviour* 6, 536–544.
Riegel, K. and Zivian, I. (1972) A study of inter- and intralingual associations in English and German. *Language Learning* 22 (1), 51–63.

Robinson, B.F. and Mervis, C.B. (1998) Disentangling early language development: Modelling lexical and grammatical acquisition using an extension of case-study methodology. *Developmental Psychology* 34 (2), 363–375.

Ronald, J. and Tajino, A. (2005) A comparison of paper and electronic monolingual dictionaries: Location, comprehension, and retention of secondary senses. In V.B.Y. Ooi, A. Pakir, I. Talib, L. Tan, P.K.W. Tan and Y.Y. Tan (eds) *Proceedings of ASIALEX 2005: Words in Asian Cultural Contexts* (pp. 255–261). Singapore: National University of Singapore.

Rüke-Dravina, V. (1971) Word associations in monolingual and multilingual individuals. *Linguistics* 74, 66–85.

Ryan, A. and Meara, P.M. (1991) The case of the invisible vowels: Arabic speakers reading English words. *Reading in a Foreign Language* 7 (2), 531–540.

Salasoo, A. and Pisoni, D.B. (1985) Interaction of knowledge sources in spoken word identification. *Journal of Memory and Language* 24 (2), 210–231.

Schmidt, R. (2001) Attention. In P. Robinson (ed.) *Cognition and Second Language Instruction* (pp. 3–32). Cambridge: Cambridge University Press.

Schmitt, N. (1998a) Quantifying word association responses: What is native-like? *System* 26 (3), 389–401.

Schmitt, N. (1998b) Tracking the incremental acquisition of second language vocabulary: A longitudinal study. *Language Learning* 48 (2), 281–317.

Schmitt, N. (1999) The relationship between TOEFL vocabulary items and meaning, association, collocation and word-class knowledge. *Language Testing* 16 (2), 189–216.

Schmitt, N. (2000) *Vocabulary in Language Teaching*. Cambridge: Cambridge University Press.

Schmitt, N. (2002) *An Introduction to Applied Linguistics*. London: Arnold.

Schmitt, N. and Meara, P.M. (1997) Researching vocabulary through a word knowledge framework. *Studies in Second Language Acquisition* 19 (1), 17–36.

Schoonen, R. and Verhallen, M. (2008) The assessment of deep word knowledge in young first and second language learners. *Language Testing* 25 (2), 211–236.

Seiko (1978) *TR-700* (pocket electronic dictionary).

Seiko (1995) *Hand-Held Longman Dictionary of Contemporary English* (pocket electronic dictionary).

Schuessler, K.F. and Cressey, D.R. (1950) Personality characteristics of criminals. *The American Journal of Sociology* 55 (5), 476–484.

Sharpe, P. (1995) Electronic dictionaries with particular reference to the design of an electronic bilingual dictionary for English-speaking learners of Japanese. *International Journal of Lexicography* 8 (1), 39–54.

Shillaw, J. (1996) The application of Rasch modelling to yes/no vocabulary tests. Vocabulary Acquisition Research Group. On WWW at http://www.lognostics.co.uk/vlibrary/.

Shillaw, J. (1999) The application of the Rasch model to Yes/No vocabulary tests. PhD thesis, University of Wales Swansea.

Shore, W. and Kempe, V. (1999) The role of semantic context in assessing partial knowledge of word meanings. *Journal of Psycholinguistic Research* 28, 145–163.

Sims, V.M. (1929) The reliability and validity of four types of vocabulary tests. *Journal of Educational Research* 20, 91–96.

Sinclair, J.M. (1991) *Corpus, Concordance, Collocation*. Oxford: Oxford University Press.

Sinclair, J.M. (2004) *Trust the Text: Language, Corpus, and Discourse*. London: Routledge.

Singleton, D. (1993) L'acquisition du lexique d'une langue étrangère. *Acquisition et Interaction en Langue Etrangère* 3, 97–113.
Singleton, D. (1999) *Exploring the Second Language Mental Lexicon*. Cambridge: Cambridge University Press.
Singleton, D. and Little, D. (1991) The second language lexicon: Some evidence from university-level learners of French and German. *Second Language Research* 7(1), 61–81.
Söderman, T. (1993a) Word associations of foreign language learners and native speakers – different response types and their relevance to lexical development. In B. Hammerberg (ed.) *Problems, Process and Product in Language Learning* (pp. 157–169). Åbo, Finland: Åbo Academic.
Söderman, T. (1993b) Word associations of foreign language learners and native speakers – the phenomenon of a shift in response type and its relevance for lexical development. In H. Ringbom (ed.) *Near Native Proficiency in English* (pp. 91–182). Åbo: Åbo Akademi.
Sökmen, A. (1993) Word association results: A window to the lexicons of ESL students. *JALT Journal* 15 (2), 135–150.
Sommer, R. (1901) *Diagnostik der Geisteskrankheiten*. Berlin/Wien: Urban und Schwarzenberg.
Stallman, A., Commeyras, M., Kerr, B., Meyer-Reimer, K., Jimenez, R., Hartman, D. and Pearson, P. (1989) Are "new" words really new? Technical Report No. 471. Center for the Study of Reading, University of Illinois, Urbana-Champaign, IL.
Stanford Achievement Tests (1973) New York: Harcourt, Brace, Jovanovich.
Stirling, J. (2005) The portable electronic dictionary – faithful friend or faceless foe? *Modern English Teacher* 14 (3), 64–72.
Stubbs, M., (2001) *Words and Phrases: Corpus Studies of Lexical Semantics*. Oxford: Blackwell.
Summers, D. (ed.) (1995) *Longman Dictionary of Contemporary English* (3rd edn). Harlow: Pearson Education.
Tang, G. (1997) Pocket electronic dictionaries for second language learning: Help or hindrance? *TESL Canada Journal* 15 (1), 39–57.
Tauroza, S. (1997) Using students' listening comprehension problems. *Perspectives* 9 (1), 167–178. Hong Kong: Department of English, City University of Hong Kong.
Taylor, A. and Chan, A. (1994) Pocket electronic dictionaries and their use. In W. Martin, W. Meijs, M. Moerland, E. ten Pas, P. van Sterkenburg and P. Vossen (eds) *Proceedings of the 6th Euralex International Congress* (pp. 598–605). Amsterdam: Euralex.
Texas Instruments (1978) *Speak & Spell* (pocket electronic dictionary).
Van Geert, P. (2007) Dynamic systems in second language learning: Some general methodological reflections. *Bilingualism: Language and Cognition* 10 (1), 47–49.
Walley, A.C. (1993) The role of vocabulary development in children's spoken word recognition and segmentation ability. *Developmental Review* 13 (3) 286–350.
Wang, M. and Geva, E. (2003) Spelling performance of Chinese children using English as a second language: Lexical and visual-orthographic processes. *Applied Psycholinguistics* 24 (1), 1–25.
Webb, S. (2007) The effects of repetition on vocabulary knowledge. *Applied Linguistics* 28 (1), 46–65.

Webb, S. and Kagimoto, E. (2007) Teaching and learning collocation. Paper presented at the 33rd Japan Association for Language Teaching International Conference, Tokyo.

Welsh, E. (1988) Second language lexical networks. MA thesis, University of London, Birkbeck College.

Weschler, R. and Pitts, C. (2000) An experiment using electronic dictionaries with EFL students. *The Internet TESL Journal* 6 (8). On WWW at: http://iteslj.org/Articles/Weschler-ElectroDict.html.

West, M. (1953) *A General Service List of English Words*. London: Longman, Green and Co.

White, T.G., Slater, W. and Graves, M. (1989) Yes/no method of vocabulary assessment: Valid for whom and useful for what? In S. McCormick and J. Zutell (eds) *Cognitive and Social Perspectives for Literacy Research and Instruction: The 38th Yearbook of the National Reading Conference* (pp. 391–398). Chicago, IL: National Reading Conference.

Wilks, C. (1999) Untangling word webs: Graph theory approaches to L2 lexicons. PhD thesis, University of Wales Swansea.

Wilks, C. and Meara, P.M. (2002) Untangling word webs: Graph theory and the notion of density in second language word association networks. *Second Language Research* 18 (4), 303–324.

Wilks, C. and Meara, P.M. (2007) Implementing graph theory approaches to the exploration of density and structure in L1 and L2 word association networks. In H. Daller, J. Milton and J. Treffers-Daller (eds) *Modelling and Assessing Vocabulary Knowledge* (pp. 167–181). Cambridge: Cambridge University Press.

Wilks, C., Meara, P.M. and Wolter, B. (2005) A further note on simulating word association behaviour in a second language. *Second Language Research* 21 (4), 359–372.

Wolter, B. (2001) Comparing the L1 and L2 mental lexicon. *Studies in Second Language Acquisition* 23 (1), 41–69.

Wolter, B. (2002) Assessing proficiency through word associations: Is there still hope? *System* 30 (3), 315–329.

Wray, A. (2002) *Formulaic Language and the Lexicon*. Cambridge: Cambridge University Press.

Xue, G. and Nation, I.S.P. (1984) A university word list. *Language Learning and Communication* 3 (2), 215–229.

Zahar, R., Cobb, T. and Spada, N. (2001) Acquiring vocabulary through reading: Effects of frequency and contextual richness. *Canadian Modern Language Review* 57 (4), 541–572.

Zhang, X. (1993) English collocations and their effect on the writing of native and non-native college freshmen. PhD thesis, Indiana University of Pennsylvania.

Zimmerman, J., Broder, P.K., Shaughnessy, J.J. and Underwood, B.J. (1977) A recognition test of vocabulary using signal-detection measures and some correlates of word and nonword recognition. *Intelligence* 1, 5–31.

Author Index

Aitchison, J. 128, 129, 130, 154
Aizawa, K. 82
Alderson, J.C. 5, 13
Altenberg, B. 125
Anderson, R.C. 3, 14, 15, 16, 17
Atkins, B.T.S. 70

Bahns, J. 95
Banay, R.G. 51
Barfield, A. 17, 95, 109, 156, 157, 158
Barkhuizen, G. 113
Barnard, H. 2
Beeckmans, R. 5, 16
Bell, H. 9, 114, 155, 156, 157, 158
Bertelson, P. 145, 146
Biskup, D. 95
Black, A. 83
Bogaards, P. 7
Bond, T.G. 100
Bonk, W.J. 95, 141
Boonmoh, A. 69, 71, 156, 158
Bradley, L. 144
Brown, S.H. vii
Bryant, P. 143, 144
Buxton, B. 4, 13, 16, 67

Castles, A. 144
Chan, A. 69
Chapelle, C.A. 13, 156
Chen, H. 151, 152, 153
Cheung, H. 146, 147, 151, 152
Chi Man-Lai, A. 95
Churchill, E. 111
Cobb, T. 56
Collins, L. 55, 56
Coltheart, M. 144
Coxhead, A 41, 56, 98
Cressey, D.R. 38

Day, R. 82, 83
De Bot, K. 111, 112
Deese, J. 25, 46
Deng, Y.P. 69
Dodd, B. 144, 145, 146, 147, 148

Eldaw, M. 95
Ellis, N. 125
Ellis, R. 113
Entwisle, D.R. 6, 38, 40

Ervin, S.M. 38, 40
Eyckmans, J. 5, 16, 17, 18

Farghal, M. 95
Fischer, I. 51
Fischer, U. 83
Fitzpatrick, T. 8, 26, 31, 33, 34, 37, 41, 43, 47, 48, 50, 51, 96, 154, 156, 158
Fox, C.M. 100
Freebody, P. 3, 14, 15, 16, 17

George, H.V. 2
Geva, E. 143
Gewirth, L. 38
Gitsaki, C. 95
Glaser, B.G. 29
Gougenheim, G. 28, 31
Granger, S. 95, 109, 125
Green, D.M. 13
Greidanus, T. 7, 38
Gu Yongyi, P. viii
Gyllstad, H. vii, 95

Haill, R. 80
Halliday, M.A.K. 137
Halter, R. 53
Harrington, M. 5
Henriksen, B. 40, 46, 95, 96, 128, 135
Hill, M. 83
Hirsch, K.W. 51
Ho, C.S-H. 143
Hoey, M. 111, 125, 131
Holm, A. 144, 145, 146, 147, 148
Hopkins, N. 5
Horst, M. viii, 56, 65, 157, 158
Howarth, P. 95
Hsu, J-Y. 95, 108
Huang, L-S. 95
Hudson, R. 111
Huhta, A. 13
Huibregtse, I. 5, 16
Hulstijn, J.H. 82
Hunston, S. 136

Ishikawa, S. 138

Jackson, N.E. 147
Johnson, R.K. 142
Jones, G. 4, 16, 43, 54, 67

Author Index

Kagimoto, E. 95
Kempe, V. 83
Kent, G.H. 38, 40
Keppel, G. 6
Kilgarriff, A. 97
Kiss, G. 25
Knight, S. 82, 83
Koren, S. 69
Krantz, G. 83
Krashen, S. 54
Kruse, H. 38, 39, 40

Lam, A.S.L. 153
Lambert, W.E. 39
Larsen-Freeman, D. 111, 113
Laufer, B. 8, 10, 54, 83, 156
Lewis, C.S. 84
Lightbown, P.M. 53, 59
Lin, A.M.Y. 142
Little, D. 6, 35
Littlewood, W. 142
Liu, N.F. 142
Luppescu, S. 82, 83

Marslen-Wilson, W.D. 149
McBride-Chang, C. 142, 143
McNamara, T. 17, 100, 106, 109
Meara, P.M. viii, xi-xvii, 1-12, 13, 16, 17, 24, 25, 26, 27, 28, 29, 30, 33, 35, 37, 38, 39, 40, 41, 43, 46, 52, 53, 54, 55, 59, 61, 63, 65, 67, 68, 81, 83, 85, 95, 96, 107, 111, 114, 128, 135, 153, 154, 155, 156, 157, 158
Melka Teichroew, F.J. 135
Melka, F. 135
Mellen, B. 153
Merten, T. 38, 51
Mervis, C.B. 111
Midlane, V. 69, 70
Milton, J. 4, 5
Miralpeix, I. 4
Mochida, A. 5
Mochizuki, M. 95

Nagy, W. 135
Nakamura, M. 68
Nation, I.S.P. 1, 8, 9, 10, 13, 29, 32, 41, 53, 54, 59, 63, 128, 154, 158
Nesi, H. viii, 67, 69, 71, 80, 156, 158
Nesselhauf, N. 95
Newton, J. viii
Nienhuis, L. 7, 38
Nissen, H.B. 40, 46
Nooteboom, S.G. 143

O'Riordan, O.L. 5
Obiedat, H. 95
Orita, M. 38

Palmer, H. 2, 11

Paul, P.V. 15
Pawley, A. 131
Pemberton, R. 141, 148, 156, 157, 158
Pisoni, D.B. 143
Pitts, C. 71
Politzer, R.L. 33, 39, 40, 43
Pollio, H. 25
Postman, L.J. 6
Prescott, M. 72
Pulido, D. 129

Qian, D. 7

Randall, M. 39
Rawlings, C. 39
Read, C. 146, 147
Read, J. 6, 7, 8, 9, 13
Revier, R.L. 95, 96
Richards, J. 128
Riegel, K. 39, 40, 43
Robinson, B.F. 111
Rodriguez Sánchez, I. 83
Ronald, J. 83, 155, 156, 157, 158
Rosanoff, A.J. 38, 40
Rüke-Dravina, V. 38, 39, 40
Ryan, A. 67

Salasoo, A. 143
Schmidt, R. 133
Schmitt, N. 1, 39, 40, 43, 95, 96, 108, 128, 129
Schoonen, R. 7
Schuessler, K.F. 38
Sharpe, P. 69
Shillaw, J. 5, 17, 18, 100, 154, 156, 157, 158
Shore, W. 83
Sims, V.M. 3
Sinclair, J.M. 130, 131, 132
Singleton, D. 6, 35, 37
Söderman, T. 6, 33, 39, 40, 43, 96
Sökmen, A. 38, 39, 40, 43
Sommer, R. 38
Stallman, A. 17
Stirling, J. 69
Strauss, A.L. 29
Stubbs, M. 126
Summers, D. 85
Swets, J.A. 13
Syder, F.H. 131

Tajino, A. 83, 157
Tang, G. 71
Tauroza, S. 142
Taylor, A. 69
Tree, J.J. 51
Tyler, L.K. 149

Van Geert, P. 112
Varantola, K. 70
Verhallen, M. 7

Walley, A.C. 147
Wang, M. 143
Webb, S. 95, 135
Welsh, E. 7
Weschler, R. 71
West, M. 2, 53
White, J. 55
White, T.G. 15
Wilks, C. 7, 8, 9, 25, 26, 27, 28, 29, 30, 33, 35, 37, 155, 156, 157, 158

Wolter, B. 37, 40, 96, 157, 158
Wray, A. 2, 109, 116, 127, 131, 134

Xue, G. 53

Zahar, R. 61
Zhang, X. 95
Zimmerman, J. 3, 14
Zivian, I. 39

Subject Index

Academic Word List 8, 41, 43, 46, 56, 57, 63, 98
Aural_Lex 5

Bank of English corpus 137-139
bilingualism
– French and English speakers in Quebec 53-54
– Welsh and English speakers in Wales 44-46

British National Corpus 18, 75, 97-98, 158

case studies
– single-subject case studies 82-94, 111-127, 155
Chaos Theory 111
checklist tests
    see Yes/No tests
classrooms
– and dictionary use 69-71
– as lexical environments 53-66
cognates
– and nonwords 4
– in word association tasks 46
collocation 95-110, 111-127, 128-140, 156
– and frequency 97-105, 108-110
– and L2 proficiency 97-110
– and word association responses 42-44, 47-48
– and word class 97-98, 104-105, 107-110
– collocational productivity 130-140
– developing use of 117-127
– errors 95-96, 97
– (productive) knowledge of 95-110
– testing 97-110
comprehensible input 54-65
computer modelling 2, 9-11, 54-55, 63-64, 156
computer-based tests 4, 6, 13, 17, 67, 85-86
concordance 95, 138-139
corpus
– and collocation research 95, 97, 130, 136-140
– linguistics 131-132
– of learner texts 56-65
– of teacher talk 55-65

diagnostic tests 5-6

DIALANG 5, 13
dictionaries 67-81, 82-94, 134
– and summary-writing 71-74
– and vocabulary growth 82-94
– bilingual/monolingual 68-69, 72-73, 78, 81, 94
– compilation of 68
– look-up behaviour 74-80, 86, 93-94
– Pocket Electronic Dictionaries (PEDs) 67-81, 158
– teacher attitudes to 69-70
– use of 67-81, 82-94
Dynamic Systems Theory 111, 127

essay data 8, 95, 111-127
Eurocentres Vocabulary Size Test 4, 43, 54, 67

Familizer 56
fluency
– measuring fluency in essay writing 112-117
form
– attention to form in language learning 128, 129, 133
– learner perception of form 34
formulaic structures 111, 116-127, 131
fossilization
    see lexical fossilization
Français Elémentaire word list 28, 31
frequency
    see word frequency

General Service List 53-54, 57, 63, 65
graph theory 7, 25, 26
guessing 3, 16, 18, 94

idiolect 125
incidental vocabulary acquisition 129-135, 140
– through listening 53-65
– through reading 61, 83-94
inferring meaning
    see lexical inferencing
input 53-56, 61, 130, 133
    see also comprehensible input
intensive language programmes 53-65
item difficulty 100-109, 158

JACET 8000 list 138, 158

L1
- reading instruction and L2 listening 141-153
- reading strategy transfer 5
- vocabulary acquisition 128-129, 132-134, 140, 155
- word association behaviour 7, 25, 26, 38-40, 44, 49-51
learner
- attitudes to vocabulary tests 8, 23, 27, 28-33, 51-52
- confidence 94
- corpus 55-65
    see also test-taker strategies
lemmas/lemmatization 18, 53-54, 57, 75-76, 84, 96-97
levels test
    see Vocabulary Level Tests
Lex30 8, 96
LexCombi 98-110
lexical density 8
lexical formulae
    see formulaic structures
lexical fossilization 128, 132-135, 140
lexical inferencing 129, 135
lexical networks 7-8, 9-10, 25-37, 65, 119, 127
- density of 26
- formation of 128, 135
- L1 and L2 25, 26
- receptive-productive connections 9-10
- self-organisation 10
lexical profiling
- and collocation 97-108
- Lexical Frequency Profile (LFP) 8-10, 54
- of classroom language 53-66
lexical richness 9, 53-66
- and classroom activity type 59-61
lexicography
    see dictionaries
listening comprehension
- and L1 reading skills 141-153
    see also incidental vocabulary acquisition
Lognostics 4, 11

mental lexicon 2, 25, 37, 39, 51-52, 128, 158
- of the learner 6-7, 9-10, 11, 39, 40, 43, 111-127, 146
- L1-L2 differences 38-39, 46
- L2 35, 40, 51-52, 97, 107-108, 111-127

modelling vocabulary knowledge 3, 9-10, 11, 26, 54-55, 64, 96, 109, 156
morpheme recognition 143
networks
    see lexical networks
nonwords 3-5, 13-17, 24, 144, 145, 147, 154

phonics in L1 reading instruction 142-144, 153

phonological awareness
- and listening ability 149-152
- and reading ability 143, 144
- and vocabulary size 147
- testing phonological awareness 144-148
placement testing 4, 67
P_Lex 9, 114-116
productive vocabulary
    see vocabulary knowledge
pseudowords
    see nonwords

qualitative data and analyses 27, 33-36, 109, 155
quantitative data and analyses 8, 29-31, 36, 37, 109, 155

Range 158
Rasch analysis 5, 17-18, 24, 100-102, 105-110, 157
- and misfits 5, 18, 105-106
reading
- alphabetic systems 143-149, 151-153
- L1 reading skills 5, 141-153
- logographic systems 143
- reading aloud 142, 145, 147, 152
- with/without a dictionary 73-74, 82-94, 129
    see also incidental vocabulary acquisition
receptive vocabulary
    see vocabulary knowledge
replication xv, 65, 157

second language proficiency
- self-assessment of 44-46
Signal Detection Theory
    see also Yes/No tests 4-5, 13, 14, 16
strategies
    see test-taker strategies
Swansea University doctoral research programme xi-xvii, 1-3, 5, 11-12, 65
syntactic complexity
- measuring 111-127

teacher talk 53-66, 142
test-taker strategies 8, 23, 27-29, 31, 35-37, 51-2
think aloud protocols 71-73, 157
transitional probability matrices 83, 86, 88-90, 94
translation tests 18-23, 86-88
t-units 113-116, 126

University Word List 53-54

V_States 83-94, 157
Victoria University doctoral research programme 2-3
Vocabprofile 56, 61, 63

Subject Index

vocabulary knowledge
- acquisition processes 111-112, 126-127, 128-140, 158
- contextualised / decontextualised 18-24, 70, 75, 92, 134, 148, 155-157
- depth of 6-7, 15, 108
- measuring changes in 82-94, 111-127
- non-linear development of 111-127
- partial 82-94, 128-140
- productive 8-10, 95-110, 111-127, 156
- receptive / productive distinction 10, 135-136, 140
- self-rating 84-94

vocabulary learnability
- of spoken language 61-63

Vocabulary Level Tests 54

vocabulary networks
  see lexical networks

vocabulary size 4, 13-18, 108, 134
- and phonological awareness 147
- estimating 13-18, 23, 154

Word Associates Test (WAT) 6-7
word association 6-8, 25-37, 38-52, 154-155
- and cognates 46
- and L2 proficiency 26, 38-40, 43, 50-51
- and post-task interviews 27-28, 31-36
- as an elicitation tool 8, 96
- categorising responses 33-35, 40, 41, 42, 47-49
- chains 7
- comparison of L1 and L2 response patterns 26, 38-52
- cue/stimulus words 40, 41-43, 46

- individual variability 26, 30-1, 43-44, 48-49, 51
- meaning, position and form responses 33-34, 41-42, 47-48
- paradigmatic, syntagmatic and clang responses 6, 33, 38, 40, 41
  see also graph theory, Word Associates Test (WAT)

word families 56-59, 61-65, 69, 84
- and variation in lexical richness 58-59

word frequency 8-9, 14, 31-32, 40, 41, 53-65, 85, 96, 114-116, 148, 155, 158

word recognition
- as part of the acquisition process 130
- errors in 148-151
- spoken 141-153

writing
- and dictionary use 67-81
- and lexical development 111-127
- assessment of 54
- learner corpus of written texts 55-65
- systems 143-146

Yes/No tests 3-6, 13-24, 154, 156, 157
- and Rasch analysis 5, 17-18
- and test-taker strategies 23
- and translation tests 18-24
- contextualised 18-24
- DIALANG 5, 13
- historical development of 13-18, 154
- reliability 15-18, 22-24
- scoring / correction formula 4, 5, 13, 15-17
- validity 13, 15, 16
  see also nonwords